With best regards
to Ed + Kitty Sasaki

— Walter Youngquist

Investing in
Natural Resources
Today's Guide to
Tomorrow's Needs

Investing in
Natural Resources
Today's Guide to
Tomorrow's Needs

WALTER YOUNGQUIST, Ph.D.
Consulting Geologist

 1975

Dow Jones-Irwin, Inc. Homewood, Illinois 60430

© DOW JONES-IRWIN, INC., 1975

This publication is designed to provide accurate and
authoritative information in regard to the subject matter
covered. It is sold with the understanding that the
publisher is not engaged in rendering legal, accounting, or
other professional service. If legal advice or other expert
assistance is required, the services of a competent
professional person should be sought.

*From a Declaration of Principles jointly adopted by a Committee
of the American Bar Association and a Committee of Publishers.*

First Printing, March 1975

ISBN 0-87094-091-0
Library of Congress Catalog Card No. 74–24463

Printed in the United States of America

*Dedicated to intelligent and profitable
investment in our natural resources,
financing the needs of today
and those of the
new economy of tomorrow*

Preface

THIS BOOK is written as a reference for individuals and institutions concerned with natural resource investments. It presents the basic facts about each resource, together with an estimate of the future, in general to the year 2000. Information includes answers to the following questions:

Where is the resource, with particular reference to supplies in the United States and Canada? What are the principal uses and markets for this resource?

How important is this resource in the economy now and how important is it likely to become in the future? What new technologies and uses are on the horizon which might increase demand?

What are the various ways in which investments can be made in this resource and the relative merits of various approaches?

To further give the reader a "feel" for the resource discussed, some supplementary material is also included occasionally, as, for example, elementary facts about the geological occurrence of certain resources as well as what particular environmental concerns may be involved in the production of some of these materials.

The political realities of the present and projected world scene suggest that resources within our own borders are the safest investments. Also, it is difficult to get information on and effectively invest in foreign resources, with a few exceptions. For these reasons the emphasis here is on natural resources in the United States and Canada. In some cases, as for example gold and chromium, where the largest deposits are abroad, note is made of foreign investment media in these materials.

North American investors are very fortunate, however, for this continent offers a natural resource investment spectrum unequalled in any other area of comparable size in the world, and, more importantly, we have the economic system through which individuals and institutions can make such investments.

This volume attempts to look at resource investments realistically. Strong points and weaknesses are given equal consideration, and there is no bias intended toward looking at resources from anything but a solid economic base, and within the realities of the social and political framework which exists. Nevertheless, the simple situation of finite resources facing an infinite demand, as populations soar and living standards rise, inevitably calls for a positive view of the increasing demand in virtually every natural resource considered.

There is, to my knowledge, no other book which is concerned with natural resource investments as this volume purports to be. It represents the sifting of a very large amount of information from a wide variety of sources, including certain unpublished industry data used as a general background for some of the discussions. My chief sources of information, however, are from the reports of the U.S. Geological Survey, the U.S. Bureau of Mines, publications of the various state geological surveys, and reports of the Canada Department of Energy, Mines, and Resources. Other helpful sources are *Science, World Oil, The Oil and Gas Journal, Scientific American, The Bulletin of the American Association of Petroleum Geologists, Mining Engineering, Engineering and Mining Journal,* and *The Northern Miner.*

This book is itself based on my previous book, *Our Natural Resources: How to Invest in Them,* published by Frederick Fell, Inc. of New York, New York. I am grateful for their permission to utilize material from that book when I was preparing the present volume. Readers might find it interesting to compare these two books to determine how my preoccupation with natural resources has evolved over the past decade.

It is not practical to cite all these references in detail, and therefore I have not burdened the reader with citations in the text. However, at the end of this volume there are listed some general references which are intended to suggest where some of these topics may be further pursued.

From what I have seen, the small investor can make good and competent investment decisions with the aid of information quite readily available to him. I would suggest the following general publications from which I too have obtained a great deal of data: *The Wall Street Journal, Barron's, U.S. News and World Report, Fortune.* The Standard & Poor's information sheets on corporations, which are in almost every brokerage office, are most useful. I would hope also that this present volume would be among the commonly used literature.

For those interested especially in mining, I would mention, in addition to *The Northern Miner,* published in Toronto; *Skillings' Mining Review,* published in Duluth; and for a local color mining paper, a subscription to *The Wallace Miner* published at Wallace, Idaho, in the heart of the Coeur d'Alene silver-lead-zinc mining district.

Demands on our natural resources will be larger between now and the year 2000 than ever before in history. Opportunities for successful investment in these resources by the informed investor have never been greater; the capital needs are enormous if we are to meet the challenge. But it also is imperative that the money we do have is used efficiently—that it is invested wisely for maximum return for all concerned. We cannot waste either our natural or our financial resources. It is to this end that this book is addressed.

February 1975   WALTER YOUNGQUIST

Contents

1

Natural Resources and History

LAWS CAN BE PASSED, political speeches can be made, and parades can be held, but in the end the clear, basic fact emerges that the nations with the natural resources are in command. Waves of human migration, the outcomes of wars, and the relative rises in standards of living around the world have all been controlled by the location and abundance of natural resources— metals, fuels, and food supplies. There is no indication that this will change.

The early peoples bartered for materials from great distances to obtain their needs, even as we do today. Obsidian for making super-sharp arrowheads came from the Yellowstone National Park area and found its way as far as Ohio. The camel caravans of the Middle and Far East went to the salt mines of India to obtain this life-essential material. The Roman road over which this traffic moved in that part of the world was called the *Via Salaria* ("salt highway"). Roman soldiers were paid, in part, with salt—thus the modern term "salary," derived from the Latin word for salt—*sal.*

The country that had the precious metals silver and gold could obtain materials for industrial expansion and for war. The Athenians used the silver from the great mines of Laurium, in Greece, to pay for building the ships with which they defeated the Persians at Salamis in 480 B.C. The Romans conquered lands to get their mines of precious metals as well as those of more common metals such as the tin at Cornwall, England. The de-

1

cline of the Roman empire coincided with the loss of gold and silver due to their use for importing luxuries rather than for balancing the imports with exports of comparable value. Ultimately the once-proud Roman currency was inflated and cheapened to the point where it became despised in much of the then known world. This is a facet of history that has modern parallels and perils.

The Huns fought for the possession of the salt deposits of Germany; Germany and France have battled over possession of the iron and coal of Alsace-Lorraine. The Allies were said to have "floated to victory on a sea of oil" in World War I. A substance called uranium, largely a laboratory curiosity until the 1940s, dramatically helped to end World War II in the Pacific.

What the future holds is hard to predict, but clearly the possession of natural resources is playing an even larger part today in the destiny of nations than in the past. Saudi Arabia's rapid rise to a position of international influence in the 1970s is but one example. With only a very small fraction of the world's population but with a very large percentage of the world's liquid oil reserves, the Arab countries now play a major role in the economy of almost every industrialized nation as well as in each of the other nations that are struggling to industrialize.

The tides of history have shifted with the rise and the depletion of natural-resource bases. This continues, and at present there are many crosscurrents brought about by the fact that our highly industrialized world is dependent on so many critical materials. No one nation is entirely self-sufficient. But as the United States, for example, no longer is able to supply all its own oil needs from its own oil wells (that critical point was passed in the late 1960s), there are alternate energy sources being developed. These include oil from shale, liquified coal, and synthetic natural gas. In some areas geothermal power, the great natural heat of the Earth, is being tapped. All of these new sources of energy require large capital expenditures and afford new opportunities for investment.

We are but an extension of the long arm of history, and the history of human society is the history of what materials there were to work with and what was done with these materials. There is no early end in sight for this scenario—the story of the development and use of natural resources, which is the realm of this book.

2

The New Investment Setting

THE FOUR BASIC ELEMENTS of the new natural-resource investment setting are (1) the world-wide scramble for resources, especially sources of energy, (2) world-wide inflation, (3) a deep and vital concern for the environment, and (4) a rising tide of nationalism.

A geologist friend called long distance the other day to read a document to me. It was not a geological report but rather a statement by a leading foreign political figure as to the attitude of their government toward capital coming into the country to be invested in natural-resource development. My friend wanted to know what I thought of the statement, not to get my opinion on the geology of the country. This illustrates the point that natural-resource investment has political as well as geological considerations.

This is true not only abroad but here in North America, as we have various political and social factions pulling at and shoving our vital resource industries. We also have become very concerned with environmental factors; much of this concern is worthwhile and constructive and it is now a fact of economic life.

True Resource Costs Must Be Paid. It is true that we have not been paying for the full cost of energy and other resources. We have been sending part of the bill to nature in the form of scars on the landscape, in polluted streams, and in many other ways. We can no longer do this. But as this situation changes it is necessary that consumers be educated to what the full cost of their standard of living really is. In addition, the high cost and risk nature of mineral exploration and development has to be fully recognized, and incentives have to be provided for people to put up the necessary capital. The easy-to-find oil has been found; the high-grade mineral deposits are being mined out.

Resources Needed, Nevertheless. Even with all the controversy that has come to the area of natural-resource development, there lies the basic fact that our livelihood is derived from the Earth. In some fashion these resources must be developed. There are trade-offs that have to be made, and the trade-offs are not so great as have been stated by some. For example, it has been estimated that 85 percent of the metal wealth of the United States has come from an area of less than 1,000 square miles. In regard to strip mining, I have personally visited several such areas in the West where modern practices are being employed. The end results are apparently quite satisfactory. In some cases even, the productivity of the reclaimed area has been improved over the original form. This does not make up for the way in which many of the West Virginia hills, for example, have been torn apart, but it does mean that a new, but workable, exploitation ethic has arrived, expensive though it may be.

Basic Freedoms Involved. There are also groups who would nationalize all our resources. Ultimately this means nationalizing all our lands, for land is the basic resource. This in turn would lead to forms of government that would submerge the individual and make the state supreme. This involves our basic freedoms, and this challenge should be clearly recognized and met.

There is no evidence that protection of the environment would be improved under total government control. Coal still has to be obtained by strip mining and holes still have to be dug to get at the copper ore. To make a roll of tissue paper a tree still has to first be cut down. There is considerable evidence from around the world that complete government control of resources leads to a very inefficient economic system, and the living standards of the citizens suffer accordingly. The Soviet Union has vast natural resources—more oil and gas than does the United States, for example—but the standard of living in the Soviet Union does not compare with that of the United States or Canada. The competition that our economic system generates promotes technological advances and efficiency. Together with a profit motive to make people work, they combine to make the economies of the United States and Canada the most productive and formidable in the world.

We need to be continually reminded of this, and hopefully in the welter of views and politics we will not forget it. Under our form of economy we can continue to draw on the financial resources of all citizens in developing the natural resources so urgently needed. In this way the public will have a concerned view of both sides of the problem—the huge cost of financing natural-resource development and the ultimate use of these resources. This is all to the good.

Invest in Ourselves. The rising tide of nationalism has made it imperative that each nation invests as much as possible in the development of its own natural resources. Self-sufficiency in all mineral and energy resources is an impossibility for any nation, but some are much better situated than are others. The United States and Canada are among the more fortunate in this regard, and, as foreign sources of raw materials become increasingly dear, one obvious solution is to invest in ourselves. We are now turning inward to take a new look at the resources within our borders. The intolerable strain that larger and more costly imports of raw materials puts on our balance of payments further insures a renewal of effort to develop our own resources.

Changes Are Inevitable. Change is the order of the ages, and therefore it is to be expected that the natural-resource investment setting also changes. Changes in social, political, and economic orders tend to come rather abruptly followed by a longer, more stable period. We have come through a rather long period of steady growth, and now we are in a time of more rapid change. The quadrupling and more of the price of gold and silver is one evidence of this. The host of environmental protection groups that have sprung up is another. The United States' loss of position as number 1 oil producer to Saudi Arabia in 1973 is now a fact of life. That we subsequently declined to number 3 world oil producer, due to rise in Russian production, also has become fact. But if history is any guide, we will adjust to these changes as they occur. Life must and will go on, and we have already begun to make some adjustments; fortunately we have the resources with which to do this

The "New Energy Economics." We have a "new energy economics" to contend with. It means that much of our industrial and transportation facilities are obsolete and must be rebuilt to different and more rigid standards. To survive in this era of new energy economics means we will have to undertake a capital-spending program both to develop new resources such as oil shale, coal liquification plants, and new and improved nuclear plants and also to build our cars, factories, and homes to new specifications. The remaining years of this century are likely to witness a worldwide capital-construction boom beyond anything ever before seen. All this will take vast quantities of raw materials, which in turn will require great amounts of investment capital.

Challenge and Opportunity of Transition. The world will survive and emerge a better world as we come to know and deal with the problems of living on a finite planet. The challenge is to make this transition into the 21st century in an orderly, wise, and thoughtful manner, drawing upon and investing in the resources needed to accomplish this and at the same time preserving our basic freedoms. I believe it will be done; it has to be done.

Ranging now from geothermal power and the atom in the breeder reactor to the prospects of lightweight lithium batteries to power electric cars (sodium batteries are a possibility also) and the advent of oil from oil shale on a significant scale, opportunities in the field of natural-resource investments have never been more numerous or diversified than they are today and will be in the decades just ahead.

3

Resource Position of the United States and Canada

THE COMBINED NATURAL RESOURCES of the United States and Canada are unequalled in any other comparable area of the world. It is very important also to note that the United States and Canada have in great abundance the ultimate resource, even beyond that of energy—the educated human mind. With our dedication to free public elementary and secondary education for all and low-cost higher education for those who can benefit from it, we have an unmatched reservoir of trained people who are able to effectively develop and use these natural resources. With abundant resources, trained people, and a relatively free and competitive economic system, the ingredients are here for a bright future. Perhaps the only remaining question mark is whether or not capital will be rewarded sufficiently to be attracted to the area of natural resources. Presumably, however, the need for these resources will insure that investment money is properly compensated.

Agricultural and Forest Lands. The Interior Lowlands and the Great Plains of the United States and Canada are by far the largest and most productive farming areas in the world. The forests of these two countries, especially those facing the Pacific Ocean, are superior to those of any other area of timber anywhere.

Energy. The coal reserves of the United States, measured in terms of Btu value (British Thermal Unit), exceed the energy

7

value of the oil of Saudi Arabia by a considerable amount. The oil shales of the Colorado Plateau and the tar sands of Canada together represent substantially larger hydrocarbon supplies than do all known oil reserves of the Middle East put together. Developing these resources, however, will take time and huge amounts of investment money, as we now have very few processing plants to handle these potentially great sources of energy. This is one of the tasks that lie before us.

The western half of the United States appears to have important quantities of geothermal resources, and the world's largest geothermal electrical generating plant is now operating in California. In hydroelectric power, the United States and especially Canada also are well endowed. In terms of the very important element, uranium, the United States and Canada together have more than half the known free-world reserves, about equally divided between them.

Minerals. Of the more important industrial metals, the rank in terms of world production by the United States and Canada is impressive:

	Rank in World Production	
Metal	*Canada*	*United States*
Copper	2	1
Iron............	3	1
Lead	4	1
Molybdenum	*	1
Nickel	1	†
Silver...........	1	3
Tungsten	6	2
Zinc............	2	1

* Minor but increasing.
† Minor.

Of the more critical metals, the United States and Canada are deficient only in chromium and manganese. However, the latter can be obtained in vast quantities from manganese nodules dredged from the floor of the North Pacific and elsewhere.

Aluminum is a special case, where abundant energy for the smelting process is nearly as important as is the raw material itself. The United States and Canada produce very little aluminum ore at present but are the world's largest refiners. Ample aluminum-rich clay deposits, however, exist in the United States. Aluminum can be obtained from them at slightly higher cost than from the conventional aluminum ore, bauxite, now largely imported.

In fertilizer ingredients, which are basic to world food supplies, the United States is the world's largest producer of phosphate and has the second largest reserves. Canada is the world's largest producer of potash and also has the world's largest deposits. The Soviet Union, however, is a close second in production.

In the minor but important minerals, the United States and Canada again are fortunate. The United States has more than 5 million of the 6 million tons of the world's known lithium reserves. Lithium is potentially important in atomic reactors of the future and in lightweight storage batteries. The United States also has the world's largest deposits of rare-earths and of boron. Considering their vast land area, the United States and Canada also have excellent water supplies.

Conclusions.   The potential mineral, energy, and renewable natural resources might of the United States and Canada is without parallel in both diversity and quantity anywhere. North Americans, as investors, are exceedingly fortunate to have such a rich and varied resource base in which to put their investment capital. The continuing flow of money from other countries, particularly Germany and Japan, into these North American resources is testimony to their importance. As we turn inward and begin to invest relatively more in ourselves and less abroad, we are assured that the potential is here for a rewarding future.

4

Investment Needs and Opportunities

IT SEEMS ALMOST REDUNDANT at this point to stress the general need for investment capital in natural resource development. The capital-intensive nature of this industry can be illustrated by many examples immediately before us. For example, the oil industry between now and 1985 will need to raise about $1.3 trillion in development funds to supply the oil needs of the free world. Only about half of this can come from profits. The rest must be new money, attracted by prospects of a reasonable return.

To develop the capabilities of 1 million barrels a day of oil from oil shale will require an investment of from $20 to $30 billion. Very large sums must be used to build plants for converting coal into liquid fuel and synthetic gas. The needs are great, but so are the opportunities.

Aside from simply investing in the presently producing deposits of natural resources such as metals and oil, there is another area of investment that, in effect, "discovers" new natural resources. This is the area of technology. At the present time there are very large low-grade deposits of nickel, copper, and other metals. There also are billions of barrels of oil locked up in the form of heavy oil (so heavy it cannot be pumped to the surface by conventional methods and equipment). Some heavy oil is now being produced by injecting steam into the reservoir rock, but much more of it remains. Solving the problem of efficiently exploiting low-grade metal deposits or heavy-oil accumulations would be worth billions of dollars.

If a technological advance can produce metal or oil from previously uneconomic deposits, this, in effect, "discovers" a new supply and is just as important as a discovery in the conventional sense. Therefore, look for investment opportunities in natural resources among companies that engage in this sort of research.

Still another area of investment opportunity is in the discovery of a new application for a previously little used resource. This resource, however, should be in reasonable abundance so that it can meet the new, larger demand. Again I cite lithium as an example; it is in only modest demand now, but new uses in batteries and in atomic reactors could greatly increase consumption. The United States has the bulk of the world's known lithium, and two companies of moderate size are the principal producers—Foote Mineral and Gulf Resources and Chemical. A breakthrough in lithium technology and use would have a significant positive impact on the earnings of these firms.

This illustrates another aspect of investment strategy. Many larger companies produce a variety of natural resources, with minor metals, for example, only a small part of overall operations. Certain smaller companies often have more of their eggs in one basket, so to speak. Also, these firms start from a smaller base so that a 10,000-ton increase in demand for their product may amount to a tripling of sales, whereas for a larger firm this might be only a small percentage increase. Putting money into smaller companies with more of their furture tied to a particular resource can therefore be a profitable approach. With regard to such investments, some of the opportunities (and pitfalls) as related to small mines and "penny stocks" of these mines are presented in Chapter 11 on "Investing in Metals and Mines."

5

Indirect and Direct Investment in Natural Resources

BY INDIRECT INVESTING is meant investment through the medium of a stock or in other ways whereby management is purchased. There is no direct involvement in the exploration for and/or the development or managing of the resource. Direct investment involves buying into a mine as such, drilling an oil well, owning timberland, or running a farm. For most individual investors and those persons handling investment accounts, indirect investment is the logical and common approach. To endorse a dividend check is much simpler than actually prospecting for, discovering, and developing the mine from which the dividend came. This is also a simple way to invest, in that one's investment is more liquid. You can usually sell a stock (particularly if it is listed) with no trouble, but peddling a used mine or a second-hand oil well sometimes is difficult. Obviously, also, if you are investing directly into some resource, you must have expert knowledge yourself or be able to draw upon such knowledge in others. If you don't know, get someone you can trust who does, otherwise stay out of the venture. It is as simple as that.

Indirect investments do not tie you down to one locality, usually. You can move your stock to where you want to live, whereas a direct investment frequently involves regular supervision and inspection to see what is going on. There should be no doubt about the fact that if you invest directly in some resource, you must take the time and make the effort to look after your investment. There are, of course, intermediate phases of this investment approach, such as forming a partnership in an oil- or gas-drilling venture and hiring an operator, but there is no easy road here either. You must keep track of what is going on or you will probably regret it. Have no illusions about the matter. Direct investment takes concentration and time.

It should also be recognized, however, that successful indirect investment also takes serious work and time. You have to continually study the matter. For the most part, however, information is available to you for the asking. There are numerous services that supply it, such as, for example, John S. Herold, Inc., for investments in the petroleum industry. Many brokerage firms put out excellent research reports and have very competent staffs to prepare the information. Deson Sze, who was born in China, is an example. He has had literally a world of experience behind him as he works in the metals research department of Harris, Upham and Company, and turns out regular reports that are part of that firm's continuing set of investor information services. These are available for the asking. Again, the North American investor is fortunate in the many good sources of information available on this very broad spectrum of natural-resource investment possibilities.

6

Renewable versus Nonrenewable Natural Resources

ONE OF THE THEMES of this book is the concept that we must gradually shift our economy toward one based much more than at present on renewable natural resources. I see this as a basic, underlying current in the investment approach of many firms and individuals today. I believe this trend will grow stronger with the continuation of problems of supply in the nonrenewable resources at what we would regard as reasonable price levels.

The renewable natural resources, of course, are principally timber and agricultural products. Underlying these is land. Companies with major land holdings in areas where climate allows a reasonable annual production of organic materials are in a fundmentally strong long-term position. More and more stock in this sort of company is being bought and locked away. Another renewable natural resource is water power, and those few utilities that are largely hydro are likewise in a good position.

It should be emphasized that renewable and nonrenewable are somewhat relative terms when viewed in the context of any reasonable time span. That is, although iron is a nonrenewable resource the quantities available are sufficient for many hundreds of years. Thus for the practical purposes of investment, iron supplies are not going to suffer from any short-term shortage. On the other hand, petroleum supplies in the United States are strictly finite when viewed against the rising demand, and we already have passed the point where domestic needs can be supplied from our own oil wells. We will never run out of oil in the United States, but we already have run out of oil at the old, low prices relative to many other commodities.

Prices will rise faster generally in raw materials that are non-renewable and therefore threatening to be in short supply. Properly timed investments in nonrenewable resources can produce a quicker and greater return than in the more abundant or renewable raw materials. However, there is, I believe, an investment balance to be achieved between these two classes of resources. Every portfolio looking toward the long-term future should surely include a broad base of renewable natural resource investments. The remainder of the portfolio should perhaps include the base metals, especially copper, and a selected scattering of the minor metals and non-metals that have prospects of exotic and new large uses. These might include lithium, boron, titanium, and several others.

7

Land

LAND IS ONE of the prime bases for fortunes made both in the United States and Canada the past 300 years. No doubt it will contribute much more wealth in the future.

There are innumerable cliches about land; one of the best known, ascribed to Will Rogers, is "They ain't making any more." Another version is "They make more people but they don't make more land." One real estate broker I know has on his letterhead a cartoon of an obviously very old gentleman with a long beard and cane over the caption, "Portrait of a man waiting for land prices to go down."

There is a great deal of truth in these messages. Land is basic—"Underneath everything lies the land." On the other hand, land not properly chosen even today can eat up a lot of money in taxes and produce little or perhaps no income. Between taxes and inflation land may not appreciate fast enough to keep even. Nevertheless, land has one proven merit over stock—it rarely if ever becomes entirely worthless. If it had any value at all when purchased, the price will not eventually go to zero as has the price of innumerable securities.

On the other hand, in fairness to stocks, they can be used as collateral for a bank loan whereas unimproved land cannot, except as an item in a financial statement. Also, with securities you are mobile. If you get tired of one area you can put all your stocks in your hat, literally, and go somewhere else. Try doing

16

that with 640 acres! Land also tends to take more management in detail than do stocks, as anyone who has fixed a fence, sprayed weeds, cleaned out ditches, or collected discarded beer bottles on his acreage can testify. I am one of them.

Also, stocks are more easily sold than is land. For listed securities, you can on any given day get at least some price for your stock and be paid five business days later. In times of depression or tight money, land is sometimes difficult to move.

The "Territorial Imperative."   Land, however, has a basic appeal. You can walk over it, kick it, feel it; there is something reassuringly substantial about land. People seem to have an innate instinct to own a piece of land. I do believe it really is an instinct, as so aptly covered in Robert Ardery's book *The Territorial Imperative* (Dell Publishing Company, 1966) which tells how animals including primates mark out their territories because a certain amount of land more or less is needed for their physical and psychological survival. People appear to have this basic need also.

Jim Kimball, columnist for the *Minneapolis Tribune,* upon his return from a vacation in northern Minnesota where he has a lake cabin, wrote:

"Joy and satisfaction is standing on a beautiful piece of land overlooking a quiet lake and saying to yourself 'This lovely bit of natural beauty is my very own.' "

Land as an Inflation Hedge.   Much has been written about this. Land and gold have been and continue to be used around the world as two common inflation hedges. How fast land has to rise in value to keep ahead of inflation and taxes is a matter that depends on just those two factors—inflation rate and amount of taxes. The old rule was that you had to have land double in price each nine years (8 percent compounded annually) to come out even. With higher inflation rates this number of years, of course, would have to decrease. Not all land by any means has met this investment criterion.

Nevertheless, there are those who with good reason have come to regard land as an internationally recognized form of money. As has already been stated, land does not go to zero in value except under very extraordinary circumstances. (I do know of one such case, however. A 200-acre farm was located on a river terrace. During a tremendous flood, the entire terrace was washed away, and now where the farm was is only air. The farm is now gravel, silt, and sand in a stream bed. Some may have reached the ocean). In the past two decades, land generally has done quite well against the onslaughts of inflation. However, with increasing taxes and with perhaps a slowing of population growth, this general fact may be altered somewhat in the future. But land surely will continue to have considerable merit as a refuge from inflation compared with many other investments, such as, for example, bonds, which some have described as "assured confiscation of your money."

In serious deflationary times, however, land can become quite a burden as taxes accumulate and even continue to rise while land values fall. Land is hard to sell then because nobody has any money. It happened in the 1930s and it could happen again.

However, the more likely trend seems to be that as population increases, the amount of land per capita will obviously decrease. This is the classic way that anything useful becomes more valuable—reduce the amount of it available per person. In parts of Europe land is rarely sold but handed down from generation to generation. It is beginning to become that way in this country. Land—good land, and especially prize recreation land such as lakeshore—is becoming "heirloom stuff," as one man put it.

Land and Leverage.   This is an advantage of buying real estate in general. You can buy it for as little as the owner will accept as down payment—perhaps 10 percent. If values rise, you can make 100 percent or more on your money rather quickly. It also works the other way, of course, if the land value goes down. But land (and all real estate) is a place where you can have a small amount of money do a large investment job for you. In inflationary times this is decidedly an advantage.

North American Land and the End of an Era.   The North American continent was the "great new land" to which immigrants came to homestead the wide open spaces that Europe had lost centuries ago. For 300 years we have rather freely tramped across this broad landscape, moving westward. Always there was more land, but now the situation has markedly changed. We have witnessed the end of the era of cheap, virgin lands. It is truly a historic development. The rules also are now changing rapidly, as zoning laws become much more restrictive and land uses are being arbitrarily set. To some extent the landowner has lost control of his land. In a few cases, zoning authorities have ruled that a landowner, after paying relatively high taxes for years on land, could not use the property for what had ultimately been planned—for example, to subdivide it. The landowner simply has had to keep it undeveloped and be locked into a situation in which the land has been designated as low value and there is little recourse. This tide of events is moving very fast, so it pays the investor considering a land purchase to look into the details very carefully.

Restrictions regarding septic tanks, road frontages, size of subdivided parcels, and many other matters all combine to make the landowner feel more of a caretaker than an owner. To some extent this has become the political thinking in the nation. There are arguments both ways; ultimately it seems certain that most of the country will be zoned in various ways in terms of land use. It is a trend that must be squarely faced by anyone investing in land. Nevertheless, the United States and Canada, when compared with the rest of the industrialized world, still have the freest land economies and the most undervalued real estate anywhere.

Zoning Information.   With this new era of the sharing of land-use decisions between landowner and the public at large have come numerous regulatory bodies. Most counties have planning commissions, as do the majority of cities of any consequence. It is important that you get a copy of the latest "1990 plan," or whatever the scheme may be, and study it for the implications it may have for land you are interested in acquiring. On the positive side of regulations, zoning not only can restrict use of land but it may also create land values very fast. In England, where land-use laws are well beyond ours, a farmer with 58 acres in Sussex discovered that his property's worth soared from $42,000 to nearly $6 million when the county council gave the go-ahead to residential construction in the area.

Other Factors in Land Values.   The statement that every piece of land is different from every other is a fair one. There are myriad factors involving land values and the physical aspects of the land. Some very good books have been written about this, a few of which I have included in the bibliography. It is not feasible to attempt to make a complete list of all things to consider here. I cite some more obvious factors, aside from zoning:

water supply—can you get drinkable (potable) water, and at what depth? What is the access to the land? Are there undesirable easements—such as a 75,000-volt power line through the place? (Many easements aren't obvious but can be found by examining the title to the property). What is the physical nature of the land—hilly, flat, bedrock at surface, or rich loam? If it is hilly, is it stable hillside or subject to landslide—some California and other hilly-terrain real estate may be even faster moving than the real estate dealer claims it will be—right down the hill into the gulch below. (If you want to see a classic example of a landslide in slow motion, go see where the city of Portland, Oregon, built its zoo.) Is the area subject to flood? In the "thousand-year" flood of 1964 in Oregon, which I witnessed, they had to open the drawbridge on the lower Umpqua River to let two houses and a barn float out to sea. It is a good idea in areas of heavy rainfall to drive around and look at the land during the wettest part of the year. In western Oregon, for example, where, as the saying goes, "Oregonians don't tan, they rust," this procedure has a lot of merit.

There are many more criteria that can be used as a checklist when considering a land purchase, but these are most of the basics. One further step is to actually go look at the land. Avoid mail-order acreage. Usually it is where things are so desolate even the jackrabbits have to carry their lunch. Be sure, also, to check the taxes and see what the assessor thinks the land is worth. He usually has a moderately good idea, though not always.

Four Basic Keys to Land Values. These are population pressures, accessibility, water, and timing. In regard to timing, land goes through certain "plateaus" in values. It remains on one for a time and then rises rather sharply to the next plateau. Land will be sold by the acre for hundreds of years as it is used for farming or forestry or grazing. Then one day it is subdivided and instead of being sold by the acre, it is sold by the lot. Ultimately some land is sold by the square foot, as in the case of commercial properties. We are not yet to the square-inch stage but we are getting there.

Land and the Future. Land, air, and water will not go out of style. Being basic to crop production and given the continuing rise in world population, regrettable though that may be, land can hardly but continue to increase in value. Historically, when currencies have finally blown up completely, the land still remains doing its fundamental job of keeping people alive. Barring a complete change in form of government, land will remain a prime hedge against inflation, and demand can only increase.

Land Investments. The subject of investing in various kinds of land is exceedingly complex, and it would be presumptuous to try to do anything but make a few general comments and suggestions in these pages. However, certain broad concepts are presented, along with some estimates of what the future may hold.

Subsequent pages deal with various categories of land and some of their individual merits and problems. However, it may be noted that you can invest in managed land through companies that hold large acreages and thus avoid the problems of personally looking after it. Some of these companies in the United States are Amfac, Arizona-Colorado Land and Cattle, Burlington Northern, Castle and Cooke (Hawaii and California land), Deltona Corporation, General Development Corporation, Horizon Corporation, Land Resources, New Mexico/Arizona Land, Northwest Cattle, Santa Fe Industries, Southern Pacific Corporation, Tejon Ranch Company, Texas Pacific Land, and Union Pacific Corporation. In Canada, the Canadian Pacific Railroad is a large landholder, and Peel-Elder is a land and general real-estate developer. Timberland companies are covered in chapter 8 on "Timber and Trees."

Successful investment in various types of land is complicated by many factors. The treatment given here to these land categories is brief, but hopefully the main points have been touched and the reader-investor can fill in the details as each situation warrants.

FARM LAND

Invest in gold? Iowa's soil produces more wealth annually than all the gold mines in the world. In the category of farm land, I presume, in effect, to include investment in all products produced on farm lands. Although these many and varied products are in themselves beyond the scope of this book, beneath them all lies the farm land.

Investing in farms has recently become a national mania, partly because of fear of inflation and partly because it is evident that world population is rather frighteningly catching up with the food-producing abilities of the land. Malthus was right, but technology, farm machinery, and hybrid crops had set back his prophecy about 150 years.

There is now little land left to put under intensive cultivation. Fertilizer is becoming expensive, and we have apparently pushed the "green revolution" in the form of high-yielding hybrid plants about as far as we can. Indeed, these crops have their own built-in fail mechanisms by being subject to certain diseases and other weaknesses as a result of giving away vitality and hardiness for the goal of production.

Nevertheless, when one looks at farm lands around the world, the focus invariably comes back to the United States and Canada with their arable, fertile lands beyond those of any other nations. Repeatedly, these two nations have been the salvation of other areas not so fortunate in food supplies. Even the Russians occasionally have had to depend on these sources for food. The fundamental facts surely justify regarding farm land as a most substantial investment—but at what price?

Along with the food shortages that have run up the price of farms, there is also the matter of inflation. Land, as already stated, has been and still is thought of by many as a form of money that is a shelter against inflation of the paper sort of money. It is difficult to know just what farm land is worth under circumstances when it is no longer valued solely for its ability to produce crops. Historically, land prices in Canada and the United States have gone through boom-and-bust cycles. It remains to be seen if we have entered the era of perpetual boom, or if a break in farm land prices will occur again. It seems probable, however, that farm surpluses, at least, will not be the problem in the future as they have been in the past—such as during the 1930s, when wheat was less than 25 cents a bushel.

With these generalizations, an approach to farm investment may be briefly examined. It is a field for experts, as soils, drainage, regional and local weather characteristics, and many other factors must be considered. For advice it is good to start with the United States Department of Agriculture's county agents. Most if not all United States farm land has been mapped by the

Department of Agriculture in considerable detail. Soil types are known and productivity records have been kept on many farms. What a farm is worth in terms of history of production can be fairly well determined. Better or poorer management, however, may make a considerable difference.

Another important consideration is size. In order to justify machinery of the sort needed to efficiently farm these days, substantial amounts of land are necessary—forty acres won't do unless it is a specialty farm of some sort such as in the intensive truck farming of California and Arizona. However, small acreages can be put together and farmed by someone who makes a business of this. Again, the county agent can tell you who farms land on shares, or under lease, and what are the going rates. In addition, there now are companies that make a business of farm management. They will look after your farmland and make decisions about crops, fertilizers, and all the rest for fixed fees, or sometimes for a fixed fee plus an incentive percentage.

Specialty Farms. We are just beginning to achieve the degree of intensive agriculture practiced in many other lands. This is possible with specialty crops such as fruits, nuts, holly, or Christmas trees, or by intensive truck farming of high value crops whereby a reasonable living can be made from a few acres. But this usually takes the careful management of an owner in residence. In a few cases small acreages of regular farm crops can be operated on shares or under contract of some sort. I do believe, however, that intensive agriculture is a coming thing, and opportunities are there for both full-time and part-time farms, especially as food prices continue to go up.

In regard to specialty farms, don't overlook the rising interest in fish farming, whereby a low swampy area can be dredged to form a small lake. Such areas, if properly managed, can be highly productive, as they have been in Asia for centuries. The U.S. Department of Agriculture offers booklets and advice on fish farming.

Summary. Overall, farm lands tend to adjust rather rapidly in terms of price to good crop years and poor crop years. More recently, however, the flight from paper money has distorted this historical relationship. Nevertheless, it would seem logical that in the long run what a farm is worth has to be related in some degree at least to its productivity. Therefore, at times when inflation has added an unreasonable increment to farm prices, it might be better to put one's money into other things. It is true that farming is so basic that there is little if any prospect that a given piece of farm land will lose any large fraction of its value. Farm land is a relatively safe but is usually a low-yield investment. It takes professional knowledge to properly buy a piece of land, and it takes skill to manage it. Both talents, however, can be bought by hiring farm management people first to evaluate your proposed purchase and then to manage it afterward. Certainly good farmland will never go out of style. It is as fundamental an investment as can be made, and it has been, for the most part, a slow and more or less steady road to increasing one's assets, though subject sometimes to severe cycles. These may be partly reduced in the future as the worldwide need for food becomes ever more severe.

RESIDENTIAL LAND

One of the profound events of this century has been the spread of the suburbs and the "move to the country." In Europe, rural land use starts right next to the urban apartment houses. Land-use pressures there are such that strict zoning is invoked to concentrate the city and preserve the countryside for farming. This trend has already started in the United States. When one combines this with the increasing costs of operating a car or of transportation in general as energy costs rise relative to other commodities, there is reason to believe that we will see in the future considerably less of an urge, or even the ability, to move to the suburbs or the country than in the recent past.

Also, zoning laws and regulations further restrict the more or less random use of country land for residential purposes than had been the case previously. Cities are beginning to put limits on how far they will extend sewer and water facilities. This further tends to concentrate population. In any case, this means that land that is now served by city facilities or that can reasonably be expected to have them in the near future is prime residential property. The days of going off into the hills somewhere and dividing up 40 acres into homesites are being severely restricted, although there will always be some opportunities for this sort of thing on a select basis.

Over the years, one of the best investments has been unimproved land on the outskirts of cities. The old rule was "start
walking out of town on main street and when they quote you
prices by the acre instead of the front foot—buy." That probably
is still a pretty good rule.

Factors in Direction of City Growth.   One of the most important factors in city growth is who has the drive, the money,
or the connections at city hall to extend sewer and water facilities into an area. But there also are some basic physical factors
that control direction of growth. Topography—the shape of the
land—controls it, for one thing. Chicago, Milwaukee, Cleveland,
and Buffalo are examples of cities bordered on one side by a
lake. San Francisco, Miami, and Seattle have ocean borders in
part. Denver and Salt Lake City have tremendous mountain
ranges behind them. In all these cases, adding 100,000 people
does not mean simply drawing another circle representing this
many persons around the city. It means a directional growth.
Sometimes this direction is quite limited, with a corresponding
rapid development in that direction.

But even communities in relatively flat areas with no strong
topographic control will show a directional growth trend. This
is noticeable to varying degrees when one flies over the Great
Plains area. In general, towns and cities in North America, other
things being equal, tend to grow directionally as controlled by
two factors: location of the main transportation arteries, which
simply means along highways, and into the direction of the
prevailing wind, which in North America is southwest. The reason for this latter factor is that the smoke, dust, and noise tend
to be carried by the winds to the northeast, and so the cleaner
and fresher environment is found in the direction from which
the wind blows, or southwest.

There are other factors to consider, however. One is how easy
is it to put in the underground sewer and water lines. Through
clay, sand, or gravel there is no problem, but if the lines have
to be blasted through bedrock that is another matter. I was once
asked to evaluate a piece of western land that had been offered
by mail to a group of Midwestern investors as a potential sub-
division. The details sounded fine. The property was on a hill
on the southwest edge of the city. The view was magnificent.
But the hill was there for a good reason—it was made almost

entirely of basalt, an exceedingly hard rock. You would have had to blast for every foot of sewer and water lines and for any basement areas.

In another instance I examined a property on a hillside. Again it was view property, but the hillside was clearly marked with the dish-shaped depressions and adjacent small mounds that are the tell-tale marks of landslide topography. If you are making any serious investment in land, it would pay to have a topographic engineer or geologist give you an opinion on any questionable matter.

Nevertheless, as our population grows there will continue to be tracts of land converted to subdivisions. Here are some simple figures that apply to this sort of situation. An acre contains 43,560 square feet; for the average house a lot of 9,000 or 10,000 square feet is ample. Allowing for sidewalk and street, about three to four houses per acre can be built. For apartments, there are usually limits set by the city as to how many dwelling units per acre can be accommodated in a given zone. Check the zoning before you buy.

Summary. Suburban or rural land for residential use may not be quite so attractive as in the past. Stricter zoning and sanitary regulations make the development of residential land a more complicated matter than it once was. In general, land closer in to town than formerly will be more in demand as transportation costs rise, especially the costs of individual, automobile transportation. The cities will henceforth probably grow more rapidly upward than outward. This will make land with existing city facilities or land located so that these facilities will shortly arrive appreciate more rapidly than in the past. Details of topography as well as soil type and rock conditions continue to be important. An expert opinion on these matters should be obtained if any substantial commitment is being made.

It should finally be noted that certain companies now specialize in buying land for investors, after presumably making all the necessary studies as to direction and rate of city growth, access, and availability of services. I have been in the offices of several such companies and what studies I saw were well done. It again shows that investment in land has become more a matter for the professional than the amateur. Still there will always be that little tract hidden away somewhere—a "sleeper" that can be made to comply with all regulations and that will show a nice profit for the investor who develops it.

WATERFRONT AND OTHER RECREATIONAL LAND

"Water is magic"—so says one real estate broker, and he is right. Push off your canoe a few yards into the lake and you are in a different world. Fly over such places as my native Minnesota and you will see how nearly every lake now has a rim of houses or cabins around it. In fact, in most areas there is little lakeshore left to be developed.

Development of lake property goes through several distinct phases. First, there is one house on the lake with considerable acreage around it. Second, the adjacent lakeside acreage is sold off and houses or cabins are put on it. Third, there is a ring of houses built back from the lake but with "lake access" to a small area on the lake that is held in common. Finally, with all lake frontage gone, including any more small pieces for "lake access," just the "lake view" is sold at a premium.

In my earlier book on natural resource investments, I detailed some of the factors necessary for good lake frontage (*Our Natural Resources: How to Invest in Them*, N.Y.: Frederick Fell, Inc., 1966). However, in the decade since I wrote that book, we have reached the point where virtually any sort of lakeshore can be sold, and it is now superfluous to discuss quality of lakeshore in detail— people are happy to get any kind at virtually any price. However, I might note that we now have a lot of artificial lakes, and there is quite a difference between these and the natural ones. If the artificial lake is small and not part of a river system, it may more closely resemble a natural lake in its behavior. But artificial lakes that are part of power and irrigation projects may fluctuate very widely in level (as much as 100 feet or more), and this can become a severe problem for the landowner. Always check to see how high up on the land the organization that controls the lake (commonly the U.S. Army Corps of Engineers, but also several other agencies) is allowed to raise the water. These lakes also are used for flood control, and in times of heavy rains the water is backed up to the highest legal level. In a few cases this was about even with the windows on the second story of the house of the fellow who didn't check this detail initially.

A natural lake, with a natural inlet and outlet, tends to maintain its level rather consistently and is substantially more desirable for building sites than is an artificial lake.

River frontage is another form of recreational land much in demand; again the supply of good acreage is limited and much has already been developed. Aside from noting the position of the historic high water in the area, the other precaution in regard to river frontage is to note which way the river channel is moving relative to the land in question. Rivers change their channels. They always have and they always will. Streams cut on the outside of a bend and fill on the inside, and the bend tends to migrate downstream. Normally this is a slow process. Yet, major changes can take place quickly during floods. You can suddenly lose a lot of land if you are on the cutting side of the bend in the river. Or the river will tend to move away from your land if it is on the inside of a bend. During the 1964 Oregon flood, I watched a full-sized house get "launched" into the McKenzie River as the bank was undercut. The house broke in half the first hundred yards and soon was just a loose assortment of planks. This might be said to have been a "rapid" depreciation of value.

Other Types of Recreational Land.   What is recreational land is somewhat a matter of opinion. Just a patch of brush in the mountains to one person may be a great hideaway cabin site to another. A steep hill, useful for very little else, can become a fine ski slope. Gun clubs, riding-stable areas, golf courses, and other types of recreational lands each have their own unique requirements.

If one wishes to pursue this matter it is first necessary to know in detail what all the characteristics are for the success of a given endeavor and then to go out and find the land. In this regard, familiarity with topographic maps is most helpful as is some elementary knowledge of how to read air photographs. I have purchased lakeshore property in Minnesota sight unseen because I could "fly" over the area in the convenience of my office in Oregon by means of stereo air photos. I could tell the type of vegetation and the depth of water along the shore with the aid of these photos. All purchases worked out well. This procedure can be applied to any sort of land, but it takes a modest amount of experience and training. Air photographs can be purchased for almost any part of the United States. The county agent or the county surveyor can usually tell you what coverage is available and who has it. For simple topographic maps, write the U.S. Geological Survey, Washington, D.C., 20242, and ask for the "Index to Topographic Mapping" for your state. This is sent free of charge and shows the names and locations of the maps and the prices for which they can be purchased.

Recreational lands often are created by the development of new roads. It is not a question of how far it is to a given locality but how much time it takes to get there. Birch Mountain Ski Resort might be five hours by the old road but only 3½ hours by the new road. That can make a lot of difference in the popularity of an area. Whenever a major new highway is built or an old one straightened or widened, the economics of the area served by the road will change. Recreational sites are some of the first to benefit.

Also useful in thinking about land is what its highest and best use might be. A marginal farm may be an ideal trail-riding area. If a barn is already there and the adjacent land is mixed woods and meadow, what was a poor investment as a farm might be a good investment as a place for boarding and riding horses, especially if it is near a large city. If you don't believe it, just try finding a good place to board and ride a horse within five or ten miles of any sizable town.

Summary. As open spaces become more crowded the demand for recreational land will grow even more rapidly than in the past. Each type of outdoor recreation has its own specific land requirements. What is a marginal piece of land for one use may be very desirable for another; imagination and foresight are the ingredients needed to make such a situation profitable. Land that has waterfront of almost any sort will continue to be at a premium. Natural lakes are to be preferred over artificial ones. Rivers have their own special problems as they continue to shift their courses.

COMMERCIAL AND INDUSTRIAL LAND

This, even more than farm land, is a complex investment problem. The requirements for various industrial and retail establishments are such that for some time now some companies have been "stockpiling" commercial and industrial sites for pos-

sible future use. More recently a host of environmental problems and restrictions have come to bear on the matter of industrial sites. The trend to more and more restrictions has placed
severe limits on locations for some industrial plants. One example is the siting of nuclear plants, with which I have had some
experience. The limitations are so severe that very few places
qualify in all respects.

Availability of a reasonably abundant supply of fresh water
is almost always a necessity. As the energy problem continues
to press in upon us, the efficiency of the steel-flanged wheel
against the steel rail—the railroad—will become more of a factor
again, and properties that have rail access will increase relatively
in value. What it costs to move five units by airplane can move
20 units by truck and 200 units by rail. This basic economic fact
cannot be ignored. Access to transportation is, along with water
supply, one of the principal requirements for a good industrial
site.

The study of possible commercial locations may involve traffic counts, shopping habits, and a variety of other factors related
to the particular commercial establishments concerned. There
are firms that make such "feasibility studies." It is a complex
matter, but commercial and industrial sites are surely some of
the prime land investments. A good long-term lease of your land
to a first-class tenant can involve you in a most pleasant sort of
exercise, that of stamping "for deposit only" on the back of a
large check each month. Or, if commercial land is sold, it is
usually sold by the square foot, which is quite a bit better than
by the lot or acre. If you are inclined toward such investments
and think you see suitable opportunities, it may pay handsomely
to investigate and ultimately invest.

UNDEVELOPED LAND INCLUDING TIMBERLAND

This sort of land is usually the least expensive, and there is
no very well defined use for it beyond its present one of relatively low unit value. Unless there is some unforeseen development such as a major new road in the area, or plans for a military
installation or industry that somehow needs just this location,
such land is quite likely to continue to be of low value and not
a very good investment. In fact, there is lots of land that does

not now pay its taxes and is not likely to for some time to come. I often wonder why such land is held at all, and from time to time much of it does revert to the county, particularly during depressions. This land is later sold for taxes, and it may go through the same cycle again.

Do-It-Yourself-Kit. There is a way, however, that undeveloped land can sometimes become a good investment, given the right piece of property and a chap with imagination and ambition. A friend of mine several years ago took over an unimproved piece of forest land, spent weekends on it with his family clearing brush, putting in roads, building campsites with picnic tables and fireplaces, and ultimately converting the acreage into a beautiful private forest camp. He did it at the right time, just as fees began to be collected in the U.S. Forest Service campgrounds and as developed space became scarce. The other day I asked him how his project was coming along. He said he had just sold it for "well up in the six figures," and the smile on his face proved it.

Another acquaintance, with an old station wagon, a chain saw, and an ax, spent evenings and weekends clearing small tracts of cutover timberland within commuting distance of a fairly large town where he lived. He first determined that the area would yield water from wells and that septic tank permits could be obtained. Choosing his acreages carefully, he bought several, built simple low-cost access roads, cleared out the likely spots where a house might be built, and on a sunny Sunday afternoon advertized three of these pieces and sold them all. Through his venture, he got a lot of good exercise, about five years' supply of wood for his home fireplace, and a handsome long-term capital gain, which in effect was his wages but paid to him at capital-gain tax rates and therefore costing him but half the normal tax. He said a rough calculation showed he made about $15 an hour on the project.

There are many opportunities like this where the small investor willing to work and with imagination can do very well, especially if he manages to buy the property with a small downpayment and thus has a leverage factor in his investment. The do-it-yourself kit consists chiefly of an ax, a shovel, and a saw, all made to run smoothly with the application of lots of elbow grease

Timberland. This is a special situation and in part is covered in Chapter 8 on "Timber and Trees." However, a note should be included about the large areas of the United States that grow trees of rather low value as compared with the well-watered and well-managed timberlands of the South and the Pacific Northwest. An example of low-value timberland where trees grow slowly is much of northern Minnesota, Wisconsin, Michigan, the New England States, and in the Rockies. The timber there is commonly used for pulpwood. It is cut on a local basis; people do it in the winter for want of something more lucrative. The pulpwood is hauled to the local paper mill and stockpiled for use the next season.

Investors should have no illusions about this sort of land. As in the case of farmland, the county agent can give you a good idea of the yield per acre. After deducting taxes and other costs, I have several times come up with a figure of about four to six percent on an investment of this sort, and it takes good management to accomplish even that. This kind of land must have a very low priority on any investment program. If you want 160 acres for your own to roam around in, that is fine, and perhaps you will make a few dollars off the pulpwood, but for the most part it is a marginal investment. Nevertheless, it is again true that it might prove to be better than many stocks and bonds. If the currency blows sky-high, as many people tell us will happen, the land will always be there. It is this fact that probably gives such land at least a portion of its currently quoted price.

Also, while walking around and enjoying their timberland, marginal though it may be, there are always things to be done for improving it. Thinning out the trees is a basic step for improving total tree growth. The low-value trees can be cut and the better ones left. Underbrush can be cut, thereby allowing more soil mosture for the valuable trees. In any event, it is again a do-it-yourself-kit situation where small investors can get a lot of pleasure and wholesome exercise and at the same time be rewarded to some degree at least for their time and effort.

MINERAL RIGHTS

This might be treated just as well under minerals, but as it is part of land transactions, I have included it here. In the United

States in general it is assumed that you own not only the surface of your land but everything beneath it down to the center of the Earth, and perhaps beyond if you can make proper arrangements with the Chinese. This is not always true in Canada, where mineral rights belong to the government in many areas.

Mineral rights not only include metallic minerals such as the ores of copper, lead, and iron, but also gas, oil, coal, limestone, sulfur, uranium, and other resources. It should be noted at this point, however, that in some areas of the West the surface rights are private and the government has retained the mineral rights to certain specific resources. In any case, the mineral rights can be separated from surface rights and sold separately. When you buy a piece of land you will want to know if you are also getting the mineral rights. If not, then this should be clearly understood by all parties. It is also possible to buy just the mineral rights and not own the surface rights. This is common practice in the oil business. The mineral rights may be owned outright by an individual different from the one owning the surface rights, or the mineral rights may be in the form of a lease from the land-owner. This lease will have certain provisions for rental payments and other matters. It should be carefully examined by someone familiar with these things.

If you own mineral rights and want to develop the resources, this will entail getting access to them on the surface. In that case there usually is a provision in the mineral rights or in the laws of the state that provides for this. Commonly, surface "damages" are paid to the surface landowner at some customary prescribed rate.

Investing in mineral rights is a very specialized enterprise. Geologists and others engaged in the oil industry are the chief participants in this business (see the section on "Oil" in chapter 9 on "Energy Resources," which describes the public land lottery for oil and gas leases in the United States). Mining claims, which are mineral rights on government land, are also bought and sold. Keep in mind that in the case of mining claims you have to do a certain amount of assessment work each year to keep up the claims unless they are patented.

8

Timber and Trees

"THE OCEANS are the mothers of great forests." This is true particularly if the land is on the side of the ocean facing the prevailing winds, as is the case of the western slope of North America. Here, along the Pacific coast of the United States and Canada, are some of the greatest forests in the world.

Very large and fast-growing forests also exist in southern and southeastern United States, where mild climate and abundant moisture combine to make for a long growing season. The relative flatness of the terrain there lends itself to tree farming in a very strict sense. The land can be cropped, plowed, and planted to trees just as with any other crop. The loblolly pine of that region can be cut for commercial use in just 20 years.

In total, the United States and Canada have usable and accessible timber resources far beyond those of any other two nations in the world.

Who Owns the Forests of the United States? America has more trees growing in its forests today than at any time in the past two decades. Three-quarters of the land that was forested when Columbus landed—about one-third of the United States —is still forested. Sixty percent of the forest areas are east of the Mississippi. New York state, for example, is 57 percent forested. Individuals own the largest share of the forests—303 million acres, or about 60 percent. The federal and state and local governments own 28 percent, and the forest-industries companies have 13 percent.

34

Investment in Timber. This can take two principal routes —investing in companies that have timber resources or becoming a timber owner yourself. Both routes of investment are considered here.

TIMBER AS A RENEWABLE RESOURCE

As has already been pointed out in this book, we ultimately must come close to a completely recyclable economy. Some resources are so abundant that there is no need for this approach with them, but as a whole the economy will gradually move toward that long-range goal of self-sufficiency of renewable natural resources. Timber and agricultural products have to be the basis for such an economy, with some products drawn also from the sea. According to Edward P. Cliff, one-time chief of the U.S. Forest Service, we are still growing more wood than we are using in the United States. So there is an even larger renewable natural resource base than we are now utilizing.

Sustained Yield. This is the goal held as the ideal for all forest management. Some companies, such as Weyerhaeuser, appear to have achieved it and others are working toward it. Certainly companies that operate on such a timber harvesting basis should merit special investor attention.

Super Trees. Aside from achieving a sustained yield, another important goal is the development of super trees, just as we have improved on strains of other plants. Most major timber companies such as Boise Cascade, Georgia-Pacific, and Weyerhaeuser are involved in genetic improvement of their timber stands. Results of these programs for much faster tree growth will begin to show up in another decade or two. Hopefully they will enlarge the earnings base of companies that are successful in thus producing more wood from the same acreage than previously.

TIMBER AS A VERSATILE RAW MATERIAL

From timber come the four basics of life—food, shelter, clothing, and fuel. This fact is hard to over-emphasize. This is not to say that trees can supply the entire population with these basics, but it can be done indefinitely for a limited population. Much research is being done to further improve this situation. Briefly, the potential in each case is this:

Food. Both sugar and protein can be obtained from wood. Protein is obtained by using the yeast method of converting wood wastes. Without too much imagination as I walk through the great Douglas fir forests of western Oregon near my home, I see sides of beef rather than trees.

Sugar can also be made out of sawdust. According to scientists at Louisiana State University, who did some of the original research, about 11 percent of sawdust is salvagable as sugar. From wood wastes Masonite Corporation has made molassas syrup called "Masonex" as cattle feed. Synthetic vanilla flavoring has been made from wood for years.

Shelter. This use of wood products needs little explanation. The range and richness of materials developed from wood products is enormous, and the American people live in the finest housing in the world largely because of the contributions of the timber industry.

Clothing. Wood cellulose is used in making rayon and related cloth fibers. Paper clothing is already a reality; the versatility of wood materials in this field is very large.

Fuel. An amazing number of houses are still heated in total or in part by wood from the back wood lot. In my own home we have two large circulating fireplaces. From my 16 acres of second-growth timber I have estimated that my house could be heated indefinitely. For several years I have heated the large office in my home with just the fireplace.

Beyond this elementary use of wood as fuel, methanol (wood alcohol) can be made from trees. With no changes in your car engine, about 15 percent wood alcohol can be added to your gasoline tank as part of your regular gasoline supply, giving slightly improved mileage as it burns. With only a few modifications your car's engine could be made to run entirely on methanol. Again, the needs of the United States, in terms of gasoline, are far beyond what wood alcohol could provide, but in a severe emergency that source of mobile energy could be used.

Grind up limbs and bark, add carbon dioxide and water, cook at about 400°C. under high pressure and the result is crude oil with a low sulfur content. The U.S. Bureau of Mines has estimated that if all the waste in the woods could be recovered, this would be the yearly equivalent of 31 million barrels of oil, after allowing for the oil that was burned to cook the wood waste. Of course, not all wood waste can be economically recovered, but this gives some perspective on what the potential is for synthetic fuel from wood.

Summary and Conclusions.   In total, there is hardly a more versatile material than wood, and the possibility of significant further advances in wood chemistry are good. Combine this with the fact that it is a renewable natural resource and the attractiveness of wood as an investment is obvious. Like any other investment, there are better times and poorer times to make commitments, but the long-term outlook surely is very favorable.

TIMBER COMPANIES

All major timber companies are integrated producers. That is, they own, manage, and harvest forest lands and process the raw materials into various finished products. There are many smaller companies that also do this to a greater or lesser extent. Some companies chiefly have cutting rights or are so situated relative to government forest land that they are in a strong position to bid competitively on timber sales there and thus supply their mills with logs. However, as the concern of this book is with investment in and not processing of raw materials, only companies with timber holdings are considered. Companies with major timber holdings include:

Company	Timberland in Acres (approximate)
International Paper	6,967,000*
Kimberly-Clark	11,600,000†‡
Weyerhaeuser	5,600,000
Mead	5,600,000‡
Georgia-Pacific	4,500,000
St. Regis	3,600,000‡
Scott Paper	3,000,000
Crown Zellerbach	2,900,000‡
Great Northern–Nekoosa	2,674,000
Union Camp	1,700,000
Boise Cascade	1,500,000
Diamond International	1,400,000
Potlach Forests	1,293,000
Westvāco	1,260,000

Company	Timberland in Acres (approximate)
Champion International	594,000
Louisiana Pacific...............	565,000
Olinkraft	560,000§
Masonite	510,000
Hammermill Paper..............	385,000
Longview Fibre................	371,000
Federal Paperboard	350,000‡
Pacific Lumber	305,000
Hoerner Waldorf	302,000‡
Brooks-Scanlon................	200,000
Pope and Talbot...............	125,000

Note: Burlington Northern has more than 1,000,000 acres of timberland in the general vicinity of its rail lines across the northwestern United States.
  * Also has 16,400,000 acres in Canada principally under government license.
  † 1,300,000 acres in the United States.
  ‡ Mixture of owned and controlled, controlled meaning that cutting rights are held.
  § Plus 100,000 acres in Brazil.

Location a Factor. More wood fiber is added to trees per acre annually in the South than in any other part of the United States. Union Camp and Westvāco have substantial holdings there. The northeastern and interior regions produce wood fiber more slowly. Scott Paper and to a lesser degree Mead, St. Regis, and Diamond International are in these areas, along with Potlach Forests, Boise Cascade, and Great Northern-Nekoosa. The remaining companies have holdings rather widely distributed or chiefly on the Pacific Coast, as is the case of Weyerhaeuser. There is no company with timber stands comparable to Weyerhaeuser and at such an initially low cost on the books.

Recreational and Residential Lands of Timber Companies.
Some of the timber companies have a good deal more going for them than just trees. As cities have grown, what were once just woods around an isolated lake or a remote stretch of ocean beach have now become choice residential and summer home sites. Other areas in the mountains are now ski resorts and cabin retreats; a few have become locations for development of year-round condominiums. Some of the companies with these sorts

of developments include Weyerhaeuser (Quadrant Corporation in the Puget Sound area), Pope and Talbot (Puget Sound area), Brooks-Scanlon (central Oregon), and Union Camp (housing and even shopping centers in the South).

Other Hidden Values. In addition to the worth of having recreational, residential, and even commercial lands evolve from their timberland holdings, timber companies also have mineral rights. Most of their lands are owned in fee. With this type of ownership the companies have rights to the minerals, which, in the South for Union Camp, Masonite, and Westvāco, include oil and gas and other mineral deposits. In the Pacific Northwest, Weyerhaeuser owns widely distributed lands that have some geothermal energy potential.

Also, in the South in particular, some land that formerly grew only trees is now being turned into regular farmland that produces much more value per acre in crops than it did in trees. Both Westvāco and Union Camp own such land.

Summary. Timber companies with substantial land holdings should be a part of every future-oriented investment portfolio. Land is basic to the production of renewable natural resources, and from timber can be produced all necessities of life. Some of these timberlands can be used instead for higher value residential and even commercial development; mineral rights are also a plus factor and include oil, gas, other minerals, and in some areas geothermal potential. Upgrading timberlands to more conventional farmlands also is increasing the productivity of timber companies.

The vast timber resources of both the United States and Canada are steadily increasing in importance, not only to their own economies but to the economies of much of the rest of the world. That these resources are renewable is of utmost importance, and it seems probable that securities of these companies will increasingly tend to be locked away in investment portfolios that are based on recognition of this fact.

TREE FARMING FOR THE INDIVIDUAL

There are mixed reports on this as a profitable enterprise, and I personally know people representing each point of view. I think it basically depends on the stand of timber involved and its size and mixture of mature and younger trees and also on how hard the individual works to manage it. A very nice income can be gained from 160 acres of trees located in a good growth area just by doing annual thinning.

Tree farming is for people with patience, as trees are a slow-growing crop. In the case of the Douglas fir, the chief tree of the Pacific Northwest slope, the mature tree ready for harvest is close to 80 years old. Therefore, one must start with a stand of trees well along, or at least with substantially mixed ages in order to realize any sort of profit in one's lifetime. In the South, on the other hand, the loblolly pine grows to harvest size in 20 years.

Some government aid is available to the tree farmer. In some circumstances, up to 80 percent of the cost will be paid for establishing forest-type trees (not including Christmas trees). The U.S. Department of Agriculture has numerous bulletins on tree farming, and its field offices will offer advice. Also, there is an organization called "The American Tree Farm System," a private organization of tree farmers started in 1942. It obtains both government and private support and will aid persons interested in this sort of enterprise.

SPECIALTY TREES

This category includes Christmas trees and such other trees as holly. Perhaps crop trees such as nut and fruit should be included. The raising of these specialty trees is more of a farming enterprise than it is of growing trees in the conventional sense. It is beyond the scope of this book to pursue the matter very far, but it should be noted that this sort of intensive land use for specialty trees can potentially provide the greatest income per acre of any type of trees grown. It is, however, a very time-consuming enterprise, to the point of being a full-time job if it is done on any sizable scale.

What are advertised as tax shelters and capital gains situations have been built on this sort of tree base. Buttes Oil and Gas Corporation organized a "Treecrop Company" with limited partnerships just as an oil-drilling venture or a real-estate syndicate would be put together. I am not aware in detail of the results of this sort of venture, of which there have been several.

No doubt careful investigation and thought should precede investment.

CONCLUSIONS

The fact that trees are a renewable natural resource, that they are a versatile source of all the basics of life, and that great timber resources exist in North America where they are not subject to the vicissitudes of foreign politics all auger well for the future of timber and timberlands as both short- and long-term investments. Improved strains of trees now being developed are only just beginning to be harvested, and the long-term potential of improved timber yields together with the probability of additional significant advances in wood chemistry and timber technology further recommend timber as an investment.

At least one company, Bohemia, Inc., has now reached the point where every part of the tree is used. Unlike even meat-packing plants where they reportedly use everything but the pig's squeal, even the bark of the tree (which formerly was waste) is now utilized. In this case it is the bark of the Douglas fir, which produces both cork equal to the best imported cork (up to now our only source) and very-high-grade waxes that also had to be imported.

The demand for wood products around the world will increasingly focus attention on the great timber resources of North America. With reasonable taxes and regulations the industry will surely prosper.

9

Energy Sources

IT HAS BEEN ESTIMATED that we Americans each have the equivalent of 300 persons working for us. (70 X 10^{15}Btu at 0.05 hp. per worker). In our modern industrial society energy consumption is the basic index of living standards. Energy also is the key that unlocks all other natural resources. Energy mines our metals and hauls the ore to the mill. At the mill more energy is used to process the ore (in the case of aluminum, a lot more). An abundance of energy allows for fewer than 10 percent of our population to be needed on the farms whereas in China 80 percent of the population must till the soil. It has been estimated that in terms of fertilizer and cultivation and insecticides each acre of harvested hybrid corn in the United States takes the energy equivalent of 80 gallons of gasoline.

Abundant cheap energy has allowed us to devote much time to things other than trying to scratch a bare living from the soil. In having this time we can conduct medical and scientific research, engage in the arts, and in general do the things that move society ahead on its many frontiers.

Energy is vital to our military posture and therefore to our national security and survival. Without abundant energy we could not provide the food supplies that the nation and the world need now and will need more of in the future. Having food and providing food is part of our national security.

How vital energy is to our economy and our most detailed

daily living habits has been forcefully brought home to us by various energy shortages, chiefly electricity and petroleum products. In many ways we are witnessing the end of an era, and in terms of cheap energy we have been living in what might aptly be called a "fuel's paradise." That paradise is now lost, and the true cost of energy will have to be paid.

Actually, there is lots of energy available, but at a price and with a time lag, as we shift from one energy source to another. In this regard, the shift from increasingly higher-cost petroleum products is overdue. The United States will never again be able to supply its own oil needs from its own oil wells. We passed that point at the end of the 1960s when the consumption and domestic production curves crossed at about 11 million barrels a day. Demand has continued to rise but domestic production has been falling, and even with our best exploration efforts the gap will almost certainly continue to widen.

It is urgent that we begin to invest in and develop alternate energy sources to petroleum, which currently supplies three-quarters of our total energy requirements. There can hardly be a more basic investment than in energy sources. At the same time, determining what will ultimately prove to be the wisest investments is a very complex decision. It involves some anticipation of new technological developments, an analysis of political factors both here and abroad (and many of these defy rational analysis and prediction), and a knowledge of the relative economics of various energy sources. Also, coming to the forefront in somewhat unpredictable ways are various environmental considerations related to the development of these resources. I do not pretend to present all the answers here, but hopefully this book will provide some of the basic facts on each energy source. The reader can use these facts to build and adjust his decisions as circumstances warrent.

OIL

About 2,000 years ago, one of the more important uses of petroleum in the Middle East was for the treatment of camel mange. Since that time oil has found somewhat wider markets and applications. The world runs on oil, as has been made so painfully clear to everyone these past few years. In the United

States, three-fourths of all energy used is derived from oil and natural gas.

Versatility of Oil. Oil is one of the most useful and versatile raw materials known. Its extreme portability as an energy source is outstanding. In this regard, nuclear fuels, which can only be used at plants that generate electricity for transmission by wire to places of use, is hard put to compete with a barrel of gasoline, which can be transported to some remote village in Alaska or to a logging camp at the head of an inlet in Labrador. Also, nuclear fuels cannot compete with oil's many uses aside from power generation. These include the manufacture of synthetic rubber, insecticides, and plastics. Grease to lubricate the wheels of industry cannot be made from nuclear fuels either. In fact, oil is such an exceedingly useful complex of hydrocarbons that it may eventually be illegal to simply burn it in the rather low-end use of space heating. That is one area where nuclear power can and will take over.

Where Is the Oil? By this time almost everyone is aware that the largest known free-world oil reserves are in the Middle East and Africa. A few simple comparisons may be worthwhile to put things in perspective. The average production per well per day in the United States is about 18 barrels; the average production per well per day in the oil fields of Saudi Arabia is about 14,000 barrels. The 48 adjacent states have an area of about 3 million square miles. In this area we have proved oil reserves of less than 30 billion barrels. Kuwait, at the head of the Persian Gulf, has an area of about 8,000 square miles, and in this small area proved oil reserves are in excess of 75 billion barrels.

It should also be noted that although there are no official figures, the Soviet Union has very large reserves of oil and natural gas, too. I am advised by reliable sources that Soviet petroleum reserves may be larger even than those of Saudi Arabia and that the Soviet Union may hold one-fourth of the world's total natural gas reserves. The geopolitical implications of this situation can hardly be overestimated as Soviet production rises and United States production tends to remain flat or even taper off.

It all adds up to the increasing value of petroleum, especially oil under control of the Western industrialized nations. The United States remains by far the largest oil producer among these nations.

Kinds of Oil Companies. There are basically five kinds of oil companies, using the term "oil company" in the usual sense of the word. These are:

1. A crude producer. This is a company that only explores for and produces oil. It does not refine or market its products. Examples are Superior Oil and the many small producing companies that sell their production to local refineries.
2. An integrated company. This is a firm that produces, refines, transports, and markets its oil. If it is a company that produces more oil than it refines, it is called a "crude producer on balance." If it refines or markets oil principally, it is designated a "refiner" or "marketer on balance." Most large companies are integrated and have familiar names such as Exxon, Mobil, Sun, Shell, and Texaco. Sometimes, crude producers have done better in terms of profitability than have refiners and marketers; at other times the reverse has been true. At present and for the foreseeable future the edge will probably have to be given to those companies that have the oil.
3. Refining company. This is usually a small organization and is only a refiner. It is set up to process locally produced crude oil from small independent operators.
4. Marketer. This company buys all its oil products and distributes and markets them through its own retail outlets.
5. Some companies may combine both refining and marketing operations but own no crude oil of their own.

The point of all this is that when you buy stock in an "oil company" you may be buying just crude in the ground or you may buy just marketing and/or refining facilities. If you buy stock in a fully integrated company you are buying all of these things. But if you want to buy natural resources you must buy a company with petroleum in the ground and, hopefully, with a lot of good undrilled acreage also under lease. When you examine such a company for possible investment, take a careful look at its "proved reserves" and "probable reserves" figures and also see where its oil leases are located.

Definition of a Few Terms. At this point, definition of some commonly used oil-industry terms is needed. A *barrel* of oil, as the term is used in the oilfields, contains 42 gallons (U.S.). To my knowledge, however, nobody has ever seen a barrel of that size. It is a theoretical unit used for calculations only. The standard oil drum you buy is a 55-gallon barrel. *Proved reserves* is oil that engineering and geological studies show definitely exists and can be recovered by existing technologies. *Probable reserves* are those that may exist near the proved reserves or in deeper zones yet largely undrilled. There is a wide range of interpretation for probable reserves. In any actual business deal, you don't pay much for them. There are also what are called *secondary proved reserves.* This is oil that can be recovered by water-flooding or steam treatment or by some method other than the ordinary flowing or pumping without further stimulation. Sometimes these secondary proved reserves are indicated separately—as they should be. It is more costly to recover oil from them than from those reserves that flow or can be pumped normally. Values given to primary proved reserves are greater than those ascribed to probable and secondary reserves.

Investing in Oil.   There are several ways to invest in oil. These include:

1. Form your own oil company and go out and look. (That is what Harry Sinclair did.)

2. Buy existing production. It is sold for various reasons—to settle estates, because of divorce problems, or because the owners do not have the technical know-how or the money to continue efficient operation. Buying oil is a very sophisticated business involving estimates of oil reserves and production costs, plotting decline curves, and factoring in a suitable dollar-discount factor. Occasionally some real bargains are found by persons who thoroughly know the business. If you have money for oil investments, be sure to get a partner or a consultant who is competent. This is a rather safe way to enter the oil business. If proper studies show the oil is there, it is virtually impossible to lose all your money—something that cannot be said for many other investments. And if a reasonable deal is made for all parties, a good profit should result. Sometimes it turns out that more oil is eventually recovered than was originally estimated. Occasionally it works the other way. But on balance, with the continual advance in producing technology, an oil field frequently will yield more than the original estimates.

3. Go into partnership with other investors and drill certain leases offered to you or that you have accumulated. In general,

the fewer the number of partners the better. Also, be sure to get a good "operator"—the person designated to run the operation for you. No amount of careful checking can be too great in picking that individual. He must be scrupulously honest and technically competent—and I put these qualities in that order of importance.

4. You can buy interests (partnership units) in drilling ventures that are managed by a general partner. The results of these drilling funds, as they are commonly called, have been mixed. They offer both tax advantages and hazards. The chief hazard is that too much of the profit is taken off by the general partner, and the losses are sustained by the limited partners—the individual investors. Some have done very well, however. You can, in some cases, buy stock in the general partner. Drilling funds have the advantage of having all the operational management and rather complex tax work done for you. They provide you with a tax form filled out at the end of the year that you can simply attach to your regular tax form and insert the numbers in the proper places. Tax accounting for oil and gas ventures is very complicated and definitely not for average persons to do themselves.

5. You can buy leases on lands that are potentially oil-bearing or gas-bearing and sell these leases later to oil companies outright for cash. Or you can sell them for cash and a small "override," which is a percentage of the oil produced, free and clear of any cost to you in terms of putting up money for drilling, producing, or other costs. This is a fine way to enjoy the oil business. If you can get a few good overrides on some long-life fields, then your chief exercise is stamping checks "for deposit only" and carrying them to the bank. I know a few people who have made it to that promised land.

In regard to leases, you can also enter the federal government land lotteries, which are held frequently by the Bureau of Land Management. The BLM will, for a small charge, send you regularly a list of land up for lease at various times. These are government leases on oil and gas for which the government will get a standard royalty on any petroleum found. This is not a competitive bidding situation. You simply fill out the application card for a particular tract and pay a small filing fee. Then all the cards for one tract of land are put into a hat, so to speak. One card is drawn and if it is yours you then have a specific time in which to put up the money for the lease. If it is any good you can usually get a commitment from somebody to buy the lease from you, so it is a relatively riskless investment. I should note, however, that a large number of applications are filed, so the chances of being a winner are rather slim. Still, it is a legal lottery in which you can play in the convenience of your own home. But to do it intelligently takes a detailed knowledge of the geology of the lands being offered. A lot of them are not very promising. However, the cost of application is small (currently about $10), and the rewards can be large. One of my geologist friends in Wyoming one day casually mentioned to me that he had just been lucky in drawing a 640-acre tract, for which he had been offered $30 an acre the same day. This figures out to about $19,000, which is a pretty fair return on a $10 lease-application investment.

6. Finally, you can invest in stocks of publicly held corporations such as Texaco, Standard of California, Exxon, Gulf, and many others.

I am reluctant to provide a do-it-yourself oil-investment kit here. Any substantial investment should be made in consultation with someone who knows the business—an experienced petroleum geologist or petroleum engineer. However, I list here a few things to consider in investing in oil stocks:

1. How much proved oil reserves are behind each share? (Note: gas and oil are found together, so gas reserves are also to be considered—see section in this chapter on "Gas").
2. How much is the oil worth in the ground at current prices? Oil in the ground is not oil at the buying point. It has to be produced and in some cases it has yet to be drilled. We used to assign a value of about $1 a barrel to proved recoverable oil in the ground. Gas prices were perhaps 10 cents per one thousand cubic feet (written *Mcf*). Those days are long gone. What value to assign oil and gas in the ground now is dependent on present market conditions, and with these changing times it is well to ask someone in the business. Putting a pencil to those figures sometimes will turn up undervalued situations. Small companies with good oil and gas reserves and perhaps a nice undrilled but prospec-

tive acreage position to go with them have frequently been good investments, as they often are bought out by larger companies at a good profit to the small company's shareholders.

3. Where is the oil located? Transportation is a factor, with producing costs being higher in remote cold country than on the Gulf Coast near a refinery.
4. What is the quality of the oil? There are many different kinds of oil, and some is worth more than others. "Low gravity" oil is heavy oil and is usually of lower value than "high gravity" oil. "Sweet crude" is oil with less than one-half of 1 percent sulfur in it and is to be desired over "sour crude," which has more than that amount.
5. What lease positions does the company hold? Some leases are a lot better than others. Only a geologist can tell how good a particular lease is. Even then it is still somewhat difficult to assign a figure to lease positions. You never really know what one is worth until it is drilled. Still a big acreage spread is worth something.
6. What are the political factors involved in the company's lease and operating positions? Obviously a lease position in Texas is safer than one in Libya or Venezuela. Many countries are firmly on the road to nationalization of all oil-company assets. This is a very serious factor to consider.
7. What are the other assets of the company besides oil? Many oil companies have coal, uranium, and other mineral resources as well as pipelines, tankers, refineries, petrochemical plants, and marketing facilities.

This list could be much longer, but it includes many of the basic considerations. An oil company's corporate structure, its assets versus liabilities, and its cash position are also to be considered but are out of the province of this discussion. Most important is a company's quality of management.

The changing scene abroad is having a major impact on oil investments. I personally favor companies with most or all of their assets in politically safe areas, which pretty much means the United States and Canada the way things are going. Perhaps I am overly cautious on this matter, having worked for an oil company in South America that was eventually expropriated without compensation. Surely one must weigh these risks against the fact that by far the richest oil fields are abroad.

To some extent a new sort of working arrangement is developing. Major international oil companies are being hired by foreign governments to provide technical know-how and transporting and marketing arrangements without themselves owning the crude oil. Actually this arrangement has been evolving for some time. In Indonesia all oil is government owned, but companies operating under contract to the government seem to be making out about as well as when they themselves owned the oil reserves. This is not true in all countries, however, so assessment of the political framework of any oil region is important to investment decisions.

Future Oil Provinces. Aside from considerable oil yet to be found in the Middle East and Africa, the greatest potential for future oil discoveries around the world lies offshore—in the South China Sea and southeastward to Borneo and beyond, in the delta areas such as those adjacent to India and the northeast coast of South America, and in shallow continental-shelf regions such as the North Sea and off eastern North America. Companies that have the technology to find and develop offshore oil are the best for future major oil investments. In actual practice the oil companies themselves do not have this capability in a strict sense. They contract for the necessary geophysical and drilling services. Companies that are leaders in offshore drilling include Global Marine, Offshore Logistics, Ocean Drilling, Santa Fe International, Sedoo International, Reading and Bates, and Zapata. In some cases these drilling companies have negotiated an interest in oil discoveries with certain foreign governments they have contracted to drill for, with the result that investments in them can be regarded to some extent as investments in oil.

Final Comments. Although there is a strong movement away from today's great dependence on oil, there can be no doubt that it will be a prime source of energy and a raw material for myriad products to well beyond the year 2000. Actually we will never run out of oil completely. The price will simply go up, so that the oil has to be used for higher-value purposes as time goes by. Investment in oil is as fundamental a natural-resource investment as can be made, but profitability will differ markedly among commitments. It is an extremely complex study and one that is subject to changing political tides, both here and abroad. Add to this the impact of technology as it allows us to develop previously uneconomic deposits and the impact of new discoveries. The result is a constantly changing picture. But in all these variables there will be many investment opportunities. Oil is a capital-intensive business; the amount of money that must be raised to provide for the oil needs of the world to the end of this century is staggering.

Investments in small domestic oil companies may prove both simpler and more rewarding for the small investor than investing in the large multinational firms. In these situations a discovery that is very little to a large company in terms of its total resources can mean a doubling or tripling of assets and income for the small firm. An example of this was the Bonanza Oil Company, which struck oil in Wyoming. The company ultimately produced 30 million barrels of oil from 540 acres, and its stock went from 50 cents to 20 dollars a share. Some small companies are both drilling contractors and producing companies in their own right. That is, they drill for others and may also drill for themselves on selected leases. Sometimes an individual has a lease but no money for drilling, so a joint venture is worked out. Many such situations have been highly profitable.

Every brokerage firm of consequence can give you a list of oil companies both large and small and recommendations on many of them. I would hope that by using the background information given here you have the basis for making some very profitable investments.

GAS

Natural gas was produced as long ago as 1000 B.C. by the Chinese, who drilled wells and piped the gas through bamboo pipelines for use in heating and lighting houses. Natural gas ordinarily is an incidental find when drilling for oil, although certain areas have more gas than others and some fields are largely gas fields with only minor amounts of liquids. Two such gas fields are the Panhandle Field of northern Texas and the Hugoton Field in Oklahoma and Kansas.

Natural gas is one of our cheapest and best fuels. Its price held down for years by federal regulations, gas was a bargain in terms of energy per penny and there had been a rush toward the use of gas. Now the true costs of energy are having to be paid, because gas is getting in short supply. Prices have gone up, encouraging the gas producers to find more of this most useful natural resource.

Some Facts and Figures.   Natural gas is sold by the thousand cubic feet, written as "Mcf." Price varies with locality. Gas produced close to major users, as in Pennsylvania, brings a higher price than gas produced in western Texas. Natural gas is chiefly methane but also contains other substances such as sulfur (in objectionable amounts in some cases, but often recoverable from such "sour" gas as a valuable by-product). When carbon dioxide, which is non-combustible, occurs in gas, it reduces the heating value (measured in Btu's). Good natural gas should have a Btu value of 1,000 or more per cubic foot.

When you start figuring gas reserves you quickly get into the trillions of cubic feet. Gas reserves of the United States are in the hundreds of trillions, but reserves have been dwindling because we have not been discovering as much gas as we are using. Some slowing or reversal of this trend may take place with the advent of higher gas prices. If America is to be reasonably supplied with gas the prices must go up. Gas has been woefully underpriced compared with oil. With the energy value of 6,000 cubic feet of gas equal to one barrel of oil, buying gas for 18 cents a thousand, as was done for so many years, was like buying oil for $1.08 a barrel. But with oil actually selling even then for more than $3 a barrel, no wonder there was a strong trend to use of natural gas!

Where Is the Gas?   For the most part, gas is where the oil is. However, this has been a problem, as oil can be much more easily transported. Now, natural gas can be liquified and transported in huge refrigerated tankers to distant areas. Algerian gas goes to Europe this way. Previously, gas in the more remote oil fields had to be flared (burned away) or pumped back underground.

Outlook.   Demand for gas will rise as long as supplies can be had at reasonable prices. It is a very useful substance, not only for heating but as a raw material for many products. Because of its dwindling reserves, the United States is basically not now self-sufficient in gas. This trend is likely to continue.

Canada has some very large gas reserves, but restrictions on gas exports are appearing, and no doubt more gas will be used in Canada, such as for the manufacture of petrochemicals, than has been the case previously. Natural gas, mostly from the Middle East and North Africa, will be imported by tanker in liquid form in increasing quantities.

Investment. Much of what has been said about investment in oil applies to natural gas. Like oil companies, there are gas companies—and gas companies. Some are strictly distributors, and others are integrated. However, as the retail gas business is a utility subject to government rate regulation, production and exploration activities usually are kept at "arm's length" from the marketing company through the medium of subsidiaries. An example of this is Panhandle and Eastern Pipeline, which owns a gas-producing subsidiary, Anadarko Production Company. For the most part, companies that have the oil also have the gas, although there are exceptions.

Again, as in the case of oil companies, brokerage firms have information on gas-producing companies. The investment picture changes so much that you can only start with certain basic facts, as given here, and then draw your own conclusions from the particular circumstances at the time. Gas reserves undoubtedly will be increasingly valuable, and any substantial gas discovery should greatly brighten the outlook of a company. Small firms that have the good fortune of finding large gas reserves are frequently bought out by larger companies, and this makes for a relatively quick capital gain for the shareholders of the merged company. There is a strong tendency to consolidate oil and gas holdings into larger companies. The economics of the industry work that way. I personally favor looking into the smaller gas-producers as investment media, because they are, like their oil-producer counterparts, simpler to analyze than are the larger, diversified corporations.

Gas has fewer production problems than does oil. It flows; you don't have to pump it. Some well service is needed from time to time but it is simpler than in oil production.

The large gas deposits yet to be discovered undoubtedly will be in the same areas as the probable future oil discoveries mentioned earlier. Because of the remoteness of these areas, most of the gas will have to be liquified to be brought to market.

Synthetic Gas. "Syngas" can be made either from coal or oil shale. The chief ingredient added in each case is hydrogen. The technologies for doing this are well known in general. The challenge is to make them more efficient. It is a matter of determining the most economical processes and then building the processing plants. The capital investment, however, will be very large. Synthetic gas will ultimately be a significant part of the U.S. energy supply but only after a large-scale commitment of both money and raw materials. This is just beginning. Present natural gas prices, however, do make syngas competitive, and a trillion cubic feet or more of it is expected to be obtained from coal annually by 1985. Chiefly it is the major oil and coal companies that will be the synthetic gas producers, and therefore avenues of investment are in these firms (see section in this chapter on "coal").

TAR SANDS

These are sands saturated with very heavy oil. They either are ancient oil fields brought near or to the surface of the Earth by uplift and/or erosion or are the results of the updip migration of oil at greater depth. They exist in many parts of the world including the United States (Oklahoma, Wyoming, and elsewhere), Venezuela, and especially in Alberta, Canada. Here the Athabasca tar sands constitute one of the greatest known reserves of petroleum hydrocarbons in the world, far outweighing the combined previously known liquid oil reserves of the United States and Canada. There are four separate Canadian tar sand deposits, totaling about 10,000 square miles. Two are near Fort McMurray, about 275 miles north of Edmonton, and one each is at Peace River and at Cold Lake. Estimates vary, but these tar sands may contain as much as 600 billion barrels of oil, of which 300 billion may be recoverable. The present high cost of foreign oil makes these deposits very attractive, and, in fact, they have been producing oil in a small way for some time. Production is now being expanded.

Process of Oil Recovery. The process of recovering the oil is simple in theory. The sands are mined and cooked and the heavy tar thus removed converted by various means to a variety of petroleum products. In actual practice, however, the problems are severe. For one, the tar sands cause constant break-downs of heavy machinery by clogging radiators and getting into other parts. For another, the large tires on some of the equipment, at last report, cost $9,000 each and are literally "eaten up" by the gritty sands. And the people who work the oil sands want high wages for the hardships encountered by temperatures that drop to 50 degrees below zero or lower at times.

Production. Ultimate output is hard to predict, but present production is almost 100,000 barrels of oil a day. Prospects are good for increasing that amount by several times.

Investment. The Sun Oil Company, owner of about 80 percent of Great Canadian Oil Sands, Ltd., (the remainder is owned by Canadian investors), is the pioneer on these tar sands and has had a plant operating for some time. Profitability, however, has been low, as technical problems had to be ironed out. Syncrude is a more recent entry and includes Gulf Oil, Imperial (an Exxon affiliate), Cities Service Athabasca, Ltd., and Arco. A major tar sand interest is in a joint venture of Shell Oil Company of the United States and Shell Canada, Ltd. The future is promising for these vast hydrocarbon reserves if some of the more vexing operational problems can be solved and if taxes and other political factors are favorable.

Other Tar Sand Deposits. The quantities around the world are very large, but problems of distance, political climate, and simply the competition from cheaper and more convenient conventional crude oil supplies have all militated against development. Now, however, the rising price of oil is increasing interest in these tar deposits. Those in Venezuela are especially large. In the United States, tar sands have been used locally for many years as road-sufacing material. No doubt an upgrading of this end use will be attempted if petroleum prices continue to climb.

GILSONITE AND SIMILAR DEPOSITS

Gilsonite is a solid bituminous material, named after S. H. Gilson, owner of the deposit where it was first discovered in Utah. It occurs in veins in shales in eastern Utah and western Colorado. This sort of solid hydrocarbon occurrence is known in many parts of the world. The material goes under a variety of names, mostly derived from geographic locations or persons. These include grahamite, uintaite, albertite, and wurtzlite. As veins, gilsonite deposits may be from a few inches to as much as 20 feet wide and are regarded as fossil or dead-oil seepages from which the gaseous and liquid fractions have been lost to the atmosphere leaving only solid residues behind.

Gilsonite has been mined locally and used for various products, including the manufacture of gasoline. For many years a plant producing gasoline operated near Grand Junction, Colorado, where gilsonite was obtained in slurry form (ground up and mixed with water) through a 72-mile pipeline from mines near Vernal, Utah.

This plant has now been sold, as the gilsonite has been found to have higher-end uses than as gasoline and is now converted into paints, varnishes, inks, automotive sealers, building materials, and plastic extenders. The mines are operated by the American Gilsonite Company. Any such deposits of solid bitumen in quantity would have merit and should be considered if an investment opportunity arises.

OIL SHALE

The term "oil shale" is applied to a rock that contains no oil and is not shale. It is actually a material called marl, and it contains organic accumulations of kerogen, which, upon heating, yields a substance like crude oil from which various conventional oil products can be made. Oil shale deposits were formed in one or possibly two ancient lakes in Wyoming, Utah, and Colorado about 60 million years ago. The richest deposits are near Grand Valley, in western Colorado.

Oil shales exist in many countries. Commercial developments have taken place at one time or another in Manchuria, Brazil, Estonia, Sweden, Scotland, and Russia, as well as in other areas. In eastern United States small quantities of "oil" were recovered from these shales well before the discovery of oil by drilling in Pennsylvania in 1859.

In western United States the Ute Indians told white settlers about mountains that burned. And the story is related of a pioneer who built a log cabin in Rio Blanco County, Colorado, and invited white and Indian friends to his housewarming. It proved to be warmer than expected, when the fireplace, built out of oil shale, caught fire and burned down the cabin.

Large Quantities in the West. There is the oil-equivalent of two trillion barrels (not million, or billion, but trillion—the only figure on this Earth that is still larger than the national debt) in the Colorado Plateau oil shales. It is estimated that about one-quarter of this amount, or 500 billion barrels, might be recovered economically, although some estimates are considerably lower. Some beds are too thin and other too deep to be mined economically.

How and When? The advent of the oil shale industry in the United States, it seems, has always been about "five or ten years ahead." This has been true for the past 40 years or more. But with the dramatic rise in oil prices that took place in the early 1970s and the basic fact that the United States can no longer supply its needs from its own oil wells, the time finally seems at hand for development of oil shales. There are two principal methods. One is simply by underground mining of the shale, and then grinding it to proper size and putting it into a rotating heated cylinder called a retort. A large number of very hot ceramic balls are added in order to distribute the heat evenly through the crushed rock, thus increasing the amount of oil recovered. This process is generally known as the Tosco Process and is employed by Colony Development Corporation, a consortium of companies headed by Arco.

The other method is through just enough underground mining to allow for the placing and touching off of explosives. Then the shattered rock is ignited, and the hydrocarbons produced in liquid and gaseous form underground are piped to the surface. Occidental Petroleum has been researching this approach.

There are a number of problems with oil shale development. One is that a certain amount of water is needed to support the oil shale facilities, which lie at the head of the Colorado River drainage. That river system is already fully taxed to support the populations downstream, and loss of water in its gathering areas would cause political and economic repercussions. Also, the capital cost of oil shale facilities is very large. I have been advised that some 20 to 30 billion dollars is the probable cost of an oil shale facility that will produce one million barrels of oil a day by 1990. So it is clear that oil shale is not an immediate large-scale substitute for conventional petroleum sources. It can only be gradually phased into our energy economy.

Investment. About 80 percent of oil shale lands are owned by the federal government. Lease sales were held in 1974 and several blocks obtained by oil company groups. However, some companies years ago obtained sizable oil shale positions of their own in the Colorado Plateau.

These private holdings are distributed among companies approximately as follows:

Company	*Thousands of Net Acres*
Atlantic Richfield (Arco)..............	20
Cities Service.......................	9
Equity Oil..........................	10
Exxon Company, U.S.A...............	11
Getty Oil...........................	24
Gulf Oil	4
Marathon Oil.......................	1
Mobil Oil	20
Shell Oil...........................	6
Standard Oil of California	41
Standard Oil of Indiana	3
Standard Oil of Ohio (Sohio)	10
Superior Oil........................	7
Tenneco	1
Texaco	19
The Oil Shale Company..............	7
Union Oil of California	30
	228

Western Oil Shale Corporation, with 76,000 acres, holds the largest single oil shade acreage position in Utah. However, these are leases and not fee ownership and are for 20 years, expiring at various times to 1987. Texas American Oil owns 44 percent of Western Oil Shale Corporation. There is an estimated 8.6 billion barrels of oil equivalent in these holdings, but there is no certainty how much if any can be recovered economically in the next decade.

The most aggressive oil shale operator in the Colorado Plateau is Colony Development Corporation, consisting of Atlantic Richfield, Oil Shale Corporation, Ashland Oil, and Shell Oil. Each has a 25 percent interest, with Atlantic Richfield the operator. A full-scale plant with a capacity for 47,000 barrels a day, has been designed which would cost in excess of $500 million. By-products would include liquefied petroleum gas, sulfur, ammonia, and coke. No firm date for construction of the plant has been set, however, due to the unsettled economic situation.

There is no early large increase in earnings likely to accrue to any of these companies from oil shale operations. It will come slowly, but those firms with large oil shale holdings have assets that could be very valuable if a federal oil shale lease sale held in the mid 70s is any indication. The winning bid was $105 million for 5,000 acres—$21,000 an acre, or nearly 50 cents a square foot.

A per-share-of-stock breakdown of possible amounts of oil from oil shale holdings for some companies shows that there are 75 barrels behind each share of Arco stock, 224 barrels per share of Getty, 73 barrels per share of Sohio, and 140 barrels per share of Union. There is no certainty, of course, when these potentials may be realized.

It does seem certain, however, that the large price rise of oil from the Middle East and elsewhere has moved up the timetable for oil shale development, and shale oil appears to be fully competitive with conventional oil sources. It might be noted that a valuable by-product of oil shale mining could be the mineral dawsonite, an aluminum ore that is present in some quantity in these deposits. This potential new source of aluminum may be available at a time when foreign sources of the conventional aluminum ore, bauxite, appear to be greatly increasing their prices and restricting exports.

COAL AND PEAT

Coal, one of the oldest fuels, was used by the Chinese 2,000 years ago. It is one of our newest fuels in a sense, as the demand for coal is now rising more rapidly than ever before.

Coal is the partially decayed remains of freshwater plants. Of total estimated world coal resources, the United States has about one-fifth. These deposits are widely distributed in what are called coal basins, which actually were and in some cases still are structural depressions in the Earth's crust. These coal basins were sites of swamps where the coal-forming plants grew. Plant remains (like leaves, tree trunks, and roots) are clearly visible in many coal deposits, especially the younger ones. Fossils found in some of the coal beds include a dragonfly with a wing-spread of nearly 30 inches and fossil cockroaches, indicating that these creatures, which unfortunately are still doing very well, have had a long and successful career.

Peat is simply the initial stage of coal formation. Peat deposits are widely distributed across northern United States and are even more abundant in Canada. They are used as local fuel supplies and in the distant future, when coal resources have diminished, might become more important economically than now.

Brief History of Coal Development in the U.S. Coal production rose rather steadily until the depression of the 1930s, when demand dropped markedly. Subsequently, coal faced severe competition from petroleum, as oil-burners were installed in homes and diesel-electric locomotives became dominant on the railroads. Now, however, as oil reserves decline and as oil from abroad has become much more expensive and led to an adverse balance of payments, interest in domestic coal deposits is rising. There has been a virtual "coal rush," especially to the West, where large strippable deposits of low-sulfur coal exist.

Kinds of Coal. Coal is classed as anthracite, bituminous, sub-bituminous, or lignite. This order is in decreasing amount of fixed carbon and increasing amount of moisture in the coal. Lignite, for example, will slack—that is, crack and shrink—when it is dried, as it contains up to 25 percent water by volume when mined. Anthracite occurs chiefly in the tightly folded rocks of Pennsylvania and West Virginia. Much of the accessible anthracite has already been mined. The bituminous coals are in the Appalachian Coal Basin, which stretches from Pennsylvania to Alabama, and also in Ohio, Indiana, Illinois, Kentucky, Kansas, Colorado, and Oklahoma. Utah and New Mexico also have sizable coal reserves; Texas has lignites. The huge Fort Union Coal Basin occupies parts of the Dakotas, Montana, and Wyoming.

Uses. Coal is used chiefly for fuel to produce electric power, for space heating, and for various industrial processes, chiefly the production of metals, of which steel is the most important. But coal also is a versatile raw material, and literally thousands of products are made from it, including dyes, chemicals, synthetic fibers (such as nylon), and pharmaceutical products.

Synthetic Oil and Gas from Coal. The technologies for converting coal to liquid fuel or to gas are well known. Hitler ran his Panzer tank divisions in part on oil derived from coal. In making both oil and gas from coal, the chief step is to add hydrogen. The U.S. Bureau of Mines and several companies are working on increasing the efficiency of this process. With luck and a large capital investment we might, by 1985 or so, produce as much as two million barrels a day of oil from coal, and one trillion cubic feet of gas annually. It is most likely that the oil or coal companies of today will be producing these coal-derived fuels in the next decade and beyond. Conoco is one such company. Certain others, such as Koppers Company, however, are involved in research and hold basic patents on some processes.

Resources. The present ratio of recoverable coal to annual demand in the United States is about 2,500 to 1; coal is by far our most abundant fossil fuel and has a Btu content far in excess of the known oil resources of Saudi Arabia. The United States, therefore, has a very important energy base in this resource. The problem is how to utilize coal effectively in our present energy economy, how to adjust our economy to coal in the future, and how to do this all in an environmentally acceptable manner.

Investment. Major coal resources are held by a number of companies, including the Consolidation Coal Division of Continental Oil, the Peabody Coal Division of Kennecott, Exxon Company (U.S.A.), the Island Creek Coal Division of Occidental Petroleum, Anaconda, American Metal Climax, Utah International (coal both in the U.S. and Australia), Westmoreland Coal, and Pittston Company. There are many others with lesser amounts. Both the Union Pacific and the Burlington Northern railroads have large coal deposits, and Pacific Power and Light has extensive coal leases, chiefly in Wyoming. Montana Power and Montana-Dakota Utilities also hold substantial coal positions.

There are some 20 fairly large and a number of small coal

companies in Canada. Major producers include Alberta Coal, Coleman Collieries, and Kaiser Resources.

The basic situation of coal is strong, and demand will surely continue to rise for the foreseeable future. There are, however, some problems to be resolved that are briefly commented upon here.

Environmental and Mining Problems. The stripping of coal is destructive to the landscape, particularly in hilly country such as in West Virginia, Pennsylvania, Kentucky, and parts of Ohio. Turning over coal-bearing strata also unearths minerals such as sulfur- and iron-yielding pyrites, which, on weathering, pollute the streams and stream valleys. The problems have been and continue to be severe in many areas. In the West the coal deposits are in relatively flat-lying country, for the most part. Reclamation of these lands is easier than in the more mountainous areas of the East. I have seen some of these reclaimed coal lands in Wyoming and Montana, and the results appear to be quite satisfactory.

Underground coal mining has been a hazardous occupation, with the problem of potential fires and the danger of explosion as well as of asphyxiation from gases. "Black lung" has been a critical problem for coal miners, and prevention calls for large investments in air-cleaning equipment. All these difficulties must be solved to keep the coal business viable. There are and will be many conflicts as a result, and though the problems will probably be solved it will be at a cost of considerably higher priced coal to the consumer. Again there is really no alternative but to ultimately face the true costs of energy, which we have so long been avoiding.

With these considerations in mind, investment in coal should still be very worthwhile; indeed, the coal mining industry needs huge inputs of capital to meet the more rigid mining specifications and to exploit new sources of coal. The combination of new technologies in coal mining and processing and the greatly increased demand for coal will create many investment opportunities.

URANIUM

Uranium was discovered in pitchblende in Germany in 1789, but it was not until the advent of the atomic bomb in 1945 that uranium received any very widespread notice. This single element has profoundly altered our lives and our outlook and will probably continue to do so to the year 2000 and beyond. The "atomic age" is a very real thing touching all of us.

Looking beyond military applications, the chief use of uranium is in the production of electrical power in atomic reactors. These reactors are of several designs, and though continued improvements and changes in them are being made, uranium will remain the basic energy source for all that will be operative for the next decade and more. Other energy sources, such as thorium and lithium, could come into prominence later.

Natural Occurrence.   Uranium is fairly widespread, occurring in several types of geological settings in small amounts. Granites contain uranium, as do black shales and phosphate deposits. Uranium originally comes out of igneous (once molten) rocks, but when these rocks are weathered the uranium in them oxidizes, becomes highly mobile, and can move considerable distances before being trapped. Finding a "uranium trap" is the role of the uranium exploration geologist. Most of the uranium deposits of the United States are in sedimentary rocks such as the sandstones and shales of the Colorado Plateau and in some of the basin areas of Wyoming. There are several uranium minerals, one of them a yellowish mineral called carnotite. Two logs discovered in Utah, were completely replaced by carnotite and in themselves were a valuable mineral deposit.

Some lignite coals in the Dakotas and Montana have uranium in them in sufficient concentration that utilities using this coal can sell the ash as uranium ore.

The largest uranium reserves in the free world are in the United States, Canada, and South Africa. Other deposits are known in Australia, Sweden, and France. The Soviet Union appears to have significant uranium reserves but the Soviet government does not choose to discuss the matter.

Outlook.   The uranium business has gone from boom to bust and is slowly coming back to what might be called a continuous modest boom. The predictions of the U.S. Bureau of Mines are that ". . . during the late seventies and early eighties, uranium prices will advance a little faster during this time, and then climb sharply and steadily during the remainder of the century reaching an estimated level of $17.00 a pound for uranium oxide in the year 2000." This prediction is in terms of constant-value dollars and relates to the price of uranium oxide ("yellowcake") in the middle seventies of about $7 a pound. So prices of uranium are likely to more than double by the end of this century. If you have any old uranium stocks from the 1950s, soak them off your basement wall and return them to your safety deposit box. They may be worth something after all.

The uranium business is coming back and this time will remain in good health for the indefinite future. Worry henceforth will be about shortages rather than surpluses.

Investment.   With the excellent future anticipated for uranium, those companies holding uranium deposits are in a good position. Kerr-McGee Industries reportedly has about 25 percent of the known uranium reserves of the United States. Other companies with substantial uranium interests are Atlas Corporation, Federal Resources, Anaconda, Homestake, Ranchers' Exploration, United Nuclear, Western Nuclear, Midnight Mines, Getty Oil, Continental Oil, Gulf Oil, Utah International, and Exxon Company, U.S.A.

In Canada, Denison Mines, Ltd., has a very large deposit, and Eldorado Mining and Refining, Ltd., holds substantial reserves. Rio Algom Mines, partially owned by Rio Tinto-Zinc, a British Company, has interests in Utah and Canada.

THORIUM

Thorium is three times as abundant in the Earth's crust as is uranium and eventually may partially displace uranium as a source of atomic energy in the breeder reactor. But in the meantime demand for thorium is very small and almost all non-energy related. These modest uses include gas-light mantles, catalysts, refractories, and alloys. It is generally assumed that thorium reactors will be developed within the next decade or two. This will markedly increase the demand for thorium. Accordingly, information is being accumulated on our thorium resources by the U.S. Geological Survey and other agencies.

Occurrence.   Thorium occurs in association with uranium or rare-earth elements. Its chief mineral form is monazite, which forms a black sand and is concentrated in both beach and stream placers after being weathered out of its original igneous rock source.

India has the largest known thorium reserves, with the United States second and Canada a close third. In the United States most of the deposits are in Idaho and Montana, along with some in the southeastern coastal regions.

Investment. Thorium investments would have to be regarded as fairly long term, as demand will probably not increase significantly for a decade or more. I am advised by the Idaho Bureau of Mines and Geology that there are numerous claims on the thorium deposits of that state but that no one company has a very large position. Ultimately these various claims, many owned by individuals, will probably be "packaged" into mineable units as the demand for thorium rises.

HYDROGEN

Hydrogen is here considered as an energy source, even though its major uses at present are not in that capacity. Some day we may achieve a "hydrogen economy" and on that basis it is discussed here.

Hydrogen, lightest of all elements, is a gas in elemental form. However, hydrogen occurs chiefly as compounds in the form of water, oil, natural gas, coal, and in all living organisms. Its current large uses are in making ammonia fertilizers and in petroleum refining, but there are many minor uses that also add up to a major amount. Demand for hydrogen has shown a strong growth curve. This curve could rise even faster when large-scale production of oil from oil shale begins, for it takes about 1,300 cubic feet of hydrogen to produce a barrel of oil from oil shale as compared with 300 cubic feet from crude oil. To produce a barrel of oil from coal, another process that is on the way, it takes about 6,000 cubic feet of hydrogen. If these synthetic fuels are produced at the highest rates forecast, the use of hydrogen between now and the year 2000 will increase at a compound annual rate of 12.4 percent.

Possible "Hydrogen Fuel Economy." One of the possibilities for hydrogen now widely written about and discussed is its use as a fuel to replace gasoline and natural gas. There are some limitations and disadvantages with hydrogen as compared with these other fuels, mostly in terms of handling problems. But there also are advantages, chiefly in the lack of pollution when hydrogen is burned. It simply combines with oxygen to form water. However, producing the hydrogen might result in pollution, for the major source of hydrogen would probably have to be large atomic plants—either breeder reactors or perhaps, ultimately, fusion plants. Radioactivity from the breeder reactor waste products could create hazards.

Hydrogen might also be produced from the capture of solar energy, which would be used to separate hydrogen and oxygen from water, perhaps on floating ocean platforms from which the hydrogen would be piped ashore. However, achieving this technology on any large commercial scale appears to be far in the future, perhaps not until the next century.

Investment. Hydrogen is presently produced in quantity by a number of companies, including Air Products and Chemicals, Air Reduction Company (Airco), Big Three Industrial Gas and Equipment Company, Chemetron Corporation, General Dynamics, and Union Carbide. Because the chief source of hydrogen is air or water, one buys into the companies that make the hydrogen rather than buying the resource itself. The outlook for hydrogen, even without much greater demands from synthetic fuel industries, is good, and investments in well-managed companies making the hydrogen should be rewarding.

GEOTHERMAL RESOURCES

Geothermal heat, or heat from the Earth, has been used by people for thousands of years. For example, hot springs have been used to heat living areas and for bathing, and natural steam vents called fumaroles have been used for cooking. More recently technology has used Earth heat to generate electric power. The first such generating plant, built in Italy in 1905, now produces more electricity than at any time since it started.

In the early 1960s, Pacific Gas and Electric Company, in joint venture with Union Oil, Magma Power, and Thermal Power, began to develop The Geysers Field in Sonoma County, California, about 75 miles north of San Francisco. Today this is the world's largest geothermal power facility. Expected development will ultimately expand the field to more than double its present size.

What Are Geothermal Resources? There are four types: (1)

Dry steam, such as The Geysers, is probably fairly rare. Here the steam is simply cleaned of rock particles and put into the turbines. (2) Wet steam, in which part of the superheated water is flashed into steam and used in the turbines. (3) Hot water, in which the heat from the water is transferred to a low-boiling-point liquid such as freon 12 or isobutane and then used to turn a turbine-generator. (4) Hot rock, which is dry and has to be fractured by some means so that water can be pumped into the rock and some of the heat transferred to the water.

Some of these techniques are still experimental. It should be noted, however, that geothermal energy can simply be used directly for heating instead of turning turbine-generators that produce electricity to be used for heating. In fact, the efficiency of directly using the hot water or steam is about twice that of using it to generate electricity. The future of direct use of geothermal resources is good. Already it is used in pulp and paper mills in New Zealand and for industrial processes in Iceland, where more than half of the population of some 200,000 also enjoy pollution-free geothermal heat for their homes.

Where Are Geothermal Resources? The distribution of geothermal sites around the world coincides with volcanic and earthquake belts—all indicating regions of instability in the Earth's crust. Oil and volcanoes don't go together very well. But those areas with volcanic terrain and little or no oil, such as Japan, Hawaii, the Philippines, New Zealand, Iceland, and the western states of Oregon, Idaho, Washington, Nevada, New Mexico, Arizona, and California (duly noting that New Mexico and California have considerable oil but not in the regions of geothermal resources), are compensated by the possession of substantial geothermal energy resources. More than 80 countries are now engaged in a search for geothermal energy, and several already have utilized this energy for years.

New Zealand generates 10 percent of its electric power from geothermal energy. In Iceland, California, Oregon, Japan, and elsewhere, geothermal waters are used to heat greenhouses where fine crops of tomatoes and other agricultural products are now being raised commercially.

Opening of U.S. Lands to Geothermal Development. After ten years of delay and debate, Congress passed the Geothermal Steam Act of 1970. Regulations for the leasing of geothermal lands were issued late in 1973, and in January, 1974, Federal lands were opened for lease applications. Those areas that were overlapped by several applications to a major extent were designated as Known Geothermal Resource Areas (KGRAs) and put up for competitive bidding. Altogether, several million acres of land in western United States have been applied for and are under exploration. A discovery by Union Oil in the Valles Caldera, a large volcanic crater north of Albuquerque, New Mexico, appears to be the second major geothermal discovery in the United States. Many other promising areas are known. In Oregon more than 1½ million acres have been applied for in which to prospect for geothermal energy.

Who Is Involved? Exploration and development of geothermal resources involves technics quite similar to those used in oil exploration. As a result the oil companies have become leaders in this effort, but a number of smaller firms that are strictly geothermally oriented as well as some individuals are making efforts to find and develop these resources.

Union Oil Company has the most experience and has completed geothermal wells in California, New Mexico, and the Philippines. Gulf Oil, Standard Oil Company of California, Sun Oil Company, Union Oil, Mobil Oil, and American Metal Climax all have taken land positions in geothermal exploration. Other companies chiefly concerned with geothermal development include Magma Energy, Magma Power, American Thermal Resources, Geothermal Resources International, Geothermal Kinetics, and Pacific Energy Company. The last two firms are closely held.

Investment. The companies just listed are obvious investment media in geothermal energy. Also, land with geothermal resources such as hot springs can be bought, or you can apply for Federal geothermal leases just as companies do. The lease applications are handled through the regional offices of the Bureau of Land Management.

One should not overlook the potential of using hot springs in special ways such as in greenhouse operations, heating homes, and in businesses. The amount of heat that can be recovered from even a relatively small hot spring is impressive, and it is likely that drilling in the area would enlarge the known resource. Homes, schools, business establishments, and one hospital in Klamath Falls, Oregon, are heated with geothermal energy. Boise, Idaho, has used this resource in a somewhat similar fashion. Ownership of a hot spring, particularly near a community of any size, has considerable potential that should be explored.

Outlook. Development of geothermal energy in the United States is just beginning. The future for geothermal energy both here and abroad in selected areas appears to be very good. Studies indicate that geothermal energy can be quite competitive with oil-, gas-, or coal-fired electrical generating plants and can even compete with some hydro sites. There is no special equipment needed, and the lead time from drilling wells to building the plant and getting power on the line is relatively short—perhaps as little as five to six years. This compares with a lead time now of 12 years for nuclear plants.

Geothermal resources appear to be somewhat less in Canada than in the United States, but some interesting, prospective areas are known in the Pacific Coast region.

SOLAR ENERGY

Solar energy is our most abundant energy source, and solar energy studies always produce some fascinating statistics. For example, only ½ of 1 percent of the solar energy reaching the United States is more than the projected energy demand of this country in the year 2000. In the form of coal and oil we use "fossil sunlight," which reached the Earth millions of years ago. Using sunlight directly in large quantities for an energy source at the present time, however, has not been accomplished. There is rising interest and it seems likely that significant developments will occur in this century. Nevertheless, as I give public lectures and talk with citizens at large and also confer with solar energy experts, it is my conclusion that the general public holds a considerably more optimistic view of what solar energy might do in this century than probably is warranted. However, some things can be done to use solar energy, and these are briefly touched on in the subsequent paragraphs.

Solar Heating. Much can be done now in the design of buildings to make better use of sunlight for heating. This involves the use of new materials, and if one were to look at the

United States in this sense it would be fair to say that 90 percent or more of our buildings are obsolete in terms of the new energy economics, especially in the way they use, or rather do not use, solar energy.

Power from Sunlight. This is likely to be a somewhat later widespread development than the use of sunlight in space heating. Various types of solar cells have been made and have been used commercially in small ways. Some recent significant advances in silicon cells have appeared. Cadmium and gallium are elements which if properly utilized, also, can produce electricity in photovoltaic cells. Cadmium sulfide is widely employed now in exposure meters in cameras. However, silicon cells promise to be the most efficient. The economics of all this, however, is still such that power would cost several hundred times that of conventional electrical power sources. Nevertheless, progress is being made, although the outlook is for no significant amount of electric power to be produced by sunlight in this century. Hopefully, this forecast may prove to be too pessimistic, but that is the way it seems at present.

Investment. A number of companies have more or less continuous research programs on solar energy conversion devices and on materials that would make the best use of the Sun's rays. These include Westinghouse, General Electric, PPG Industries, Honeywell Corporation, Bell Telephone, the Clevite Division of Gould, Inc., the Centralab Semiconductor Division of Globe-Union, Inc., and the Spectrolab Division of Textron, Inc.

A number of small companies work on these matters from time to time, and there is always a chance that they will perfect something that, in effect, can become the "Xerox" of the 1980s or 90s. This is something to continually look for, as the potential for profit in some major breakthrough in solar energy conversion devices is enormous.

FUEL CELLS

These are not a direct natural energy source in themselves as is oil, for example, and in fact many fuel cell designs use petroleum products as their basic raw materials. But no discussion of energy sources would be complete without mentioning them. Their chief attractions are that they are more efficient in the release of energy from sources such as oil than are many other devices and that they also are largely non-polluting in operation and, unlike the internal combustion engine, operate at low temperatures.

Fuel cells have been used in a variety of ways, including on spacecraft. They can operate on hydrogen, oxygen, gasoline, kerosene, natural gas, ammonia, alcohol, methanol, and a number of other substances. From these they produce electricity.

There are no large-scale fuel cells in operation, but research is being conducted toward this end. Fuel cells may someday power our automobiles.

Investment.   There are no fuel-cell manufacturing companies as such. All three major auto manufacturers—Ford, GM, and Chrysler—are working on them. Exxon Corporation has a continuous fuel-cell study program. Allis-Chalmers, Union Carbide, General Electric, Texas Instruments, and others conduct research. Texas Instruments has delivered a 100-watt fuel cell to the Army. General Electric has produced an experimental 1,100-watt cell. Watch for further developments in fuel cells. Their 60 to 70 percent efficiency, in effect, makes them virtually a new power resource, because they will allow our presently known energy resources to last a good deal longer than they would without the fuel cell.

WIND

Wind is really solar energy in action, as it is the Sun's heat that causes motion of the atmosphere. However, wind is usually thought of as a distinct energy source. First caught by sails to move boats, use of winds is ancient history. Later, but still going back many centuries, the windmill in various forms produced usable energy. The windmill appears to have been invented in Persia thousands of years before Christ. In 1700 B.C. the Babylonians used windmills to pump water for irrigation. Use of windmills spread to Europe about the 11th century; using windmills to grind corn was a Dutch idea about the 15th century. By 1850 the use of windmills in the United States represented about 1.4 billion horsepower-hours of work annually, the energy equivalent of burning 11.8 million tons of coal. By 1870 the amount of power produced by windmills had been cut in half, however, due to the advent of the steam engine driven by fossil fuels. Now, as these fossil fuels become more scarce and expensive, the windmill and its variations is getting renewed attention.

Wind is a renewable resource in the sense that more is generated all the time. On the other hand, it is not a constant energy source in any given locality, and one cannot ship it in to provide a steady supply. It is either there or not and nothing can be done about it. The somewhat unreliable nature of this resource is one of its major disadvantages. Fairly costly methods of storing wind-generated electricity would have to be devised. Also, the number of sites with good wind power are limited. By their nature, windmills are large and not necessarily very attractive against the skyline atop some mountain or high ridge and therefore have some ecological drawbacks if one includes the scenery in ecology.

Present Technology.   Windmills have long been used for small, local sources of power where reliability was not an overriding factor. Windmills are not very efficient, generally, and do not have to be built to very rigid specifications. On the other hand, large windmills of the sort that could generate appreciable electric power have to be very carefully engineered. The technology is reasonably perfected, but the capital costs are large. A number of designs are being tested, and the technical details are still in a state of flux. Both the National Science Foundation (NSF) and the National Aeronautics and Space Administration (NASA) are conducting research.

The Future   Both the NSF and the NASA state that by the year 2000 a major development program in American windpower could yield 1.5 trillion kilowatt-hours of electricity annually, equal to the total electricity consumed in the United States in 1970, and that costs could be competitive with electric power from nuclear sources. A number of fairly exotic ideas have been proposed, including a line of windmills floating on platforms offshore. Ideas for storing windmill-generated power include large flywheels that would store power through inertia—that is, they would keep spinning after the windmill stopped. Another is the idea of using windmill-generated electricity to produce hydrogen, which could be stored as a fuel.

The foregoing are the more optimistic views on the matter. There is another view, as expressed by Dr. Ernest Peterson of the Department of Atmospheric Sciences at Oregon State University, who writes in *Science* (August 9, 1974) as follows:

To produce 160 billion kilowatt-hours a year (assuming an average wind of 20 knots) would require more than 15,000 wind generating units. The cost of installation of the units alone, not counting the cost of the offshore platforms, would thus be in excess of $15 billion. If these wind generators were placed in a line on platforms 100 meters apart, the line would stretch for 1500 kilometers, which is about the length of the entire New England coast.

Only 15 modern coal- or nuclear-fueled power plants will supply the same amount of electricity as 15,000 wind turbines, and their cost of installation is at least 5 times less. Also, electricity can be produced at will at conventional power plants, whereas the wind is unpredictable.

There is no doubt but there is plenty of power in the wind. The real problem is in economically extracting this power, and since the fundamental technology for building wind machines has already been developed, reasonable estimates of the cost of extracting wind power can be made. My analysis indicates that large-scale generation of electricity by harnessing the wind even as a supplemental source of power, is not feasible economically.

So this is the other point of view. I am personally inclined to go along with Dr. Peterson. I believe that large-scale generation of electricity from wind is a long way off and may never be a serious reality. Still, one has always to qualify such a view with the thought that some new invention or technological concept could change matters. When I discussed this with several persons one day, we concluded that the best place to build an experimental model windmill might be on Capitol Hill in Washington D.C., where the power source would be the most consistent.

Investments. This is a case where one would invest in the technology to invest in the resource. At the present time there are no companies significantly committed to windpower work. Therefore, the interested investor would have to pursue the matter on his own. From time to time small companies have been formed to develop windpower stations but their history has usually been short and unsuccessful. Some time, however, it might be different.

TIDES AND WAVES

Anyone looking at the "restless sea" can hardly but be impressed with the vast amount of energy involved in moving all that water. But success in harnessing that energy has largely eluded us up to now. Only recently, near St. Malo on the Rance River in France, has there been a successful tidal power station installed. Now producing about 240,000 kilowatts, it is a generating station of modest size. But the cost of the energy is zero and its never-ending supply makes it attractive.

Interestingly enough, when you analyze the source of tidal and wave energy, you find that the Sun plays an important part in both, just as the Sun produces coal and oil and natural gas through organic processes. The waves are the result of wind, which is Sun-produced, and the tides are a combination of the pull of the moon and the Sun.

Tidal power has a number of limitations. Only in far northern and southern latitudes are tides great enough to be a significant energy source. The Soviet Union, for example, has announced plans for building several tidal-power plants in the Arctic Ocean. I have been in Frobisher Bay in southeastern Baffin Island (just west of Greenland) and seen the impressive 50-foot tides there. But the outlet for power developed there would be limited. In any case, there are only a few sites in the world where configuration of the land together with a sufficiently high tide would make tidal power feasible. The Bay of Fundy, lying between Maine and Nova Scotia, has been studied for years in this regard but nothing has been done. Cook Inlet, Alaska, and San Jose Gulf in Argentina have also been investigated but no action has been taken.

Investment and the Future. At the present time there appears to be no tidal-power investment medium. Such projects as might be developed would be very expensive and so probably would have to be financed by the government. However, it is not beyond the realm of possibility that some one or some company could develop a totally new concept in capturing tidal power and capitalize on it.

Waves. As waves occur everywhere as opposed to high tides, which have a limited geographic distribution, the potential here might appear to be worldwide. The problem has been that no economic technology has been developed to obtain energy from waves on any large scale. Very small floating power plants have been built, particularly by the Japanese, which make use of wave motion to produce electricity. But even these have the limitation that wave action is not steady nor consistent. Calm days occur everywhere at times, and at other times storm waves are very large and destructive. The prospects for developing significant amounts of energy from wave action appear remote, and it is not an investment outlet of consequence. Again, as with tidal power, one has to allow for the possibility of some new technology. But aside from that rather slight possibility, wave energy can probably only be admired as part of the ocean scenery as the waves dash on the shore.

EARTH'S MAGNETIC FIELD

Being a naturally occurring force like the wind, the Earth's magnetic field presumably has to be classed as a natural energy resource. This force, like the tides, is of Earth-size, but so far the problem of how to harness this force has not come even close to being solved. The total amount of energy is large, but at any one point on the Earth's surface it is very small. Perhaps it may some day be utilized by a technology yet unknown. I offer in defense of even bringing up the idea at all that 50 years ago if you had told people they could eventually invest in a satellite that would orbit the Earth and be used as a relay station for television programs ("what's television?"), you would have been laughed off the floor of the New York Stock Exchange, where Comsat (Communications Satellite Corporation) is now traded and in the not too distant past made some people a lot of money.

Imagination, technology, the Earth's resources, and investment capital are the ingredients of economic progress in the world of today—and tomorrow.

10

Metals—Past, Present, Future

METALS HAVE BEEN so important to the progress of the human race that we have even used metal names to designate certain periods of history such as the Copper Age, the Bronze Age, and the Iron Age. We are told we now live in the Atomic Age, but uranium is hardly an industrial metal, and we will continue to live in the Iron Age for some time to come. If one wishes to acknowledge aluminum, it could be suggested that we are now in an Iron-Aluminum Age.

Metals have been the raw materials for implements of agriculture and for implements of war. The possession of metals has been a prime objective of nations and continues to be so.

At the present time we are using metals more rapidly than ever before, and no early lessening of this trend is foreseen. Eventually however, other materials will have to be gradually substituted as our metal resources diminish, and we will have to recycle our metals much more than we are now doing. We are now beginning to recycle, and in the case of copper we continue to keep in use most of what has ever been mined. It is estimated that about 85 percent of all the copper ever produced in the world is still in use today in some fashion. Scrap iron is used as part of the charge for blast furnaces in increasing amounts. Aluminum too is being recycled, with the particular advantage in that primary aluminum production is very energy-intensive; the reuse of once-smelted aluminum effects a marked energy savings—if you can collect the aluminum scrap without too great an expenditure of energy.

Some metals last almost indefinitely. Platinum is one. It is not used up in its major use for crucibles in chemical work and as a catalyst in oil refining; the total supply grows slowly as new metal is put into industrial use. On the other hand, recovery of mercury in any significant quantities is difficult. It cannot be reclaimed easily from mercury vapor lamps, and recovering mercury from broken thermometers is not likely to be a lucrative enterprise.

Zinc, used chiefly as a coating on steel, is difficult to reclaim; lead, however, in storage batteries and other forms, is recoverable and substantial quantities are reused. But in spite of competition from scrap the primary production of metals is still increasing and probably will do so to the year 2000 and beyond.

11

Investing in Metals and Mines

"He found a gold mine" is the classic symbolic expression for the lucky fellow who struck it rich. Investing in mines has been a fever, one might even say a disease, that has plagued and pleased men for generations. Owning a mine is an ambition of more people than you might suspect. I meet them almost every day. Some of them own the mine to their regret; others have done very well.

Definition of "Ore." Before proceding further, it is important to understand one fundamental term in mining—ore. Ore is not a geological term; it is economic. An ore is a metalliferous mineral or aggregate of metalliferous minerals from which a metal or metals can be extracted *at a profit.* Therefore, what is ore today may not be ore tomorrow if the price of a metal goes down. Conversely, what is a marginal mining situation with no ore in it by technical definition today can become a going mine with lots of ore if the price of a metal goes up. Ore bodies, in effect, expand and contract as the price of the metal changes. For example, it was estimated for one mine that a 2-cent rise in the price of copper would enlarge the ore body by 24 percent.

Keep in mind also that what is an ore at one place is not necessarily ore at another location, even if you have the same metal content. That is, a ½-of-1-percent copper deposit on some island in the Arctic Ocean would not be economic, but deposits with less than that percentage of copper are mined in

78

some operations in the United States and Canada. An actual example of a high-grade mineral deposit that because of its location has lagged in development is the rich iron deposit on Baffin Island, west of Greenland. The "ore" is 68 to 70 percent iron and can be fed directly into open-hearth furnaces. But the major problem is that the Arctic shipping season is only two months long, too short to make a large-scale investment pay at present. Later on no doubt this deposit will be a valuable asset to its owners but at the present time it apparently does not qualify as an ore. Having been on Baffin Island myself in a snowstorm in early August at sea level, I can testify as to the short summer. A group headed by Anglo-American Corporation is the owner of this deposit.

Some mineral aggregates may have smelting problems—the metal may be hard to get out of the rock. It may have a tough silica bond or undesirable amounts of impurities that are costly to remove. The rock can show a good metal content but by the time you mill it and ship it to the nearest smelter (which may not be too near) and pay the smelting costs, the returns (called "smelter returns") may be very modest or even non-existent. The whole matter is an economic one, so be sure to put a sharp pencil to any mine operation in which you think you want to become involved firsthand.

All these factors tend to add up to the conclusion that, for most investors, buying stock in a well-established mining operation is the most satisfactory way of investing in metals.

"Mineral" and "Rock" Defined. These terms also should be understood by the investor. "Mineral" has a number of different meanings—how it is used legally is sometimes different from how it is commonly used by geologists. For example, "mineral rights" include oil and gas, but these are not minerals by geological definition. For our purposes here a mineral is defined as a naturally occurring inorganic substance with a fairly definite chemical composition and physical structure. A quartz crystal would be one example; a piece of pyrite ("fool's gold") would be another. A rock is a mineral aggregate, such as, for example, granite, which is composed chiefly of four minerals—quartz, feldspar, hornblende, and mica. There are exceptions to this, of course. Limestone is a rock, but pure limestone is essentially all one mineral, calcite. Quartzite is virtually all quartz.

Stages of a Mining Boom. We may or may not have seen
the last mining boom in North America. We went through a
uranium rush in the 1950s and there was a metals rush (mostly
copper and silver) in Ontario when the great deposit near Timmins was discovered in 1964. The chances are there will be
other discoveries and we will have mining booms and rushes
again of sorts. Or higher metal prices or new uses for metals
not now in great demand can create a rush.

My observations of mining rushes and booms (the two are not
quite synonymous but are used interchangably here) indicate a
general sequence of events like this:

1. The initial report of discovery sets off the staking of hundreds of mining claims in the area; most are located with little
or no regard to the geology. Prospectors (and for the moment
everybody in the area becomes a prospector) simply try to get
as close to the original discovery as possible. Haste is of the
essence.

2. Many small companies are subsequently formed and stock
is issued to obtain money, presumably for exploring and developing claims. These are "penny stocks" and usually sell for a
few cents to a dollar or so when issued. Some penny stocks go
up ten times or in a few cases even 100 times or more their initial
offering price, moved chiefly by rumors (not uncommonly
started by those who own the claims). Most drop back to zero
sooner or later. Stocks are issued in some instances where the
company is rarely or never heard of again after the first few
months. This has been especially true in Canada where regulations historically have been rather loose (Canada is taking steps
to tighten up this situation a bit). Unless you are on the location
(and even then it is difficult) you cannot have more than a random chance of picking a winning stock. For most people it is
better to stay out at this stage, but to sit on the sidelines is
difficult when the "get rich quick" psychology sweeps through
the investment community. In mining discoveries the pressure
is almost overwhelming. A good example of how fast a cheap
speculative mining stock can move at this stage came out of the
Timmins copper-silver strike. On rumors that the company had
discovered a rich ore body, the stock of Windfall Oils and Mines,
Ltd., (I like the name!) rose from 56 cents to $5.60 in two weeks.
When Windfall later announced negative results, the price of

the stock fell *in one day* from $4.15 to 80 cents (Windfall had become Downfall). If you were an investor in this stock who lived in Houston or Chicago or Los Angeles you would probably not be able to move fast enough to protect yourself. The local boys would have already "unloaded."

3. Most of the smaller companies collapse after a few months or at the most a year or two. Firms with good claims usually sell out to established mining companies. A few companies have sufficiently large and good-quality holdings to justify developing the properties themselves. To show how things get concentrated in this third stage of a mining boom, it is noteworthy that a single set of mining claims ultimately assembled in the uranium rush in Canada are now reported to have more uranium reserves than all the other uranium deposits in Canada put together.

4. A few large, chiefly old established companies emerge with most of the newly-found resources. Only a small percentage of the newly-formed companies persist after the initial sorting out of a few years takes place. After trying to develop and run their own mines, many of these companies for lack of capital will ultimately sell out to better established organizations. However, the bigger firms don't always come out ahead on such deals. They can make a mistake and pay more for a property than it is worth. A classic example is the uranium deposit found by Vernon Pick, an ex-electrician from Minnesota. This mine in the Colorado Plateau was eventually sold to Floyd Odlum as head of Atlas Corporation. The price was $7 million. The mine was exhausted after only about $2 million worth of uranium had been recovered. When asked how he felt in his conscience about having sold this mine to Odlum, Pick is reported to have replied "He's over 21." Maybe you can do better than Odlum in picking winners among newly-discovered mines, but I doubt it.

When and How to Get In. My view is that the best way to get in on a mining boom, if you do not have expert firsthand knowledge of the situation, is through stage 4—buy into an established mining company that puts some of its retained earnings into carefully examined new mining areas. Better yet, have investments already in good mining companies and wait until they discover or buy into new properties, which any well-managed mining company can and must do from time to time to stay alive. Searching for new ore is a constant concern.

Here it is important to buy quality. Invest in firms with good management records and they will look after your interests. Mineral exploration, for the most part, is a high-cost and very sophisticated procedure. Only the better-financed and more-experienced companies can really compete. In Canada, International Nickel has an excellent record in this regard. In the United States, Kennecott, among others, is aggressive and capable. They operate through several exploration subsidiaries, including one called "Bear Creek." I have, in my own consulting work, run across Bear Creek's work, and was well impressed. There also are other mining companies with good staffs and a few that haven't done very well in spite of having considerable resources with which to work.

In spite of the foregoing, there are some examples of small mining companies that have struck it rich. This is a facet of investing in mines that intrigues many people and some comments on it are in a later section on "Penny Stocks."

Information Sources and Quotations. There is always an abundance of information currently available on mines and discoveries. Anyone seriously interested in such investments would do well to subscribe to some of these sources. Beyond what brokerage firms can give you, good sources of information include *The Northern Miner,* 77 River Street, Toronto, Canada, M5A 3P2. A six-month subscription to *The Northern Miner* will give you a very liberal education in the mining business and will probably also give you at least a mild case of "mine investment fever." The same organization also publishes the *Canadian Mines Handbook,* a very useful tabulation of all mining operations of consequence in Canada. In the United States, *Skillings' Mining Review,* 210 Sellwood Building, Duluth, Minnesota 55802, is an informative weekly publication and has an extended list of mining-stock quotations. Somewhat more technical but still very readable are *Engineering and Mining Journal,* P.O. Box 430, Hightstown, New Jersey 08520, and *Mining Engineering,* 345 E. 47th Street, New York, New York 10017. Both are monthlies and carry excellent detailed articles on mining discoveries and developments. *The Wall Street Journal* and *Barron's* at various times carry articles on metals and mines and quotations on some foreign mining issues as well as certain stocks on Canadian exchanges. The Vancouver, Toronto, Spokane, Denver, and Salt Lake City papers all have mining stocks quoted, but chiefly local issues.

Before discussing some details of mine investments, it should be mentioned that you can directly invest in several metals by buying futures on the commodity market. Metals in which such markets are now made include copper, mercury, platinum, silver, and gold. The commodity market futures operation is a specialized business and decidedly not for amateurs, although lots of amateurs try it. Most brokerage firms have commodity departments and can introduce you to this rather hazardous but potentially very profitable business.

MAJOR DEPOSITS

Metals tend to occur either in very large or in relatively small deposits. All the other copper deposits in Utah don't begin to add up to the tremendous amount of copper ore that Kennecott has at Bingham Canyon. Anaconda's Berkeley pit in Montana accounts for more than 90 percent of the copper produced in that state. Molybdenum occurs in many localities in small amounts, but the deposit at Climax, Colorado, is by far the largest deposit in the United States. Iron is a very widely distributed element but the Hull-Rust Mine and a few others in the Lake Superior region produce the great bulk of the iron mined in the United States.

There are, of course, intermediate-sized deposits, but in general this rule holds true—there are a few large mineral deposits and many small ones. Either can be profitable, but it is well for the investor to recognize the scale of things when thinking of metal occurrences. When it comes to the principal industrial metals, a few major companies tend to dominate the field, and much of their dominance comes from the possession of a few very large mines.

Obviously, the chief approach to investing in major ore deposits, unless one is fortunate enough to buy into a small mine that subsequently proves to be very large (this does happen but not often), is to buy the shares of major mineral producers. In most instances, reserves are present to last the companies for many years. See what they say about this in their annual report;

check it through other sources. The principal way to make your dollar work harder in this sort of investment than it otherwise might, is to take advantage of the cyclical swings in prices that securities of these companies show related to the movements of the metal prices. These cycles, however, are being somewhat subdued by the rising demand for and the tighter supply of some metals; nevertheless, they will continue to occur to varying degrees.

SMALL DEPOSITS

There are thousands—even hundreds of thousands—of small "mines" in existence. I will not attempt to define a "mine," for it has been used for everything from virtually a gopher-hole on up. It must be clearly stated at the outset also that far more money has been put into the ground in search of metals than has been taken out. But you usually don't hear about the diggings that simply struck dirt instead of "paydirt." The diggers silently slip away to dig again somewhere else. Mark Twain once defined a mine as "a hole in the ground, owned by a liar." Unfortunately, there is considerable truth in that statement.

Now that you have had the bad news, let's look at the good news. Some small mines have made fortunes for their owners. "Pockets" of gold either in vein or placer form have been worth many thousands of dollars. Silver can occur in large amounts in small areas. Small mines that have the more common but still relatively high-unit-value metals in them can often be worked at a profit. These metals are chiefly tungsten, mercury, antimony, and perhaps a few others, including chromium (if you could find a good chrome deposit in North America).

Beware of "Mine Fever"—Get Good Advice. If you are considering an investment in a small mine, get some good advice *first* from someone who is competent and knows the situation in detail. As a consulting geologist I am asked rather frequently to give advice on mining properties. Regrettably I quite often am called in not to treat the patient but to perform an autopsy. Unfortunately people usually seem to think about getting good advice after they are involved in a mine and things go wrong, and not before. "Investigate first—then invest," is the simple often-ignored rule.

I was once called in as consultant to a company formed by a group of apple-growers to buy some mining claims. They bought the claims and subsequently built a beautiful little mill in which to process the ore. These people were as nice a group as you could wish to know, but they were out of their element in the mining business. I did meet most of them at a special (and rather sad) stockholders' meeting when I came to explain the situation. I would have been glad not to have had that consulting job. The company had difficulties. They had purchased these claims and built this fine mill but there was just one problem— there wasn't any ore. This situation is sometimes known as putting the cart before the horse.

Believe it or not, this deal had been based on a single piece of rock that had been picked up and assayed. It showed commercial amounts of the metal (in this case, tungsten). My geological investigations showed that a few more pieces of rock might be found to have some tungsten but to be a valid mine the deposit has to be measured in terms of hundreds of thousands or even millions of tons of ore. This "mine" had no ore.

It may seem elementary to you to say that the company should have first done some core drilling to outline the ore body, if any, and to determine the average quality ("tenor") of the ore. Only then, if the ore deposit was good enough, should the mill be built. The fact was, however, that on the basis of one piece of rock, hundreds of thousands of shares of stock were sold to individuals, and a first-class mill built by people who in their own business would be cautious and careful. They caught "mine fever" and were carried away. I had been paid for my geological investigations; for going to the meeting I finally decided to settle for my travel expenses and a crate of apples.

I have seen this phenomenon many times. It is not just the desire to try to get rich quick. This might be satisfied, one way or another, by a night at the gaming tables. It is a special sort of disease. People want to say they own a mine. If you are tempted to get involved in a small mine, by all means get good advice—early. Contact a reputable geologist or mining engineer. Pay him to write a report, and make him sign it. If you do get involved in a small mine, or just want to know more about mining in some detail, a very fine little publication is "Mining Explained in Simple Terms" published by *The Northern Miner,* in Toronto. It is a booklet costing a couple of dollars and well worth the price.

"PENNY STOCKS"

No discussion of investing in mines would be complete without some comment on "penny stocks." These are stocks in small companies, selling generally for a dollar or less and traded on regional stock exchanges, over the counter, or sometimes just between individuals. Trading these securities is a fascinating game, and every once in a while an incredibly big winner turns up. For years the stock of Lucky Friday sold for less than a dollar; at one time it was around five cents a share. Then the company broke into a rich silver vein and Hecla Mining ultimately bought them out in an exchange of stock that brought the equivalent of about 60 dollars a share. A few people had "faith" in Lucky Friday. In one instance the faith was rewarded to the extent that a couple ended up with "his" and "her" Cadillacs along with a half million dollars or so. But this is the exception rather than the rule. Let me tell you about one of my experiences.

Story of a "Hot Tip." What happened was this: It was midwinter in northern Idaho and I was a young professor teaching in a College of Mines. One day a student came in and said, "I know a fellow who knows a fellow . . . ," and so on. The gist of this "hot tip" was that a mine existed high on a mountainside in northern Idaho. In the valley below another mining operation had just cut a rich vein of silver ore that trended right toward this other mine, now covered with 15 feet of snow. It was said that the vein "probably goes through the other property but they just haven't reached it yet." Few people knew about all this, so now was the time to buy. This mine had stock selling at the fantastically low price of 1½ cents a share. How much could I lose? Just the idea of owning 1,000 shares of stock for $15 total investment was attractive, especially as that was about what I had saved from my first year of teaching so far. And think if the stock only went to $1 a share! We couldn't check on the geology of the area because of the snow, but we each bought 1,000 shares anyway. When the snow did melt we went back into the mountains and found a big fault—a break in the Earth's crust—between our mine and the mine with the rich silver vein. The geology showed that the vein clearly terminated against the fault.

How much could I lose or did lose? I lost everything, which is a pessimist's way of viewing it. I prefer to think I only lost $15, but I got my money's worth in experience and at that price it was pretty cheap. I also got a pretty certificate that I now have framed on my office wall to remind me not do so such things again. The frame is very nice and well worth the 75 cents I paid for it.

Assessable Stocks. You should know that some mining stocks are "assessable." The idea behind this is that the mine operators don't know just how much money they will need to develop the mine, so the stock is issued for enough money to get things started. Then, as money is needed, they "pass the hat" among the shareholders by assessing the stock—perhaps a few cents a share. If you don't pay your assessment your stock reverts to the company, which can sell it to somebody else. There is nothing wrong with the theory, if it is run honestly, but sometimes the assessments go to pay for the company president's new car, which, obviously, is necessary for him to conduct the company business (which could be in Tucson or Miami Beach during the winter). There are a variety of other ways in which assessment money doesn't pay for drills and dynamite as it should. So be wary of assessable stock. If you do get into an assessable situation, my recommendation is that you be very "hard-nosed" about the matter. Ask for a full accounting at the annual meeting and check to see if what is told you is correct. I am reluctant to say so, but the "penny stock" type of mining business has some very fast operators in it.

Some stock is "fully paid and non-assessable." That may or may not be a better deal in the long run. In such instances, the company, when it runs out of money, may just have to issue more stock, which accounts for why in some cases you will find a small hole in the ground against which ten million shares of stock have been floated. These general remarks, by the way, including the matter of fast operators, also applies to the oil business, but I think perhaps to a somewhat lesser extent. There are legal remedies but they cost money and take time. It is easier to stay out than to try to get out. Incidentally the most wonderously capitalized small resource company I have ever heard of was an oil company—PODCO, which stood for Philippine Oil Development Company. When it finally expired there were 693 million shares outstanding. It would take some oil field to pay a dividend on that capitalization! They never found it. The only things "drilled" and that "produced" were the stockholders.

Saga of the Sunshine Silver Mine. But "penny stocks" do have their success stories. Some real bonanzas have been hit, and the Sunshine Silver Mine in the Coeur d'Alene district of northern Idaho is an example. The story, told over and over again, has probably sold more stock in other mines (good and bad) than any other legend in recent years.

The Sunshine Mine was organized on a group of claims in 1921 and financed largely by apple growers in the Yakima, Washington, area. Stock was sold initially by salesmen who heard there was a good apple crop that year and descended on these growers, disposing of the Sunshine stock at ten cents a share and very happy to get rid of it at that figure. It remained at a low price until the late 1920s when a few good ore stringers were cut and the stock went up to about $3 a share in 1929. In the depression, from about 1930 to 1932, the price fell to 70 cents. After that it worked up gradually to the year 1936 when excellent ore was hit and the stock went to $25 a share. Since then the price has varied considerably, but in any case the apple growers in the Yakima Valley who bought it for ten cents made fortunes. For many years the annual meeting was held in Yakima because the apple growers, who had the majority of the shares, didn't want to go to snowy northern Idaho in winter. Later, as the stock became more widely distributed, the annual meeting was moved to Spokane. And what about the stock salesmen who sold the Sunshine stock for ten cents a share? They continued selling other stock and most of them made just a bare living, if that.

The Sunshine Mine has been the largest single silver-producing mine in the United States. Its total production has been greater than the amount of silver taken from all the mines in the famous Comstock Lode in all its history. No doubt there will be other "Sunshine Mines" discovered and the rags-to-riches story of a penny stock and its lucky shareholders will be repeated. The odds against this, of course, are long, but as one fellow told me, "Shucks, I've spent money in my younger days on things worse than penny stocks," and proceeded to list a few items that certainly proved his point; I have omitted the list here, fascinating reading though it would be.

PROSPECTING

This ancient art is on the rise again, and the price increase of gold has been a major impetus; the larger demand for metals in general also has encouraged people to take to the hills in their spare time and on weekends to see what could be found. It is a good pursuit that every so often pays off; in any event it pays off in healthy, wholesome exercise, sometimes for the whole family.

Prospecting by amateurs is done chiefly for gold and silver, but uranium, tungsten, and other materials are also searched for.

Basic Equipment. The most useful piece of "equipment" is at least some knowledge of the geology of what you are looking for. Don't look for giraffes in Alaska. I have included, in a very elementary way, some notes on the geological associations of many of the natural resources discussed in this book. But beyond this, and you surely should go beyond, there are many good books on geology and for the prospector. I have listed a few at the end of this volume under the heading "Prospecting."

Beyond knowing what you are doing, to some degree at least, the basic equipment involves a gold pan or even a portable sluice box, if you are after gold, and a geology hammer, an acid bottle, a "black light," and a Geiger counter (or a scintilometer, which for all practical purposes is merely a more expensive and sophisticated Geiger counter).

Some state geological surveys have published excellent books, maps, and pamphlets just for the prospector. Check with your state survey. Also, many colleges and universities offer night school courses for the amateur prospector, and these can be a most pleasant use for one evening a week during the winter. For a number of years I taught such a course called "Rocks and Minerals," and between the nature of the subject and the many interesting and fine people who took the course it became my favorite lecture series.

The U.S. Geological Survey also publishes many useful maps,

and your state survey may direct you to such items as would suit your specific purpose and interest. Also, these state geological surveys usually provide rock and mineral analyses at modest cost to the citizens of the state. They will tell you if you have found a gold mine—or not.

What Are the Results? Who can predict? The Midnight (uranium) Mines Corporation northwest of Spokane was so named because a uranium deposit was discovered accidentally while prospectors were looking for tungsten ore (which fluoresces under a black light) during the dark of the moon at midnight. I know at least a few people who claim to be making modest incomes by panning certain "secret" stream gravel areas for gold. In the 1950s Vernon Pick, an unemployed ·electrician whom I already have mentioned, had just decided to "take off and do some prospecting" when he found that uranium deposit he sold for $7 million.

I am sure the impact of the amateur prospector will continue to be felt by the mining business in both the United States and. Canada. If you are inclined that way, do look into the matter further and perhaps you and I will meet in the field some day. There are claims to be staked and fortunes still to be made, I am sure.

12

Major Industrial Metals

THE INDUSTRIAL METALS are aluminum, beryllium, chromium, copper, iron, magnesium, manganese, molybdenum, titanium, tungsten, and vanadium. Over the years this list has been gradually enlarging as metals such as aluminum, long regarded as a laboratory curiosity, came in great demand either through new uses discovered for them or through the discovery of a process for producing them cheaply, or both. The importance of these metals cannot be overemphasized. Civilization is literally built with them, and there is no early prospect that they will be superceded in the economy by other materials. They are basic, and so are investments in them.

The demand for these metals tends to reflect national and international business cycles, but the long-term growth of population and the ever-rising aspirations of world populations for better living standards insure increased use of these exceedingly useful raw materials.

ALUMINUM

Background. Aluminum is the third most abundant element in the Earth's crust, making up nearly 9 percent by weight. It is the most abundant metallic element, more common than iron and, because of its lightness, with a more desirable weight/strength ratio. Aluminum, however, is never found native as an

91

element but always in compounds, and where it is tightly locked in with other elements. The result is that aluminum has been known as an element only since 1827, whereas many other metals such as gold, lead, copper, and silver have been known for thousands of years. Aluminum at one time was regarded as a precious metal available only to the very rich. Napoleon III is reported to have had a tableware set made of it.

Because aluminum enters into a very tight bond with other elements, it was not until a Frenchman named Heroult and an American named Hall perfected the Heroult-Hall aluminum reduction process that aluminum could be produced relatively cheaply and in quantity. Even if discovered earlier, however, this process could not have been used because it was dependent on large amounts of electricity, which were not obtainable previously. Thus one technological advance, in this case the development of large generating facilities, leads to other discoveries, in this case the Heroult-Hall process. That these discoveries and developments tend to pyramid on one another has been a chief factor in the exponential growth of our economy and standard of living this past century. Aluminum also is an excellent example of the fact that energy is the key that unlocks all other natural resources.

The great surge in air transport during and after World War II provided a major impetus for the development of the aluminum industry. The use of aluminum in many kinds of construction has also accelerated since that time.

Present Demand and Uses.   Demand for aluminum shows no signs of abating and remains on a strong up-curve. Other countries are behind the United States in aluminum use but are beginning to catch up, further increasing demand. The uses of aluminum are so well known that there is little point in recounting them here.

Sources.   Aluminum ores are the result of the extreme weathering of clays derived from the aluminum-compound minerals, chiefly feldspars of igneous rocks such as granite but also from clays in limestone such as on Jamaica and Haiti. The chief ore of aluminum is bauxite, and because it is relatively insoluble it occurs in tropical areas of heavy rainfall such as on the north coast of South America (Surinam) and in the Caribbean. Aluminum-rich clays occur also in many other parts of the world.

There are some very large deposits in the United States, in the southeastern states and in the Pacific Northwest especially, that can be used as aluminum ores at a cost currently about 25 percent above the cost of producing aluminum from bauxite. Anticipating possible problems with foreign sources, the major aluminum companies have already examined and leased some of these deposits. There is no real problem in the supply of raw material for aluminum except that the grade of ore has a considerable range. This is an important consideration, for a very large amount of electrical energy is required in smelting aluminum. Higher-grade ores use substantially less electricity than do the lower grades. The United States has only relatively small deposits of high grade ore, chiefly near Bauxite, Arkansas. Most aluminum ores are imported to areas such as the Pacific Northwest and to British Columbia, where power has historically been relatively cheap.

Outlook and Investment. In recent years in the United States, the rate of growth of aluminum production has been three times faster than the average rate of growth of all other metals. A 5- to 7-percent annual growth rate in aluminum output can logically be forecast to the year 2000—if the electrical energy is available. With cheap hydroelectric sites now almost fully developed in the United States in particular, and in Canada to a lesser extent, the problem of power to produce aluminum is rapidly becoming a critical issue in communities used to low electric rates. The Pacific Northwest now has this problem and it will remain with us for some time to come.

There is another problem, that of the capital cost of an aluminum-producing facility, including the bauxite mining operation, the transportation of the ore, and the aluminum reduction plant together with the power facilities. This makes it difficult for existing companies to meet the rising demand and even more difficult for a new company to enter the field. The federal government has assisted at times with loans and tax concessions. This whole problem of aluminum plant costs will persist and be a negative factor on an industry that otherwise could look forward to a very high demand for its product. Nevertheless, the list of aluminum producers has been slowly growing and now includes Alcan Aluminum, Ltd., Alcoa, Reynolds Metals, Kaiser Aluminum and Chemical Corporation, Anaconda, Ormet Corporation (a subsidiary of Olin Corporation and Revere Copper and Brass), and American Metal Climax. Most of these companies are integrated and have their own supplies of raw materials, although some are in politically unstable areas and may not be too reliable.

In Australia, Comalco Industries has recently become a major bauxite producer based on huge deposits at Weipa on the Cape York Peninsula, Queensland.

If the problems of power supplies can be solved, the outlook for the aluminum industry is very bright. Difficult problems do lie ahead but they can be worked out. The result, however, may be wide swings in the price of aluminum companies' shares, with corresponding investment prospects and pitfalls.

Comment. Aluminum smelters have some environmental problems not only with the smelting processes themselves, which now are pretty well controlled, but by the impact that an aluminum plant has on the demand for electric power in a region. The power-producing facilities may cause environmental difficulties. The mining of aluminum ore is like most other open-pit operations, and reclamation of the land can be accomplished but at some cost. The combination of increased power costs and the new environmental standards will serve to raise the cost of producing aluminum substantially and may dampen its use to some degree. However, it will still have considerable relative advantages over other metals, which face somewhat similar problems with regard to the environment and energy needs (though not so severe as does aluminum).

BERYLLIUM

Background. Beryllium was discovered in 1797 and first produced in 1828 in France and Germany. It was not used extensively, however, until 1926 when the hardening effect of beryllium on copper was discovered. A 2-percent addition of beryllium to copper makes copper six times stronger. More recently beryllium has been used for nuclear, aerospace, and military applications. Beryllium is lighter than aluminum and has a high melting point (1,278° C).

Present Demand and Uses. The current demand for beryllium is small and is expected to grow at perhaps a 4- or 5-percent annual rate. Most beryllium is used as an alloy in copper, but it also is alloyed with other metals to impart qualities of hardness and high tensile strength. As an oxide, beryllium with its high melting point, high thermal conductivity, and low electrical conductivity is used as an insulator. Beryllium has certain qualities that lend it to use in nuclear energy plants. This use will grow but the quantities involved are not large.

Sources. Virtually the only source now for beryllium is the mineral beryl, which occurs chiefly in coarse-grained granite-like rocks called pegmatites and as vein deposits formed from hot waters. An emerald is a rich green, relatively clear variety of beryl. About 95 percent of the beryllium used in the United States currently is imported although more than half the known beryllium reserves of the world are in this country. The world's largest single deposit is in western Utah and is owned by the Brush Wellman Corporation. Other deposits are known in the United States and also in Argentina, Brazil, India, South Africa, and other areas.

Outlook and Investment. The use of beryllium is projected to increase at about the same rate as the gross national product, but new uses for it can reasonably be expected to be found and it could be in significantly greater demand in the decades ahead. At the present rates of consumption, however, there are both ample domestic and foreign sources. As holder of the world's largest deposit, Brush Wellman Corporation is in a strong position. Kawecki Berylco Industries, formed some years ago by the merger of Kawecki Chemical with Beryllium Corporation, also has beryllium holdings. Both of these beryllium companies are listed on the New York Stock Exchange.

CHROMIUM

Background. The French chemist Louis Vauquelin discovered chromium in 1797 and gave it the name derived from the Greek word "chroma," meaning color, because of the brilliant hues of its compounds. It remained a laboratory curiosity for more than a century until its various merits were recognized. Chromium achieved widespread use only in the present century, with total world production expanding from about 175,000 tons of chromite in 1906 to more than 6 million tons at present.

Chromite, an oxide of chromium, magnesium, iron, and aluminum, is the only mineral source of chromium.

Present Demand and Uses. Chromium demand is strong, but fortunately for the United States, which has very little, a little goes a long way. As an example, chromium is used in plating to prevent corrosion and for decoration (as on auto parts), but the coating is rarely more than 0.00002 inch in thickness. The chief use of chromium is in alloys. It hardens and toughens steel and is an important part of stainless steel. Most stainless steel contains 18 percent chromium, but some cutting tools and wear-resisting alloys contain as much as 33 percent. Chrome is used in many other ways but it can be replaced in some uses by titanium or aluminum. Sometimes, however, there is no alternative.

Sources. The United States is the world's largest user of chrome, but it has produced very little and reserves are small and low-grade. They consist mostly of pod-shaped deposits in certain types of rocks (called basic or mafic rocks by geologists) in the West (Oregon and Montana) and in Alaska. It is unlikely that major chromium deposits will be found in the United States; Canada might have a slightly better chance, but to date the known reserves there are less than those of the United States. South Africa has about two-thirds of the world's known chrome reserves, with Southern Rhodesia about another fourth; the Soviet Union is a very poor third, followed by Turkey, Finland, the Philippines, and India with minor amounts.

Outlook and Investment. As a very useful metal in our industrialized society, chromium will have a steady and strong demand. Unfortunately, there is no easy way for North American investors to participate in this anticipated high demand for chromium, as this continent is woefully deficient in the metal. In Africa, Southern Rhodesia Chrome Mines, Ltd., and African Metal Corporation, Ltd., are major producers.

COPPER

Background. No metal has a more useful and distinguished history than does copper, and there is every reason to expect its future will be similar. Because copper may occur in native form—that is, a pure copper—and because in this form it is malleable, early humans fashioned tools from it. In North America, native copper came largely from the deposits of Upper Michigan and on Isle Royale in Lake Superior, where the Indians worked them. It is reported that these deposits were later rediscovered accidentally by white men when a herd of pigs fell into a prehistoric mine pit dug by the Indians, who used the copper for spear points and knives.

Copper has been known and used by people for more than 6,000 years. It was first mined on the Sinai Peninsula. Later, large deposits were found on the island of Cyprus, and the metal there was so highly prized as to be the cause of a number of bloody conflicts. Copper was used to make pipes to carry water to the Pyramids during their construction. Columbus' ships were copper bottomed (a use still important today, as it prevents barnacle growth). Copper and tin form bronze, and copper and zinc form brass, both widely used alloys.

Copper possesses a number of unique properties that make it especially valuable in our modern industrial society. One is its ability to transmit heat (as used in car radiators, for example), a second its electrical conductivity (in wires), and a third the fact that it resists corrosion. Silver is a better conductor of electricity but cannot compete with copper, of course, due to its higher price, although the copper from the Upper Michigan area (Copper Range Company mines) has silver in it. The company does not remove the silver but sells the copper with the silver content at a premium.

Copper has long been one of the most interesting and profitable metals in which to invest. More than $300 million in dividends came out of the Upper Michigan area at a time when the dollar was a respectable amount of money. The oldest company of any kind in the world still operating today is said to be the Great Copper Mountain Mining Corporation in Sweden. It is reported to have been in business continuously since the year 1288.

Present Demand and Uses. Copper is the workhorse of the rapidly growing electrical industry. Continued growth of electrical power consumption around the world assures the importance of copper's future, although it also is exceedingly useful in other ways. The value of copper production, among the metals, is second only to iron. Copper does have to compete to some extent with aluminum, but in total it has qualities that simply cannot be duplicated by any other metal. The most important competitor to newly mined copper is scrap copper, for copper can be readily reclaimed—only about 15 percent of newly mined copper is lost before it is used a second time in some fashion. It is estimated that some of the copper now being used in the world has been in use for a thousand years or more in various forms.

Sources. The United States has for many years been the world's principal copper producer, supplying about one-fourth of the world total. However, the United States has more recently become a net copper importer, with Canada being the largest single outside source and Peru and Chile following. The United States, on the other hand, exports copper to Germany, Italy, France, Japan, and a number of other countries.

Abroad, copper comes from western South America, Africa, and Europe. Australia has small amounts. Estimates of copper reserves, identified and hypothetical, indicate the United States has 23 percent of the world total, South America 17 percent, Africa 14 percent, the Soviet Union 12 percent, and Canada 11 percent.

Geologically, copper occurs in a wide variety of situations. More than 160 minerals contain copper, but the principal minerals are chalcopyrite, cuprite, chalcocite, bornite, azurite, and malachite. About two-thirds of the world's copper is found in vein deposits and more importantly in the United States in what are called porphyry deposits (pronounced poor-fur-ee). These are large bodies of igneous rock, in a broad way like granite but more technically called quartz monzonites. The copper minerals are scattered through the rock and so the whole rock must be mined. Porphyry coppers are the chief source of copper in western United States, and copper contents as low as 4/10ths of 1 percent in the rock are now being mined. The exploitation of these porphyry coppers was dependent on the development of massive earth-moving machinery. At the Bingham Canyon, Utah, Kennecott mine, more than five times the amount of material involved in digging the Panama Canal has now been moved.

About a fourth of the world's copper occurs in sedimentary rocks, such as, for example, the floor of the ancient shallow sea that covered part of Germany and left behind some 20,000 square miles of what is called the Kupferschiefer (copper shale). Smaller amounts occur in volcanic rocks as massive sulfide deposits, and a minor quantity exists as native copper.

Outlook and Investment. Copper mining has been highly cyclical in the past, but the outlook for the future appears to be one of greater stability in demand relative to supply. There will be no copper shortage in the sense that we will run out of copper, but there are likely to be chronic shortages of copper at present prices relative to many other commodities. That is, the demand for copper is likely to increase faster than for many other materials and so the price will go up. This demand will come chiefly from the electrical industry as nations try to electrify everything they can, using the atom as a power source and thus reducing the need for utilizing the finite fossil fuel resources of this globe. Many countries have neither coal nor oil, and importing uranium for nuclear plants is a logical way to produce power and electrifying the country. This has already started, as the United States and other Western nations begin to export their nuclear know-how and equipment to less-developed areas.

Perhaps we have not yet seen the end of copper price cycles, but the combination of the projected supply and demand curves suggest that a relatively more stable and strong market will characterize copper henceforth than has been the case previously. The U.S. Bureau of Mines estimates that the demand for copper in the year 2000 will be two to four times what it is today in the United States and that demand in other countries will grow even faster.

There are several routes for investment in copper. One is to buy stocks of major mining companies. Copper company securities have fluctuated even more widely than has the price of the metal itself. Strong moves will no doubt occur again and can be seized upon at the proper time for both long-term and short-term speculative profits. Given a sound company, with substantial reserves, buying its stock at any reasonable levels by historical standards should involve little risk. Stocks of copper companies are favorites of banks and trusts operating under the "prudent man" concept. Copper stocks generally pay good dividends, and most of the major copper companies have sizable reserves. Adjustment to the nationalization of foreign holdings of American companies has now taken place in most copper stock prices. This unsettling element is now largely behind us or has been discounted in the price of companies whose holdings still exist abroad but may be in politically unstable areas such as Africa.

Reserves of the Copper Range Company (White Pine Mine, Michigan) are stated to be at least 25 years and perhaps as much as 100 years at present production rates. Kennecott does not issue reserve figures, but a calculated guess based on the amount of money they have invested in the Bingham Canyon operation, their major single holding, indicates that they probably have reserves for 40 to 50 years at present mining rates.

Major American copper producers include American Metal Climax (which has African holdings also), American Smelting and Refining, Anaconda, Copper Range, Cyprus Mines, Inspiration Consolidated, Kennecott, Newmont Mining (through wholly-owned Magma Copper), Phelps Dodge, and Utah International. Cities Service, an oil company, also has important copper holdings in southwestern United States.

In Canada, major producers include International Nickel, Falconbridge Nickel, Ecstall Mining (subsidiary of Texas Gulf), Noranda Mines, Gaspe Copper Mines, Ltd., Hudson Bay Mining and Smelting, and Sherritt Gordon. Smaller companies with expanding production include Brenda Mines, Bethlehem Copper, and Gibraltar Mines. Roan Consolidated Mines is listed on the New York Stock Exchange and has large copper properties in Zambia.

A second way to invest in copper is by buying into small copper-mining companies—not the approach for the cautious investor, but an avenue that intrigues some persons because of the very substantial fortunes that have occasionally been made by this "penny stock" route. Canada has more of these situations than does the United States. It seems fair to say that Canada has not yet been so thoroughly explored as has the United States, so the chances of additional copper discoveries there are greater than south of its border. Copper has a high enough unit value so that a rich small mine can be very profitable, and therefore this kind of situation lends itself to speculation by small investors. The fluctuations of some of the penny stocks are astronomical at times and call for the investor to be alert and wary, but it also is a fascinating business. Again, as mentioned earlier, *The Northern Miner,* of Toronto, is the best single continuous current source of information on Canadian mining companies.

A third way of investing in copper has been to grub-stake a competent prospector or prospecting group and let them pursue promising leads and ultimately stake the property. This era has passed to some degree in the United States more than it has in Canada. If a copper property is found, however, the sale of it to a going copper concern rather than development of it by the initial investors is usually the wiser course of action.

Finally, there is a futures market in copper, where a small amount of money can obtain a large leverage position. This, like the silver futures and other commodity futures markets, is for the sophisticated investor, and the ride can be very fast—either way.

Comment. Foreign influences still continue to make copper prices fluctuate considerably, as overseas supplies come chiefly from Chile, Peru, Zambia, and the Congo—areas that are known for abrupt political changes. The cutting off of production or the resumption of production in these areas has caused large and rapid changes in world copper prices. It can be assumed that this will continue to be the case. Nevertheless, the position of copper in future world trade seems certain to be strong overall, and it should be one of the major investment considerations for anyone interested in natural resources.

With regard to investing in "copper mines" that people may want to sell you, keep in mind that a little copper staining goes a long way in rocks along fractures. You can have the finest-looking copper-green outcrop in the country and still have very little copper. Copper in various mineral compositions is colorful and eye-catching, and therefore much time and effort has been spent in staking claims and digging holes in green and blue rocks. It is great exercise and I have visited many of these workings at the request of persons who, after a time, began to see the realities of the situation. Usually, only a well directed core-drilling program will establish the presence of a significant copper deposit. Don't put your money on the table because of a pile of green-stained rocks.

Also, copper occurs in veins and veinlets in many places. A

given sample from a vein can be very rich (veins can run 10 percent or more copper), but one usually cannot economically pursue small veins by underground mining. Underground mining is expensive for several reasons—the great amount of rock that has to be taken out along with the copper vein, the cost of timbering the mine, the water problems (mines fill up with water if they're not continually pumped out in most cases), and the cost of the greater amount of hand labor needed in digging rock out of small places than in open-pit methods.

The most notable underground vein-type copper mine in North America was that of Anaconda at Butte, Montana. Eventually, however, with the development of huge earth-moving machinery and more efficient copper recovery methods, it too was converted into an open pit operation—the Berkeley pit. The veins are rich and closely enough spaced so that the whole rock mass can be mined. The percentage of copper therein is equal to a porphyry-type copper deposit that has the copper initially scattered all through the rock. So again, beware of vein-type deposits. Selected samples will give a high analysis, but copper has to be mined in substantial quantities to make it profitable, and veins usually do not lend themselves to this sort of operation. There are exceptions; it always pays to check into the situation anyway.

IRON

Background. The earliest recorded use of iron was around 2000 B.C. by the Egyptians, who used iron found in meteorites in some of their weapons. History does not record when iron smelting was discovered, but it was probably by accident in some large charcoal fire. By 400 B.C. iron was in common use. The first iron-making in the New World was sponsored by Sir Walter Raleigh in 1610 at Falling Creek, Virginia, where "bog iron ore" (limonite, a hydrous iron oxide in swamp deposits) was smelted. This operation came to an unfortunate and sudden ending when all the iron workers were killed by Indians in 1622.

Major events since that time in the United States have been the discovery of the great Lake Superior iron ores in 1845 and the development of the Bessemer steel process in 1850. More recently, as the high-grade hematite deposits (60 to 70 percent iron) have been worked out, the development of the process to convert the huge low-grade taconite (20 to 30 percent iron) to concentrated iron ore pellets has been of major significance.

With the aid of some tax concessions given in belated recognition of the huge investment and technical problems involved, the iron ore industry remained in Minnesota instead of moving out toward foreign deposits, which they would have had to do otherwise. Large open pits have now replaced almost all the earlier underground iron ore operations, although much early iron mining was also by open pit methods such as at the Hull-Rust mine at Hibbing, sometimes called "the Grand Canyon of the Midwest."

Present Demand and Uses. We may be in the Atomic Age in one sense, but we are still in the Iron Age for all practical purposes in terms of metal use. This is likely to be the case for the foreseeable future. There is no metal more vital to our modern industrial society than is iron and its many alloys. It would be superfluous to list the various uses of iron. Demand will grow with growth of the economies of the world, though an increasing amount of iron scrap also will be recovered and recycled.

The United States has been consuming about 25 percent of the world's primary supply of iron and produces about 13 percent. However, iron ore reserves are sufficient in the United States to supply all domestic uses, so imports would not be needed. Small price differentials (which are important when huge amounts of a material are used) and the advantages of ocean shipping serve to make foreign iron ore deposits competitive with domestic supplies.

The process of pelletizing taconite into iron ore is more costly than simply mining the higher-grade hematite and shipping it, but the hematite deposits are now largely exhausted. However, there is a compensating factor in that taconite pellets provide a uniform-quality charge to the blast furnaces. The resulting increase in efficiency partially offsets the higher cost of the pellets.

Sources. There are sufficient world supplies of iron ore to last hundreds of years at the present rate of consumption. Measured reserves of iron ore that can be exploited profitably at current prices are sufficient for well into the 21st century at present production rates. The Soviet Union is credited with having the largest deposits, with Canada next, closely followed by the United States and South America (chiefly Venezuela, Brazil and Peru). Africa, the Far East, and Australia also have large amounts of iron ore.

Iron occurs in many minerals, but the most common ores are, in order of richness, magnetite, hematite, and taconite (more a rock than a mineral). Limonite is a local minor ore, and siderite, an iron carbonate, has been important in England. Magnetite occurs in igneous rocks and has a 72.2 percent iron content, but mining costs usually are high for this sort of deposit compared with lower-grade ores from open pit operations. The famous Kiirunavaara iron deposit at Kiruna, Sweden, is a magnetite body about 4,000 meters long and about 90 meters wide. The bulk of the deposits in the United States, and many of those in other parts of the world, are sedimentary in origin. Those of northern Minnesota were deposited in the bed of a very ancient, shallow sea, possibly precipitated by iron-secreting bacteria. Algae also grew in these iron-rich waters and some of the algal structures are still preserved in the Biwabik iron formation. While working in that area one year I collected some large pieces of these fossil algae in the iron ore and cut them into bookends, a purpose for which they are admirably suited, being quite heavy. It stirs my imagination as I look at these iron-ore-algae bookends in my office to visualize these algal beds growing quietly in a shallow sea a couple of billion years ago in what is now the northwoods country of my native state.

The hematite deposits of northern Minnesota were formed by the localization of weathering processes due to fractures and other geological features. This caused a local enrichment of the low-grade taconite deposits, upgrading them to hematite through the leaching out of the more soluble waste materials and leaving behind the less soluble iron compounds. These hematite deposits have been likened to raisins in a large loaf of bread made out of the low-grade taconite.

Taconite is a siliceous iron-bearing rock, wherein the iron is in two forms. One of them is magnetic and can be separated from the taconite matrix by crushing and then running the material through a magnetic separator. A large amount of iron, however, is bound up in a silica compound that is non-magnetic and that to date has resisted any large-scale economic recovery of the iron. This problem is being worked on by the U.S. Bureau of Mines and others, but meanwhile the siliceous iron is simply being stockpiled toward the time when technology will make this an ore also—keeping in mind again that "ore" is an economic term and means that a metal or metals can be extracted *at a profit.* Technology often can turn what is useless material today into a valuable mineral deposit tomorrow.

Outlook and Investment. The obvious outlook for iron is that its use will grow with the growth of world economies; additional reclaiming of scrap in the United States especially may moderate the demand somewhat, but the continual solid growth in use of iron is assured for the indefinite future. Most major iron ore companies are integrated—that is, they have mines, transport facilities, and smelters and turn out finished products, as does U.S. Steel, Bethlehem, and others. A few companies are strictly iron ore producers, such as Steep Rock Iron Mines in Canada and Hanna Mining Company in the United States. In some cases iron ore properties are mined on a royalty basis, and smaller companies and even individuals have held these over the years. An example is Mesabi Trust, whose certificates are traded on the New York Stock Exchange. The ore is mined by and sold to Reserve Mining Company, which is a joint operation of two steel companies. The royalties are almost 100 percent paid out to the certificate holders, as per the legalities of the trust. An interesting provision is that the price of the ore is adjusted annually according to the cost-of-living index of the Bureau of Labor Statistics, so that the trust certificate owners are protected against inflation. The trust certificates represent ownership in a 9,700-acre taconite property in northern Minnesota. This fact together with the cost-of-living escalation clause combine to make this an income situation that is both bomb-proof and inflation-resistant. There is not much an A-bomb or any other bomb can do to 15 square miles of taconite. Another nice fact is that the reserves are estimated to be good for at least 40 years at present rates of mining. Great Northern Iron Ore is another iron mine royalty situation.

Iron mining is very competitive in that there are ample supplies. No one has a corner on sources, unlike with certain other Earth materials that some select areas of the world are blessed with but that most other areas are not. The result is that simple availability of the iron is only part of the story; freight rates and distance to markets and taxes and other political factors all enter the picture.

Investing in iron ore is done chiefly in the major iron and steel companies, most of which have interests both here and abroad. U.S. Steel Corporation is in a premier position. In Canada, Dominion Foundries and Steel, Ltd., is a major producer. Quebec Cartier Mining Company (wholly-owned subsidiary of U.S. Steel Corporation) is a very large producer as is Iron Ore Company of Canada (owned by Labrador Mining and Exploration Company) and Wabush Mines (owned by The Steel Company of Canada).

LEAD

Background.   Lead has been used by the human race for approximately 6,000 years and is the fifth most important metal in our present economy. The Greeks used lead in building construction. The Romans made lead water pipes, which has led to the conjecture that one of the things leading to the downfall of the Roman empire may have been lead poisoning. The Latin word "plumbum," meaning "heavy," was given to lead. From the use of lead in pipes we have derived the name "plumbing."

Lead also was used in early coinage, indicating that the lead quarter has had at least an ancient if not an honorable past. The Chinese, who seem to have a number of distinguished "firsts," also have the dubious distinction of being the first to make lead money. Later, when silver coins came into use, the government forbade working the lead mines to prevent counterfeiting. Greek and Roman governments used various amounts of lead in their coins. When a bit impoverished they sometimes simply coated lead coins with silver. They had not yet figured out the handy device now used by obviously more advanced civilizations of just printing paper money.

Lead, with copper and silver, probably was one of the first metals smelted, as it has a low melting point. Because of its common occurrence and the relative simplicity of its reduction and combination with other metals, lead was used by many ancient peoples.

Present Demand and Uses. Lead has many uses, chiefly in storage batteries, ammunition, cable covering, pipes, paint pigments, and as a gasoline antiknock additive (this last use is being phased out to a degree). Demand for lead in storage batteries may be expected to triple or even quadruple between now and the end of this century, but other uses will show less rapid growth. Even the use of lead in batteries also could be somewhat diminished by the development of lightweight sodium-sulfur and lithium- or sodium-water batteries. Demand for newly mined lead also has to meet the competition from scrap lead—a third of the lead now used in the United States is reclaimed. In total, the use of lead may grow about as fast as the economy, unless some major new application is discovered. As lead compounds are toxic in varying degrees, lead has some environmental problems.

Sources. Both Canada and the United States are major sources of lead. Although the United States actually imports appreciable amounts, recent huge discoveries in the Viburnum Trend or "New Lead Belt" in the Mississippi River Valley are sufficient to make the United States independent of foreign supplies. Lead will not be in shortage until at least the year 2000 and probably well beyond.

Accordingly, unless new deposits would be very rich, as compared with those now known (and those known are quite good), a new lead deposit would not be a particularly significant event for a company, although ultimately, of course, any good-grade metal deposit of size will be worthwhile. Some lead deposits, however, carry substantial quantities of silver, and that metal combination in a newly discovered ore deposit would be welcome.

There are some potentially large and somewhat unusual lead deposits that might be developed in the foreseeable future, and as these deposits also contain other metals of higher value the lead could simply be a cheap by-product. These deposits are in the form of brines and muds in the bottom of the Red Sea, which some company may eventually perfect the technology to exploit economically.

Outlook and Investment. The immediate and longer term outlooks for lead are for fairly steady but moderate growth in use, with supplies ample for foreseeable needs, particularly in

North America. By and large, the same companies that mine major amounts of zinc are also lead producers, as lead and zinc are commonly associated geologically. These companies include American Smelting and Refining, American Metal Climax-Homestake Mining (joint operation in Missouri), Hecla Mining, St. Joe Minerals, NL Industries (formerly National Lead), and Texas Gulf. Kennecott Copper also has major lead holdings in Missouri. In Canada, Brunswick Mining and Smelting, Pine Point Mines, Ecstall Mining (subsidiary of Texas Gulf), Noranda Mines, Cominco, and Hudson Bay Mining and Smelting are major producers. There are many small companies that also mine lead.

Very large lead deposits are known in the Broken Hill area of New South Wales and at Mount Isa, Queensland, in Australia, and it is usually possible for North American investors to buy stock in companies developing some of these deposits. Your brokerage firm can no doubt give you further information, and I know of some that buy and sell Australian stocks for their customers.

MAGNESIUM AND MAGNESITE

Background. Magnesium metal was first produced in Germany in 1886, but prior to that time magnesite, a natural magnesium carbonate, had been used as refractory material to line furnaces. By 1931, German manufacturers had developed a worldwide market for magnesium alloys, but the advent of World War II cut off magnesium supplies from Germany. Subsequently the United States increased its production of magnesium, including development of a process to obtain it from sea water. Prior to producing magnesium directly from sea water, it had been obtained from brines trapped in the rocks of the Michigan Basin, residual from ancient seas in Michigan. Dow Chemical pioneered this process.

Present Demand and Uses. Magnesium is the lightest of all structural metals (but not the lightest metal, which is lithium). It is widely used as an alloy in aluminum and as a structural metal by itself. About 80 percent of the magnesium metal is used for structural aluminum and magnesium alloys in aircraft and missiles, machinery, chemical products, tools, and various consumer products. It is also used for cathodic protection of other metals. One of the world's largest users of magnesium metal has been Volkswagenwerk, A. G., and each Volkswagen automobile contains about 42 pounds of the metal. New applications are being found at a rather steady rate, including uses in batteries, in photoengraving plates, and in various military applications. Magnesium compounds collectively called basic refractories are indispensable in the production of steel and other metals, as they are used in the lining of furnaces. About 30 pounds of magnesium in magnesium compounds is used for each ton of ingot steel produced, and this use accounts for about 80 percent of the magnesium used today.

Sources. Magnesium is the eighth most plentiful element in the Earth and, in various forms, makes up about 2.06 percent of the Earth's crust. Magnesium occurs in 60 or more natural materials, but only four—dolomite, magnesite, brucite, and olivine—are used commercially to produce its compounds. At present, dolomite is the only domestic ore used as the principal raw material for making magnesium metal. Sea water and brines from wells (waters from ancient seas) are also principal sources of magnesium, the third most abundant element dissolved in sea water, averaging about 0.13 percent magnesium by weight. A cubic mile of sea water contains about six million tons of magnesium—an amount more than has been produced in the entire history of the world. Magnesium also occurs in quantity in certain saline lakes, including Great Salt Lake, Utah.

Of the four magnesium minerals, dolomite, magnesite, brucite, and olivine, dolomite is by far the most widespread. It is actually in rock-like form like limestone and covers many square miles of the Earth's surface. There is no shortage of magnesium. Quantities are very large in nearly every country. The prime cost in obtaining magnesium is the energy required to process the raw material. Therefore, discovery of a new source of magnesium would not be particularly important to an individual or company.

Outlook and Investment. Demand for magnesium and its compounds will increase rather steadily to the next century. Its chief competitor, outside of its use in refractories, is aluminum, which at the present time is cheaper and easier to fabricate. Technical advances both in production and fabrication of magnesium may serve to make it more competitive in the future, and the fact of its virtual unlimited supply will give it an advantage over other, less abundant substitute metals. However, aluminum is not in this category, being itself very common and substantially more abundant than magnesium.

Investment opportunities in magnesium-producing companies at present include Dow Chemical, by far the leading producer (almost entirely from sea water), American Magnesium Company, and NL Industries, which produces magnesium from the brines of Great Salt Lake. Dominion Magnesium produces this metal in Canada.

Other opportunities for investment in magnesium would be largely in the areas of technology designed to reduce extraction costs either from sea water or from the common magnesium-bearing rocks. In compounds, Basic Inc. produces magnesium in the form of refractory materials and has a large mine near Gabbs, Nevada.

Comment. The direct environmental impact of magnesium production is modest. Lands mined for magnesium ores can be reclaimed fairly easily as the areas are not large. In the case of recovery of magnesium from sea water, there is no polluting effect from the discharge back into the ocean of sea water that has had its magnesium removed. There is an indirect impact on the environment, however, through the large amounts of energy required to obtain magnesium from either its rock or sea water source. In this respect magnesium is similar to aluminum.

MANGANESE

Background. Manganese is a metal similar to chromium and iron. It was used for centuries in glassmaking to remove objectionable tints and produce a colorless product. This was the only application for manganese until the latter part of the 18th century when Scheele, a Swedish chemist, prepared chlorine by heating manganese dioxide with hydrochloric acid. From then until about 1850, manganese ores were used extensively in the manufacture of chlorine.

Manganese has been used in the manufacture of iron and steel since about 1839, when it was found that addition of manganese improved malleability. It came into more general use in steel-making with the advent of the Bessemer process. The addition of manganese greatly improves the forging characteristics of steel made by this process and enables steel to be rolled hot without cracking or tearing.

Present Demand and Uses. Currently manganese is used in the production of nearly all steel and cast iron. It is used as a scavenger in molten steel to remove sulfur and oxygen, which make steel brittle; it is used also as an alloy. Manganese is also employed in the chemical industry in dry batteries. More than 90 percent of manganese used in the United States is by the steel industry, and despite much research no substitute has been found. About 13 to 20 pounds of manganese is consumed per ton of steel. Demand obviously parallels the production of iron and steel.

Sources. Manganese production in the United States has been sporadic, and the odds are that as you read this page there is no U.S. current production. Manganese occurs in several geological circumstances, including bedded deposits in shales as at Chamberlin, South Dakota. It occurs also in slightly higher-grade deposits in the Cayuna Iron Range of Minnesota, and in Maine, Montana, Arizona, and New Mexico. But the total amount of ore in the United States that would yield a currently acceptable concentrate of manganese by presently known methods (35 percent) is probably no greater than 1 million tons. The United States has been importing virtually all of its supplies. South Africa has the world's largest deposits, closely followed in amount by the Soviet Union. Brazil, India, and Australia have deposits and supply the United States. The United States uses about 13 percent of world production, and the government at times stockpiles manganese as a strategic material.

Manganese ores around the world, however, are believed to contain at least 1 billion tons of the metal, much larger than the high end of the projected world demand to the year 2000.

It should be noted that very large manganese deposits exist on the ocean floors in the form of manganese nodules. So far these have not been exploited, but several companies have plans to do this. At least one firm, Hughes Tool, has had an experimental ship in operation for some time. Economic recovery and processing of these nodules (not only for their manganese content but for their nickel, cobalt, and copper also) could prove very rewarding.

Outlook and Investment. There is no substitute for manganese in modern steel making, and consumption will rise with steel production. Investment in manganese in North America is virtually precluded by the absence of any substantial high-grade deposits. Bethlehem Steel does hold some manganese ores of sorts in the United States and has substantial deposits abroad. Abundant foreign supplies indicate that manganese prices probably will not rise from current levels relative to other commodities.

MOLYBDENUM

Background. Molybdenum was discovered about 200 years ago, but it is a metal of fairly recent entry into the industrial scene, chiefly after World War I. The Germans knew about molybdenum's unique quality in toughening steel and called this fact rather forcefully to world attention in World War I when they built the famous cannon "Big Bertha"—110 feet long and weighing 42 tons. It was made of tough molybdenum steel, which withstood the force of the blast that sent 264-pound artillery shells into Paris 76 miles away.

Present Demand and Uses. Molybdenum has a number of useful qualities, including a high melting point (2,620° C—the fifth highest melting point of all metals), a very low coefficient of thermal expansion, resistance to acids and oxidation at ordinary temperatures, and a high thermal and electrical conductivity. It strengthens steel, allowing bridges and other structures to be built using much less steel than otherwise, thus significantly reducing both weight and cost. It is also used in many other ways including in chemicals, as a vital trace element in fertilizers, in lubricants, in catalysts, in pigments, and in the manufacture of high-speed cutting tools. In some uses it can substitute for nickel, chromium, columbium, tungsten, vanadium, and boron. There are essentially no competitive substitutes for molybdenum in certain critical applications, and its several unique qualities are of particular value in propulsion applications (especially space propulsion) and in nuclear power generation equipment. The United States uses about 40 percent of the world supply, but this percentage (but not quantity) will probably decrease as other countries become industrially more developed, particularly in steel production.

Sources. The United States produces three-fourths of the free world's supply of molybdenum and has slightly over half the world's identified resources. By far the largest single deposit is at Climax, Colorado. Other major sources are the copper producers of western United States, where molybdenum is associated with the porphyry copper deposits. About 95 percent of the world's molybdenum is found in porphyry-type rocks and other disseminated deposits. Canada produces about 15 percent of the world's supply and the remainder comes chiefly from the Soviet Union and China.

Outlook and Investment. The outlook for molybdenum is good. The supply available is also potentially large, so no shortages are expected at reasonable prices into the next century. Accordingly, whereas the demand will be strong, the price will probably not rise above the general level of other commodities. It will be a steadily growing and substantial business. Investing in molybdenum is a simple situation, the obvious answer being to "buy Mount Moly," American Metal Climax's deposit in Colorado. It is the world's single largest source. Molybdenum Corporation of America (now called Molycorp and 18 percent owned by International Mining Corporation), Kennecott Copper, Duval Corporation (99 percent owned by Pennzoil United, Inc.), Newmont Mining (through its Magma Copper operation in Arizona), Phelps Dodge, and Anaconda are also substantial producers. In Canada, Noranda Mines is a major source along with Molybdenite Corporation of Canada. Placer Development, Preissac Molybdenite Mines, and Cadillac Moly-Mines also are producers.

Comments. Environmental effects of molybdenum production, when chiefly molybdenum is mined, are modest. A relatively few acres are involved per unit of production and the amount of land area that has to be reclaimed is minimal. The copper mines that also produce molybdenum disturb somewhat greater areas. Some air pollution occurs from the smelting of molybdenum ores and this may lead to the shifting of smelter locations in the future.

NICKEL

Background. Ancient people apparently used nickel before they knew what it was, as they utilized nickel-iron meteorites as a source of material for weapons. Nickel has been identified in Chinese coins dating back to 800 B.C. and in Greek coins of 300 B.C. Pure nickel was discovered in 1751. The name, incidentally, comes from the fact that the miners called the nickel arsenide they were mining "Old Nick" because the arsenic in it caused skin irritations and forced the miners to wear rawhide gloves and boots for protection. Nickel was mined only in a small way until the large deposits of New Caledonia began production in 1875. The great nickel deposits of the Sudbury area, Canada, were discovered about 1890, and International Nickel Company of Canada, Ltd., was formed in 1902. Nickel is one of the several most important metals today and is likely to remain so.

Present Demand and Uses. Historically the demand for nickel has been rising more rapidly than that for most other metals, as new uses have been found for it. Over 90 percent of nickel is used in metal form, principally alloys, where its ability to resist corrosion and to impart strength is very useful in many consumer goods. Nickel is also used in dyes, batteries, pigments, as a catalyst, and in insecticides. It is one of the strategic metals for war.

Sources. World nickel reserves (but not all mineable ore at present prices) are estimated at about 150 billion pounds, but this figure is probably conservative. Using this number, however, Cuba is credited with 36 billion pounds, New Caledonia with 33 billion, Canada and the Soviet Union each with 20 billion, and the United States with 400 million. In terms of mineable ore, Canada appears to have the largest deposits, located in Ontario and Manitoba.

The only source of nickel in the United States is at Riddle, Oregon, where Hanna Mining Company operates a mine and smelter.

Nickel occurs both in sulfide primary ore from hot solutions, as at Sudbury, and as a residual ore resulting from the weathering of certain types of rocks with a low nickel content. The nickel minerals are more resistant to weathering than are the other, valueless materials. As a result the nickel is concentrated on the surface to the point where it becomes an ore. This is the origin of the deposit in Oregon and of several nickel deposits now being explored and developed in Central America, Colombia, the Solomon Islands, and Australia.

There also are some very large low-grade sulfide deposits (hard minerals in hard rocks) in what is called the Duluth Gabbro of northern Minnesota. Some 6.9 billion pounds are estimated to exist there but the difficulties of extraction have not yet been solved economically; International Nickel and others are working on the problem.

Outlook and Investment. The demand for nickel seems likely to grow at least as fast as the general world economies, and perhaps faster. It is an exceedingly useful metal with wide applications. However, large new deposits are being brought into production and this would indicate that the price of nickel will stay in line with commodities in general. There are ample nickel resources to take care of world demand to the year 2000. In North America, the Canadian companies of International Nickel, Falconbridge, and Sherritt Gordon Mines are leading nickel producers. As already mentioned the only U.S. producer is Hanna Mining, whose operations are chiefly in iron ore.

Interests in what appears to be a very large nickel deposit in Western Australia are held by Union Oil, Homestake Mining, and Hanna Mining, together with an Australian company, Poseidon N. L. Kaiser Aluminum and Chemical is a partner in a New Caledonian nickel venture.

TITANIUM

Background. Titanium, discovered in 1790, was not used commercially, as an alloy in steel, until more than 100 years later. As a metal by itself it was not used until 1948.

Present Demand and Uses. Titanium's strength compared to its weight exceeds that of steel, especially at higher temperatures. This fact favors the use of titanium in aircraft and aerospace engines and other structures. Also, it is now possible to cast titanium rather than having to machine it to form. This has reduced the cost of making component parts. Titanium also is resistant to corrosion and has numerous applications in the chemical industry. It continues to be used in dioxide form as a pigment in paints because of its superior covering qualities and chemical inertness. This use accounts for about 90 percent of current titanium consumption in the United States. Demand for titanium is strong, and considering how recently titanium in all its various forms has come to be utilized, it seems likely that this strong demand will continue.

Sources. Although estimated to be the ninth most abundant element in the Earth's crust, titanium is obtained commercially from just two minerals, ilmenite and rutile. South Africa has the largest titanium reserves; Norway is next, followed by the United States, Canada, and the Soviet Union, with about equal amounts. Australia has substantial deposits. When the factor of current economics and technology is applied, however, Norway comes out first, with the United States and Canada following. Titanium minerals are obtained both directly from mining igneous rocks, in which they were originally formed in the Earth's crust, and also as placer deposits—old beach and stream deposits. Some of these beach deposits are now submerged and the titanium minerals are recovered by dredging. Ilmenite deposits form the so-called "black sands" of Florida, Georgia, and New Jersey. Titanium deposits are known in igneous rocks from Virginia and New York.

Outlook and Investment. The future for titanium appears to be good if not excellent, but the lower-cost, easily developed deposits are not likely to meet the demand to the year 2000. Higher-cost deposits will have to be brought into production. There is indication that substantial titanium deposits exist yet undiscovered in offshore areas. Companies that can solve this ocean prospecting and mining problem will have obtained a valuable resource. NL Corporation, with mines in the United States and Norway, controls about 50 percent of the world reserves of ilmenite, the principal ore mineral for titanium. Western Titanium N. L. is a major producer in Australia as is Consolidated Goldfields of South Africa (but in Australia), Conzinc Rio Tinto, and NL Corporation. Titanium reserves in Sierra Leone, Africa, are 80 percent owned by PPG Industries and 20 percent by British Titan Products Company. Canada has substantial deposits, and Quebec Iron and Titanium Corporation, approximately two-thirds owned by Kennecott Copper Corporation, is an important producer. Titanium Metals Corporation of

America, owned jointly by NL Industries and Allegheny Ludlum
Steel, is the only producer of titanium metal that is fully integrated from mine to semi-finished titanium products. NL Industries, with about 50 percent of its worldwide sales coming from
titanium operations of various sorts, is the most heavily invested
firm in titanium in the world. In other firms, titanium is only a
small part of total operations.

TUNGSTEN

Background. The name tungsten comes from two Swedish
words, "tung" and "sten," meaning heavy stone. The metal was
discovered in the 1780s. The first important use of tungsten was
as an alloy of steel in the middle 1800s, which accounted for
most of its use before 1900. Afterward, with the advent of electric light bulb production in quantity and mass production of
consumer steel goods such as cars, tungsten came into its own
because of its exceedingly high melting point (3,400° C) and the
fact that it has the highest tensile strength of all metals (maximum 590,000 pounds per square inch). These properties make
tungsten invaluable in the production of high-speed metal-cutting tools, which keep their sharp edges at high temperatures,
and as filaments in electric lights.

Present Demand and Uses. Tungsten, because of its dis-
tinctive properties, has many uses basic to our rapidly diversify-
ing technology. It will be an increasingly important, if not a
critical, commodity in world trade.

Sources. Of known and estimated world resources of tungsten, about 80 percent are believed to be in Communist countries—60 percent in China and 20 percent in North Korea and
the Soviet Union. Tungsten geologically occurs along contacts
of granitic rocks with limestones and dolomites and in veins in
both the limestones and dolomites and in granites. It also occurs
in porphyry deposits that contain molybdenum. Although more
than 20 minerals carry tungsten, only wolframite and scheelite
are important as ores.

In the United States the chief tungsten deposits in hard rocks
are in California, Colorado, Nevada, and North Carolina. However, there are substantial additional domestic resources in the
brines of Searles Lake, California, and at the mine-dump tailings

at American Metal Climax's mine at Climax, Colorado. The Searles Lake brines are partially controlled by American Potash and Chemical, now a unit of Kerr-McGee. Canada has only small known tungsten deposits, but prospects for discovery of additional reserves are fair to good.

Outlook and Investment. The United States has been producing not much more than half of its tungsten needs historically and is likely to continue to be a net importer of this critical metal. The United States now uses about 20 percent of world tungsten production. Known domestic tungsten ores will probably not last until 1990. Increased prices seem certain. This will stimulate exploration both here and abroad and more deposits can be expected to be discovered. Tungsten comes from about 50 mines in the United States, but the great bulk of production is from the single mine of Union Carbide Corporation at Pine Creek, near Bishop, California, where tungsten is the major and molybdenum the minor product. At the Climax mine of American Metal Climax, molybdenum is the major product and tungsten the minor. Ranchers Exploration and Development Corporation owns the Tungsten Queen Mine in North Carolina, which is one of the larger deposits in the United States but has been worked only intermittently.

Canada Tungsten Mining Corporation has been the principal producer in Canada. There are a number of other small properties that produce from time to time, depending on market conditions. American Metal Climax has a sizeable tungsten property straddling the Yukon-Northwest Territories boundary.

Comment. Western United States in particular has many small tungsten prospects, and the chances of finding additional deposits are good. Even relatively small deposits would be worthwhile in view of the rapidly rising demand and expected higher prices for the metal. This is a situation where prospecting in the old classic sense might still pay off, particularly as tungsten's two ores, scheelite and wolframite, both have the property of fluorescing under a black light and therefore are easy to identify. One approach to tungsten prospecting has simply been to go out in the dark of the moon with a black light and walk areas where granite comes in contact with other rocks. The best rocks for tungsten mineralization are limestones and dolomites along these granites. The tungsten minerals give a bright yellow fluorescence. A note of caution, however, is in order. Both rattlesnakes and scorpions are nocturnal and also fluoresce, with the result that scorpions are sometimes known as "Arizona scheelite." If it buzzes or stings, don't stake a claim.

VANADIUM

Background. Vanadium was first discovered in Mexico in 1801 but was not recognized as a new element until 1831. The vanadium content of the Earth's crust is more than that of copper, lead, or zinc. Vanadium, however, is distributed through a wide variety of rocks and tends not to concentrate and form ore bodies easily.

Present Demand and Uses. Principal use of vanadium has been in steel alloys and more recently in jet engines and in nuclear plant construction. Demand is strong and expected to rise more rapidly than the growth of population.

Sources. Vanadium is presently recovered chiefly as a by-product of uranium mining, but small amounts come from vanadium ores as such, which are vanadium-titaniferous magnetites. Some vanadium is obtained as a result of phosphate mining. It is also known in asphalts and crude oil and in oil shales. These latter sources could become commercial in the future.

Outlook and Investment. A growth rate in consumption higher than that of any other ferrous metal has been predicted for vanadium to the year 2000 in the United States. Foreign consumption is predicted to have a similar trend. Projected domestic requirements to the year 2000 exceed the estimated amount of vanadium available from currently producing domestic reserves by 300,000 to 400,000 tons. Additional sources in carbonaceous shales and other deposits will be sufficient to bridge this gap but probably at relatively higher prices. Those companies with uranium deposits in sandstone (the form of most of the uranium deposits of the United States) are those that hold vanadium reserves (see section on "Uranium"). Some oil companies also have the metal, as do firms that mine phosphate containing vanadium. They include FMC Corporation and Stauffer Chemical, with their vanadium-bearing Idaho and Wyoming phosphate deposits. In Canada, Petrofina Canada, Ltd., recovers a small amount of vanadium from crude oil.

ZINC

Background. Zinc has been used for many centuries, first only as an alloy but later as a metal by itself and as a component of chemical compounds. Zinc, in alloy form as brass, was known by the Greeks and Romans, who melted copper and zinc minerals together. Zinc as a distinct metal was not known until the Middle Ages, and modern zinc smelting began in Belgium in 1806. At present, zinc is the fourth most important metal in world trade, after iron, aluminum, and copper. Zinc has had a phenomenal rise in use during the 20th century. Half of all the zinc produced in the world up to 1970 has been since 1950. When all production between now and the end of this century is added up it will surely total substantially more than all the zinc used in the world from the beginning of history to 1970.

Present Demand and Uses. Although subject to business cycles to some extent, the demand for zinc is increasing and is likely to continue that way for some time. Zinc is used chiefly in three ways, which account for about 90 percent of the total: for zinc-base alloy die castings, for galvanizing iron and steel, and in the manufacture of brass, a compound of zinc and copper. Zinc has competition in some of its uses, such as in die castings, where both plastics and aluminum can be substituted. But zinc seems to have no significant competition in its major use for corrosion protection of a wide variety of iron and steel products. Zinc also is an important trace element for plant growth and is used in fertilizers. Some zinc can be reclaimed but not nearly so extensively as lead.

Sources. United States zinc consumption has grown consistently since the 1940s but mine production has been relatively static, resulting in increased imports to the extent that the majority of U.S. supplies are now obtained abroad. Canada is a major source. The distribution of estimated major zinc reserves around the world shows that the United States is credited with 34 million tons, Canada 25 million, Eastern and Western Europe each with 14 million, Asia 10 million, and Australia with 9 million.

In the United States the major deposits are in Tennessee, the tri-state mining district of Kansas-Oklahoma-Missouri, and in Idaho and Washington. In Canada major deposits are in British

Columbia and at Pine Point on Great Slave Lake, Northwest Territories. In the past both New York and New Jersey have been substantial producers.

The chief ore mineral of zinc is sphalerite, a zinc sulfide, but zinc occurs in at least 55 minerals. Its geological associations are very similar to lead; it occurs in beds of sedimentary rocks such as in limestones in the Mississippi Valley region, in vein deposits, as massive igneous deposits, and in the form of zinc minerals left in fractured and other porous rocks from hot zinc-bearing solutions.

Outlook and Investment. The outlook for zinc is good, and any new discoveries of size and quality would significantly enhance the future of the company concerned. The United States and Canada are fairly well supplied with zinc reserves, but there is competition from large imports of foreign, less-costly sources. At higher prices zinc in much larger quantities can be produced domestically, and it would appear from rising nationalistic trends abroad that higher prices will result. Zinc should do as well as if not better than many other commodities to the end of this century.

A number of companies mine zinc, including American Metal Climax, American Smelting and Refining, Gulf Resources and Chemical, Gulf and Western Industries, Hecla Mining, Kennecott, and St. Joe Minerals. In Canada, Cominco, Hudson Bay Mining and Smelting, and Pine Point Mines are major producers. Texas Gulf, based in New York, has substantial Canadian zinc production, and there are numerous smaller companies.

Large lead-zinc deposits occur in Australia. In fact, Mount Isa Mines of Australia (52 percent owned by American Smelting and Refining) seems likely to become the world's largest single lead-zinc-silver producer. It is possible for investors to purchase shares of companies developing these deposits. Check with your brokerage firm.

Comment. Potentially there are at least two large undeveloped zinc deposits that are a challenge to technical ingenuity. Companies that can solve the problems of their development economically will have "discovered" very significant zinc supplies. Both these deposits are on ocean floors. There are an estimated 1½ trillion tons of manganese nodules on the ocean floor with 0.05 percent zinc, which amounts to about 750 million tons of zinc. To put this in perspective, the United States has been using about 1½ million tons of zinc per year. Also, in the Atlantis Deep II in the Red Sea, hot brines from submarine volcanic activity have deposited an estimated 2.9 million metric tons of zinc. There also are substantial low-grade zinc deposits on land that can be brought into production if prices rise or if more-efficient recovery methods can be devised. The rising demand for zinc, together with the chance for technological advances in mining and processing both on land and on the sea floor, will no doubt result in investment opportunities in the years ahead.

ZIRCONIUM

Background. Zirconium is not well known to most people and is sometimes thought of as a relatively rare element. Actually it is more abundant in the Earth's crust than nickel, copper, lead, or zinc. It was first discovered in 1789 but it was not until 1925 that the pure metal was isolated.

Present Demand and Uses. Zirconium has a number of useful properties. Two of them are extreme resistance to heat and a very high degree of inertness to attack by air, seawater, alkalies, and acids. Both qualities combine to make zirconium a very useful material in the construction of nuclear reactors, particularly for making the tubing in heat exchangers. Zirconium has many other uses, including in paints, abrasives, ferroalloys, and pharmaceuticals.

Despite all these fine qualities, demand for zirconium is moderate. Although its specialized uses such as in nuclear reactors are growing rapidly, this tends to be offset by slower growth of zirconium in its major uses, with which it competes with other materials. The net result is that growth of zirconium production is only about 3 to 4 percent a year.

Sources. The principal source of zirconium is the mineral zircon. It is a primary mineral in granitic rocks but cannot be obtained from granite economically. Zirconium is resistant to weathering and tends to accumulate in beach sand deposits in many parts of the world. Both the east and west coasts of the United States have such deposits. The 5 million tons of zirconium in the mineral zircon recognized in the United States is a large resource base. At the present time, however, zircon is recovered only from sand-type deposits as a by-product or co-product of the recovery of titanium minerals. The rate at which zircon is recovered, therefore, is dependent on the demand for titanium from these relatively low-grade deposits. So for the period to the year 2000 only about 1.2 million tons of zirconium are projected to be actually available. If, however, the demand for zirconium should rise sharply, the situation could be reversed, with titanium minerals becoming the by-product of zirconium mining. This is a good example of how price determines the amount of "ore" that is available.

Of the identified zirconium resources of the world, the United States has somewhat more than one-third and the Soviet Union and Australia each about one-sixth. Australia has been and continues to be a major producer.

Outlook and Investment. Zirconium has such a wide variety of uses—although for the most part each is quite small—that the demand for it will probably grow with the gross national product, or about 4 percent a year. However, it has a number of qualities that, with the occasional sudden shifts in demands of technology, could cause it to be substantially more popular. Only one company in the United States, the E. I. du Pont de Nemours and Company with mines at Trail Ridge, Florida, and at Folkston, Georgia, has been consistently mining zirconium. Canada does not produce zirconium, although minor occurrences are known. Australia has been recovering zircon, the ore of zirconium, from beach sands for a number of years, largely for export.

13

Minor Metals

THE LIST OF MINOR METALS is fairly long and includes some that are unfamiliar to many people. Some of these unfamiliar metals, nevertheless, are in daily use by nearly all of us. An example is selenium whose light-related electrical properties are the basis of the process on which the Xerox Corporation was built. Another example is germanium, which is used in transistors and has revolutionized the communications industries.

Antimony	Germanium	Scandium
Arsenic	Hafnium	Selenium
Barium	Indium	Silicon
Bismuth	Lithium	Sodium
Cadmium	Mercury	Strontium
Cesium	Radium	Tantalum
Cobalt	Rare-earths	Tellurium
Colombium	Rhenium	Thallium
Gallium	Rubidium	Tin
		Yttrium

Other materials, now relatively obscure, may come into prominence as discoveries of new uses greatly increases the demand for them. Such a material could be lithium, lightest of all metals, which has interesting possibilities in storage batteries of the future and in atomic reactors. Cadmium, because of its ability in photovotaic cells to convert light to electricity, may become more important as interest focuses on how to harness solar energy.

These minor metals offer especially interesting investment prospects, as many of them, such as lithium and berrylium, are known in quantity in only a few deposits and are controlled by a few companies, some of them not very large. Accordingly, an accelerated demand for these metals could have a very positive effect on an investment in one of these firms.

Any new discoveries could be significant in adding to the world supply of some of the rarer materials. Companies making such discoveries should benefit much more than if, for example, another deposit of a common material such as iron ore were located.

It will pay the serious investor in natural resources to become familiar with these minor metals, their potential uses, and the companies that hold them.

ANTIMONY

Background. Antimony, although not very well known to most people, is nonetheless one of the oldest continuously used metals. A vase found at Chaldea, cast in antimony, dates back to about 4000 B.C. Natural antimony sulfide (its mineral name is stibnite) was used in Biblical times as medicine and as a cosmetic for eyebrow painting. Antimony was used as an alloy in printer's type as early as the 15th century, but the use of antimony did not increase substantially until the beginning of this century, when the low-cost and abundant supply of Chinese antimony became available. However, this was largely cut off by the Japanese invasion of China in 1937 and by World War II. Fortunately, however, in 1935 the world's largest antimony deposit, the Gravelotte Mine in South Africa, had been put in production. This source met the demand formerly supplied by China.

Present Demand and Uses. The principal use of antimony is as an alloy of lead and other metals. About 48 percent of the metal now goes for use with lead in storage batteries. Other applications include power transmission, communication equipment, printing (type) metal, solder, and ammunition. In compounds it is used as a fire-retardant, in chemical and plastic products, and in glass and ceramics. Nevertheless, the demand for antimony, on the whole, is modest. There is no particular basic use that makes it critical although its high melting point makes it suitable as an alloy for the skin of high-speed sub-stratosphere aircraft and in the nose cones of space vehicles. However, titanium competes with antimony in this last use.

Sources. Mainland China appears to have more than half the world's supply of antimony, with Brazil, South Africa, the Soviet Union, and Mexico well behind. The United States currently can supply only about 15 percent of its needs. Most of this antimony comes as a by-product of mining other metals, notably copper, lead, and zinc. However, California and Idaho have antimony mines as such but they have had a sporadic operational history.

Outlook and Investment. The outlook is for a fairly slow growth in antimony demand. World production can keep up with consumption at reasonable prices. If, however, foreign supplies were cut off, the United States would not be able to supply its own needs, which amount to about 40 percent of world production. Therefore, a new domestic source would be welcome and could be quite profitable. It is within the realm of possibility that one may be discovered.

Consolidated Durham Mines of Canada is the largest antimony producer on the North American continent. Cominco also produces antimonial lead in quantity (much of it used in storage batteries). The Sunshine Mining Company, from ores of its own mine and those of Hecla Mining and Silver Dollar Mining Company, all in the Coeur d'Alene district of Idaho, recovers antimony as a by-product of its milling operations. U.S. Antimony Corporation has a mine in Montana.

At times, when mainland China has cut off supplies, the price of antimony has skyrocketed, as happened in 1969 when it went from 45 cents to $2.85 a pound. Antimony, being of relatively high-unit value, can be a profitable small-mine operation, so the opportunity to look at an antimony prospect should not be passed by.

ARSENIC

Background. Arsenic has a rather checkered history and until fairly recently the demand has been modest at best. The advent of more intensive agriculture and the use of insecticides has increased the use of this highly poisonous substance.

Present Demand and Uses. Despite its rather grim history, arsenic does have a place in our economy. Its use will grow, although more slowly than most other commodities. Arsenic is usually sold as a compound, arsenic trioxide, commonly called "white arsenic." The value of white arsenic per pound is usually less than the price of lead or zinc, to put it in economic perspective. It is a low-value material under present market conditions and is likely to stay so unless some totally new and substantial use for it is found. Arsenic has never been considered a strategic material and there has never been a government stockpile program for it.

Arsenic is used principally in five ways (in order of decreasing quantity): agricultural chemicals, chiefly pesticides but also herbicides and defoliants; glass and glassware production; industrial inorganic chemicals—catalysts and reagents, and in treating animal hides; in soldering as an alloy; in a few medicinal chemicals.

Sources. Most of the arsenic now used in the United States and Canada is imported simply on the basis of price. Arsenic is produced almost entirely as a by-product of the smelting of base-metal ores, notably copper. Being of such low value, it apparently does not pay most smelters to recover it; arsenic actually is regarded as an unwanted item in ores. Only American Smelting and Refining Company recovers it in the United States.

Although we import most of our arsenic, there is an ample supply available in the United States and Canada for the foreseeable future. The supply of arsenic, in itself, however, is inelastic in that it is a by-product of other metal mining; therefore, like silver, the potential supply of arsenic is controlled by the mining activity in other metals.

The major outlet for arsenic compounds being agricultural chemicals, there is now considerable competition from organically-derived pesticides and herbicides. Reduced use of arsenic compounds is also due to their persistence in the environment. Arsenic pesticides also are rather corrosive and difficult to handle and this inhibits their use.

Outlook and Investment. Unless some substantial new use is found for arsenic, the outlook is for relatively slow growth in the demand for it. If such a use were discovered and one wished to invest in arsenic, one would simply buy the stocks of the base-metal companies (lead, zinc, and copper chiefly).

BARIUM

Background. Barium seems to have escaped notice until about the last century. Most of the interest in barium has come from the rise of the petroleum industry, where the chief ore mineral of barium, barite, a barium sulfate, is ground up and used as a weight control in drilling muds. This use accounts for more than 70 percent of barium currently produced. These drilling muds lubricate and cool the drill bit, plaster the walls of the drill hole to prevent caving, carry cuttings up the well bore to the surface, and restrain high gas and oil pressure in their formations to prevent blowouts. The heavy specific gravity of barite—4.2—makes it especially useful for this last purpose.

Present Demand and Uses. Demand for barium as barite fluctuates principally with petroleum-drilling activity around the world. The lesser uses of barium are more steady and include the glass industry, where barite makes the glass more easily worked and increases its brilliance, as a flux in magnesium smelting, as an additive to greases, in pharmaceuticals, in the refining process of the sugar beet industry, in paints, in the white sidewalls of automobile tires, and in many other ways. In general, demand approximates the growth of the gross national product, or about 4 percent annually.

Sources. Barium, in its principal mineral form of barite, occurs as vein deposits from hot solutions, as residual deposits from weathering of rocks containing these vein deposits, and as bedded deposits in siliceous siltstone and shale. The origin of this third type of deposit is not known. The United States has about 40 percent of the total world known deposits of barium; mainland China is next with 13 percent, followed by the Soviet Union, West Germany, and other countries with substantially lesser amounts. The United States can supply its own needs at present, but imports about 60 percent. Most U.S. production comes from Missouri, Arkansas, and Nevada. In Canada about 90 percent of production comes from the Walton deposit in Nova Scotia. It is operated by the Dresser Minerals Division of

Dresser Industries, Inc., which is also a major producer in the United States, together with the Baroid Division of NL Industries.

Outlook and Investment. The close tie of barium sales (in the form of barite) to the petroleum industry means that oil and gas drilling activity will control barium sales for many years to come. However, projections indicate that good quality barium deposits may be exhausted before the end of this century, suggesting that higher market prices will mark the course of barium for at least the next decade. A discovery of additional high-grade barium deposits in North America would be worthwhile. There are two major companies, cited in the preceding paragraph, and several smaller companies that mine barium in North America. However, in the case of the two largest firms, barium is only part of their product mix, so the fortunes of these companies are not tied entirely to barium. The future should show a continuing and rising demand for barium at prices that may rise more rapidly than the average of other commodities.

BISMUTH

Background. Bismuth-lead and bismuth-tin alloys were used during the Middle Ages; in some fashion that I cannot quite visualize, it was discovered in 1597 that bismuth nitrate was useful in treating intestinal disorders. I suppose if one has a bad enough stomach ache, one will try anything. In any event, its use as a stomach and intestinal remedy is well established, and bismuth compounds are promoted through television ads and are sold in every drugstore across the land. Beginning in 1883, as a by-product of the Pattinson method of de-silverization of lead bullion, bismuth metal with a 99.995 percent purity has been commercially available. As long as we eat so much of it, it is nice to have it pure.

Present Demand and Uses. Bismuth has a broad-based demand in many industries, although in relatively small quantities. About 45 percent goes into alloys of aluminum, iron, steel, and lead, and pharmaceuticals and cosmetics account for about 40 percent. The addition of bismuth gives lipstick, body powders, eye shadow, and nail polish a pearly luster. There are literally thousands of other uses for bismuth but none very large. Bismuth faces many substitutes but nevertheless has had a fairly stable demand history.

Sources. Nearly all bismuth is recovered as a by-product from other mining operations, chiefly lead, zinc, copper, and molybdenum. About 60 percent of United States requirements are imported, although potential domestic sources are ample to meet all projected needs to the year 2000.

Outlook and Investment. The outlook is for a fairly slow growth in demand of about 2 percent annually. There are no companies in North America producing bismuth as a principal product. It all comes as a by-product of other metal production. UV Industries produces most of the bismuth in the United States. In Canada, again as a by-product, Molybdenite Corporation of Canada, Preissas Molybdenite Mines, and Cadillac Moly-Mines produce most of the bismuth. To invest in bismuth one would have to invest in the companies mining copper, lead, zinc, or molybdenum.

CADMIUM

Background. Cadmium is a relatively rare metal and was not discovered until 1817, in Germany. For 60 years after its discovery there was no commercial interest in cadmium, but now there is a moderate to strong upward trend as new uses are being found for it and established uses are growing.

Present Demand and Uses. The United States uses about one-half of world cadmium production. Cadmium is a silver-white, soft, malleable metal that, with its compounds, has a wide range of industrial uses, chiefly electro-plating, in certain types of batteries, and as a silver alloy in electrical contacts. Cadmium sulfide, in photovoltaic cells, has the interesting property of being able to convert sunlight to electrical energy, an application used in light meters on cameras and in other light-sensitive equipment.

Sources. Cadmium occurs chiefly as a trace element in zinc deposits. No cadmium deposits as such are known. Therefore, the supply of cadmium is dependent on the reserves and rate of production of zinc. It is recovered from fumes in zinc smelting operations, and those companies that produce zinc are or could be cadmium producers. The United States has an estimated one-fourth of the world's cadmium supply; western Canada has large quantities.

Outlook and Investment. The demand for cadmium is likely to continue to grow rather strongly, particularly as some of its special properties become more widely applied to the making of electrical equipment and devices. Cadmium's ability to convert sunlight to electricity in photovoltaic cells may give it a good future in solar energy developments. As cadmium is produced only from zinc deposits, however, there is no direct way at present of investing in cadmium except as one would buy zinc producers' stocks. In North America, Gulf Resources and Chemical, American Metal Climax, Texas Gulf, Inc., St. Joe Minerals, American Smelting and Refining, Cominco, Hudson Bay Mining and Smelting, and Noranda Mines, through their zinc operations, are cadmium producers. Abroad, Rio Tinto-Zinc's mines in various parts of the world produce cadmium.

CESIUM

Background. Cesium was discovered in 1860 but was not commercially used, in early radio tubes, until after 1920. The sophisticated technologies following World War II have led to increased use of cesium in small quantitites in a variety of ways.

Present Demand and Uses. Cesium is used in photomultiplier tubes, infrared lamps, scintillation counters, and in a variety of experimental projects including magnetohydrodynamics (a potential new energy source) and in the concept of ionic propellant engines.

Sources. The chief source of cesium is a mineral called pullucite, of which the United States has very little. Small quantities of cesium occur in the potash deposits of New Mexico but have not been exploited. A fairly large reserve is known at Bernic Lake, Manitoba. Some deposits exist in Africa, mainly in Southern Rhodesia, from which the United States gets most of its supply.

Outlook and Investment. Forecasting the future for cesium is complicated by the fact that more than 75 percent of it is presently used in research and development laboratories. If the research produces major new uses, cesium demand could greatly increase. The U.S. Bureau of Mines has forecast a probable use of between 10,000 pounds and 37,000 pounds annually by the year 2000 in the United States, but the maximum figure could be off very much. These figures suggest an average expanding consumption of about 1 to 2 percent a year.

No company in the United States or Canada at present mines cesium. The Penn Rare Metals Division of Kawecki Berylco Industries produces cesium compounds from imports and has produced cesium metal.

COBALT

Background. Cobalt is hardly a household word, but it has been known since at least 2250 B.C., when used in Persia to color glass a "cobalt blue." Cobalt colors are in ancient art objects of the Far East, and cobalt blues are recognizable in Byzantine and Renaissance art works. The metal was isolated in 1735, but it did not come into significant industrial use until about 1900, when it began to be employed in plating and alloys.

Present Demand and Uses. Demand for cobalt is increasing and likely to continue. Cobalt is used in high-temperature steels as an alloy in the aircraft industry, in permanent magnets (which contain about 35 percent cobalt), in chemical products, and in paints and ceramics for its coloring qualities. It also has wide application in the radio, television, and communication fields. The United States is the world's principal consumer of cobalt but produces very little.

Sources. The Congo has about a third of the world's known cobalt; New Caledonia, Zambia, Cuba, and the Soviet Union follow in that order. Canada has some reserves. United States reserves are estimated to be only about 200 million pounds, in the Blackbird district of central Idaho. The economics of this deposit are such that foreign supplies remain very competitive. A very large potential source of cobalt is in the manganese nodules that lie on the ocean floor in many areas, notably about 500 miles south of Hawaii in a broad east-west band.

Cobalt is produced largely as a by-product of other metal mining, chiefly copper. However, by selectively choosing the ores of copper or other minerals containing the cobalt in minor quantities, the amount of cobalt produced can be varied somewhat. The cobalt produced in Canada is a result of silver and nickel mining and this is true also in New Caledonia.

Outlook and Investment. Cobalt probably will continue in good demand but subject to competition from other minor metals in its chief use as an alloy. However, like many materials, it has certain unique qualities for which it will always be used, one being its rich blue color in compound form. As cobalt is recovered almost entirely from other mining operations, there is no direct way to invest in cobalt, unless a cobalt mine is discovered. The Blackbird Mine in Idaho is about as close to this as has been located to date in the United States, and it is marginal. In Canada, International Nickel, Sherritt Gordon Mines, and Falconbridge Nickel all recover cobalt from their nickel-mining operations and are the principal producers.

COLUMBIUM

Background. The United States, in a roundabout way, gave the name columbium to this silver-grey, corrosion-resistant metal. The English chemist Hatchett discovered it in 1801 while he was analyzing some black sands from Connecticut and named it in honor of the United States, often referred to then as Columbia. A German chemist thought he had found a new element in 1844 and named it niobium, but it proved to be columbium. However, the name niobium is still occasionally used. Little commercial application was found for columbium until the 1930s, when it was combined with steel to make columbian-carbide high-speed metal-cutting tools.

Present Demand and Uses. Columbium is used chiefly as an alloy with steel. It also is used in permanent magnet alloys, electronic components, and in minor other ways. Vanadium can be substituted for columbium in some alloys.

Sources. There is no current United States source for columbium; it is obtained chiefly by imports of raw materials that are processed to obtain tantalum and other refractory metals. Columbium is associated geologically with tantalum, chiefly in pegmatite deposits. There are some potential domestic supplies in Colorado, where an estimated 140 million pounds exist in rock with an average grade of about 0.24 percent columbium oxide. There are also some placer deposits in Idaho that contain over 20 million pounds of columbium, and there are large but very low-grade deposits in Arkansas, Oklahoma, New Mexico, Arizona, and Montana. The most promising domestic supplies are those of Idaho and Colorado but they would take a substantially higher price than at present to make them economic. Brazil, Canada, the Congo, and Nigeria chiefly supply the world market.

Outlook and Investment. Columbium is not regarded as a strategic element and its use will grow only slowly as is now foreseen. In North America, St. Lawrence Columbium Metals Corporation produces columbium from the Oka Mine near Montreal. Other deposits in Quebec are also known. Molycorp, based in the United States, produces columbium in Brazil through a partially owned mining affiliate.

GALLIUM

Background. Discovered in 1875, gallium was first recovered commercially in the United States in 1943 and continues to be extracted in very small quantities.

Present Demand and Uses. Demand is measured in kilograms (2.2 pounds), and the amounts used world-wide are about 1,000 to 1,500 kilograms annually. Uses are chiefly in electronics, particularly semi-conductors (transistors). There are also potential uses in lasers and in other sophisticated electronic equipment. Developments in these fields are only in their early stages, so that the demand for gallium could greatly increase.

Sources. There are no gallium ores as such. It is extracted as a by-product from aluminum and zinc ores. Due to the small demand, only a small amount of the potential gallium available is now recovered. Both the Aluminum Company of America and Eagle-Picher Industries produce gallium metal, but it is, of course, an exceedingly minor part of their operations.

Outlook and Investment. Gallium is a small but very useful part of certain sophisticated electronic equipment, and its value in laser work might ultimately lead to much greater use. However, the outlook at present is that it will remain a very minor metal in trade. There is no direct way of investing in gallium, as it is a by-product of zinc and aluminum operations and a very small part of these at best.

GERMANIUM

Background. In 1871 a Russian scientist predicted a missing element between silicon and tin in the periodic table. In 1886 a German scientist discovered it and named it in honor of his country. Germanium remained not much more than a scientific curiosity until the early 1920s, when it was used in treating anemia. More recently it has been found to have very useful electrical properties, particularly valuable in transistors. Availability of high purity germanium has, in many ways, revolutionized the communications industry and has permitted miniaturization of radios, television, hearing aids, and telephone dialing equipment, and it has also resulted in major advances in astronautics, missile guidance, and worldwide communications.

Present Demand and Uses. The uses of germanium are many and critical, and their general scope has just been listed. The major single use of germanium is presently in a single-crystal high-purity metal used principally in the manufacture of transistors, diodes, and rectifiers; this end use constitutes 90 percent of total demand but will probably drop percentagewise as other uses increase.

Sources. Germanium is recovered as a by-product from lead-zinc ores and from certain coals. World and U.S.–Canadian reserves are really not well known, as no very systematic attempt has been made to determine them. The largest potential source seems to be in some coals. It is estimated that in the United Kingdom about 4 million pounds of germanium yearly may be present in stack gases, flue dusts, and ashes at plants burning germanium-bearing coals. The world supply is apparently well beyond any demand requirements during this century.

Outlook and Investment. Germanium demand will grow about with the growth of the economy. It has some competition in the electrical field from silicon, also used in transistors. Investing in germanium directly is not possible as there are no ores as such, nor is any company engaged primarily in its recovery. Eagle-Picher Industries has a germanium-recovery operation at a zinc smelter in Henryetta, Oklahoma.

HAFNIUM

Background. Hafnium has only recently been of serious interest to industry, and the U.S. Bureau of Mines and the Atomic Energy Commission have both been conducting tests on this metal. Its use still continues to be largely experimental.

Present Demand and Uses. Domestic demand can be measured in the thousands of pounds. It is still being researched in the laboratory, but its ability to capture neutrons makes it an interesting metal for possible use in nuclear reactor control rods. It also may have possibilities as an alloy.

Sources. Hafnium occurs with zirconium in zircon in a ratio of about 1 to 50. It is extracted from that source exclusively at present (see section on "Zirconium").

Outlook and Investment. Hafnium use may grow substantially from its present very low level but at best does not seem likely to be in large demand very soon. There is no direct way of investing in hafnium. It is recovered as part of the zirconium mining process; firms which have zirconium have hafnium. There appear to be ample world-wide reserves even if the demand were to greatly increase.

INDIUM

Background. Indium, a silvery-white, soft metal, has been used commercially only since about 1934 although it was discovered in 1863. Production is measured in ounces, and it is used in very small quantities, chiefly in the electronics field.

Present Demand and Uses. Transistors, diodes, and rectifiers are the largest users of indium, but demand is moderated by competition with other materials that have similar properties. It is also used in a few specialty alloys, such as, for example, high-speed silver-lead bearings. Because indium has been commercially available for such a short time, about 25 percent of it is still used in research and development laboratories.

Sources. Indium is produced from ores mined for other metals, chiefly zinc, and is recovered principally as a by-product of zinc refining. United States supplies of indium, based on zinc resources, are estimated at 47 million troy ounces of recoverable metal. This seems ample for foreseeable needs.

Outlook and Investment. Moderate growth in uses, but in very small quantities, is projected for indium. American Smelting and Refining has been the chief and at times the only producer of indium in the United States. This metal is relatively more abundant in the lead-zinc ores of the Missouri-Kansas-Oklahoma (tri-state) mining district than in other lead-zinc areas. Companies having holdings there, such as Eagle-Picher, are potential producers of it. In Canada, Cominco produces indium as a by-product of its British Columbia zinc operations at Trail, but, of course, this is a very minor part of total operations.

LITHIUM

Background. Lithium is the lightest metal known, and was discovered by a Swedish chemist in 1817. The first commercial mining of lithium minerals in the United States was in 1899. The United States now is the world's largest producer and consumer of lithium.

Present Demand and Uses. Current demand is modest but could possibly increase greatly if breakthroughs in development of lithium batteries and other lithium-based products materialize as some expect. Lithium is used primarily in compounds, and its applications include multipurpose greases, air-conditioning equipment, ceramics, welding and brazing materials, laundry bleaches, and synthetic rubber.

Sources. Lithium comes primarily from two geological sources—coarse-grained granite-like rocks called pegmatites in the southeastern States and in the West, and brines of salt lakes such as Searles Lake, California, and Great Salt Lake, Utah. Lake sources are now becoming dominant over the pegmatite rock source. There are an estimated 640,000 tons of lithium in Great Salt Lake, more than double the known reserves in the rest of the United States. The United States has most (about five-sixths) of the known lithium deposits of the world, and United States reserves have been estimated by the U.S. Geological Survey to total more than 5 million tons (this is an estimate of possible reserves, not "known" reserves). Quebec and Manitoba also have some deposits, with Quebec Lithium Corporation holding the most important known reserves.

Outlook and Investment. The outlook for lithium is somewhat unpredictable. It will surely show a steadily increasing demand, especially with the possible advent of the electric car in quantity, because of its potential use in batteries. The use of lithium might also increase in a variety of other areas now under research. Particularly interesting is the possibility of lithium's use in nuclear reactors to generate electric power. It is estimated that only one-half of the lithium in Great Salt Lake could produce enough electricity to supply the needs of the United States for 1,400 years.

The company having the largest lithium holdings is Foote Mineral. Lithium Corporation of America, a subsidiary of Gulf Resources and Chemical, also has substantial lithium deposits and has interests in lithium recovery from the brines of Great Salt Lake. Total resources of lithium in the United States are several hundred times current needs, but this could change markedly with new uses.

MERCURY

Background. The first recorded mention of mercury, also called quicksilver, was by the Greek philosopher Aristotle in the 4th century B.C., when it was used in religious ceremonies. Until the 16th century, consumption was small and chiefly for medicinal and cosmetic purposes. But after 1557, with the introduction of the Patio amalgamation process for the recovery of silver, mercury was widely used in Peru, Mexico, and other silver-producing areas. The invention of the barometer in 1643 and the thermometer in 1720 put mercury into scientific usage. Three great mines dominated world mercury production prior to 1850—the Almaden Mine in Spain, where production began in 400 B.C., the Idria Mine in Yugoslavia, where mercury was found in 1470, and the Santa Barbara Mine in Peru, which began operation in 1566. Mercury is known in 25 different minerals, but most of it comes from a red mineral, cinnabar, a mercury sulfide.

Mercury is the only metal that is liquid at room temperature, and so it has many unique uses. It is also a highly mobile element even in the Earth's crust, and in some mines mercury will literally come out of the rock and form small pools on the floor; in some mercury deposits droplets of mercury can be seen with the aid of a hand lens.

Present Demand and Uses. Mercury has no substitute for some uses, particularly in electrical apparatus and industrial-control instruments. It is also used in batteries, in pharmaceutical preparations, in dental supplies, in agricultural chemicals, and in a host of other ways including the making of chlorine, a very important industrial chemical. Demand, however, tends to be in a state of flux because of the increasing concern about the effect of mercury in the environment. Mercury poisoning has in some instances become a severe local problem, such as in Japan.

Sources. All mercury deposits are formed by rising hot solutions. It occurs in a great variety of rocks, but at comparatively shallow depths from a few feet to a little more than 2,000 feet. Half of the United States mercury mines that have produced 100 flasks (a flask weighs 76 pounds) or more are less than 200 feet deep. Mercury is mined independently of other metals and not as a by-product. Most of the large economic deposits are in regions of relatively recent volcanic activity—recent in the sense of being no older than perhaps 60 or 70 million years, or back to the beginning of the Tertiary Period. These younger volcanic rocks tend to be found along the edges rather than in the interiors of continents, thus the occurrence of mercury deposits in western United States (California and Oregon), western South America, Spain, Italy, and Yugoslavia. Spain has the largest identified resources. The United States has only small amounts. Canada has modest production.

Outlook and Investments. The outlook for mercury is clouded by serious environmental concerns. It is highly toxic in small amounts and tends to be residual and cumulative. Nevertheless, mercury is vital to a variety of products, and ways will have to be found to successfully handle it. Only one mercury-mining company in the United States has more or less consistently operated, the New Idria Mining and Chemical Company, which has mines in the Coast Range of northern California. Aside from that company (listed on the American Stock Exchange), there is no easy way for the average investor to put money into mercury. Cominco of Canada has a small mercury operation at Pinchi Lake, British Columbia, but operation has been discontinuous and, of course, is dwarfed by Cominco's other mining interests.

Mercury mining, however, can be a small but profitable venture. Because most mercury deposits are shallow, and because the process of recovering mercury from the ore is simple—just heat it and then condense the mercury vapor fumes—mercury mining can be done with only a few persons and with a relatively modest capital investment. The real risk is in the toxic effects of mercury. Mercury poisoning has many effects—including having your teeth fall out and your skin turn green. Ultimately, mercury can invade the central nervous system with fatal results. Mercury must be handled very carefully, and the haphazard mercury mining operations of the past will not serve the present from what we now know of mercury poisoning.

The unit value of mercury is high, although the price takes some truly mercurial leaps and drops, bigger than does the price of virtually any other industrial metal. With a high unit value, a small mine can be quite lucrative if run properly. However, the environmental problems with mercury may continue to overhang that market in varying degrees for some time to come.

RADIUM

Background. This famous radioactive metal was discovered by Pierre and Marie Curie in 1898 while they were studying uranium. They noted that even after all the uranium had been extracted from ore samples, the samples were still radioactive, indicating the presence of still another material. Radium has served us for more than half a century but is now being supplanted by a variety of artificial radioisotopes.

Present Demand and Uses. Used largely in medicine but also in luminous paints, radium is now losing its position to more abundant and more specifically useful radioisotopes. Present uses do not appreciably dissipate the supply of the world's radium, with the result that demand has fallen off rapidly and leveled somewhat since the 1950s.

Sources. Radium appears to be present in infinitesimal quantity in practically all rocks of the Earth's crust. Only pure limestones and quartz sands seem to be barren of this material.

No known radium deposits as such are known in the free world. Most of the radium produced in the past has come from high-grade carnotite (an ore of uranium) deposits in Colorado and rich pitchblende deposits in Canada, Czechoslovakia, and the Congo. Small amounts have been produced elsewhere. Radium is unique in that only its radioactivity is used. It can be extracted from uranium ore, but at present this is not being done in the United States. Most radium recently has come from a plant in Belgium that obtained its raw materials from the Congo.

Outlook and Investment.   Demand for radium will probably not exceed 24,000 milligrams annually by the year 2000. There are ample sources widely distributed to meet these needs. Demand for radium in radiotheraphy is likely to be the most important use. As the stock of radium grows, and as it is not destroyed when used, the need for additional supplies will decrease, and it could be that the demand for new amounts will be essentially zero by the year 2000. It is unlikely that any significant quantity of primary radium will be produced in the world for the rest of this century. Present world inventories are estimated at 3,000 grams. Radium is circulated among users, and a few firms are in the business of leasing it to customers in need. One can conclude that whereas radium is radioactive, investment possibilities therein are inactive.

RARE-EARTHS

Background.   The rare-earths are treated collectively, as they occur in the same general deposits and are commonly mined together. Also, economic deposits exist at only a few places in the world and are under control of a very few companies. Most of the rare-earths still have only limited use at best; a few currently find extensive use, such as, for example, europium, an element used to improve brightness and trueness of colors in TV picture tubes. Familiarity with these rare-earth elements for the most part will but be an impressive addition to your vocabulary. For the record, the rare-earth elements are cerium, dysprosium, erbium, europium, gadolinium, holmium, illinium (also called promethium), lanthanum, lutetium, neodymium, praseodymium, samurium, terbium, thulium, and ytterbium. Scandium and yttrium are also close to, but not strictly in, the rare-earth group and are treated separately in this volume.

Present Demand and Uses.   Petroleum refining is the largest market for rare-earth elements. Glass-making is another major application. Properties of many rare-earth elements have not yet been fully exploited, and new uses being found have markedly increased the demand for a given element, such as that already cited for europium. Similar developments could occur in the future.

Because rare-earth elements tend to be mined and milled together, although the demand for each is quite different, large surpluses of certain ones exist.

Sources.   Some members of the rare-earth group are relatively abundant in the Earth's crust but mineable concentrations are uncommon. The largest single known deposit of rare-earths in the world is at Mountain Pass, San Bernardino County, California, but there are large potential resources also in the monazite sands of northwestern and southeastern United States. Elsewhere, India, Australia, the Soviet Union, and Brazil have sizeable deposits.

Outlook and Investment.   Demand for rare-earths is expected to parallel the growth of the gross national product to the year 2000. Even with the most optimistic use forecast, there are ample reserves in the United States to take care of all needs. Molycorp (18-percent owned by International Mining) owns the Mountain Pass rare-earth deposit and as a premier position in this resource. Denison Mines in Canada produces or has produced some rare-earths.

RHENIUM

Background.   Although the existence of rhenium was predicted in 1860, it was not discovered until 1925. To date, the major portion of rhenium produced has been used in research on its properties and possible applications.

Present Demand and Uses.   Aside from still being used for research on itself, rhenium is also employed in thermocouples, in tungsten and molybdenum alloys, in electronic equipment, and as a catalyst.

Sources. Rhenium has been produced from copper and potash residues, and more recently Kennecott Copper Corporation has been obtaining it in flue dust from molybdenite roasters. There is evidence that the Soviet Union has been producing rhenium for a decade or more, but details are not available. Little is known about world reserves, but they are estimated to total about 1 million pounds, of which the United States has 400,000 and the Soviet Union 350,000. Chile, Peru, and Mexico have most of the rest.

Outlook and Investment. The U.S. Bureau of Mines estimates that by the year 2000, rhenium demand in the United States might reach as much as 3,000 pounds annually. There is obviously no foreseeable lack of rhenium and its very limited use precludes it from serious investment consideration barring some quite unexpected technological advance which would require rhenium in larger amounts.

RHUBIDIUM

Background. Although found in 1861, rubidium had almost no industrial applications until the 1920s, when small amounts were used in photoelectric cells. Since that time demand has increased slowly but is still very small.

Present Demand and Uses. Rubidium demand for the entire world is a few thousand pounds annually at present. Some research is being conducted on possible new applications but the results to date have been modest. Rubidium salts containing radioactive rubidium are used to trace the flow of blood and in minor other pharmaceutical forms. It is also used in various ways in photoelectric cells.

Sources. Rubidium is associated with certain pegmatite rocks. The largest deposit in North America appears to be at Bernic Lake, Manitoba, where it is in a purple mica called lepidolite. Reserves there are estimated to be about 1,000 tons which, under present demand, would supply the world for many years. Small amounts occur in the potash deposits of New Mexico but have not been exploited. Elsewhere, especially in Africa, additional deposits are known. Actually, rubidium is found in very small traces (in the range of 10 to 100 parts per million) in a great variety of places such as the potash deposits just mentioned, in brines from oil wells, and in many scattered mineral deposits.

Outlook and Investment. The outlook for rubidium, unless some quite unexpected new use is discovered, is modest. No company mines it as such, but here and there around the world small amounts are recovered from other operations, but none in the United States. Penn Rare Metals Division of Kawecki Berylco Industries in the United States produces rubidium from imported raw materials.

SCANDIUM

Background. Scandium was discovered in 1879 but because of its scarcity and lack of an outstanding property, it was known for years only in a few experimental laboratories. In the 1950s the U.S. Air Force included scandium in its materials research program, which resulted in the systematic study and cataloguing of its properties. But no useful properties that could lead to any significant commercial application were found, except for a minor use of the radioisotope scandium 46 for the tracing of fluid flows in oil wells.

Present Demand and Uses. Because scandium has no particularly useful qualities, there is virtually no demand for it. However, this in itself is a distinction as it is hard to find a metal that is not good for something.

Sources. Scandium has been obtained from the rare mineral thortveitite in Norway and Malagasy and from residues in the processing of certain tungsten ores. It also has been recovered as an impurity from processing uranium ores. Some western phosphate rock contains very minute amounts of scandium, but because of the large size of these phosphate deposits they appear to be one of the greatest known scandium sources. However, nobody seems to care so far.

SELENIUM

Background. Discovered in 1817, selenium remained a laboratory curiosity until 1873, when it was discovered that resistance to the passage of an electric current through selenium decreased markedly if a light was shined on it. This established the technical basis for the development of the photoelectric cell and ultimately the development of xerography. Without selenium, the Xerox company could not have gotten started; the people who made fortunes in its stock owe part of their luck at least to selenium.

Present Demand and Uses. The use of selenium in photoelectric cells and in xerography takes about 23 percent of the total supply. Selenium coats the metal cylinders from which the photographic image is transferred by static electricity in the Xerox process. About four pounds of selenium are required for each 100 square feet of effective surface. Replacement of the selenium may be required after 50,000 to 500,000 copies have been made.

Selenium has a wide range of chemical applications, but manufacture of certain pigments takes most of the output; the pigments are used to color plastic, paints, enamels, inks, and rubber. Selenium is also used in pharmaceuticals, in the control of dandruff, and in the manufacture of deodorants. One has to have a certain amount of respect for a minor metal that is useful in things ranging from xerography to dandruff medicine to photoelectric cells. To top it off, it was discovered in 1957 that selenium is required in the nutrition of animals including humans. Selenium's use in fertilizers could greatly increase demand.

Sources. Selenium is primarily obtained as a by-product of copper refining; 90 percent of the production in the United States is derived from the anode mud deposits during electrolytic refining of copper. Blister copper contains about one pound of selenium per ton, but actual recovery is somewhat less. Selenium may be more abundant than is apparent from studies so far, but it appears that the principal problem is that selenium is widely dispersed over the Earth. Selenium accompanies sulfur in volcanic gases and appreciable amounts of it apparently have been deposited over every square yard of the Earth's surface by these gases. Through this process, selenium tends to become a dispersed element, but other geological processes, fortunately, have tended to concentrate it somewhat.

Outlook and Investment. Selenium demand should continue to grow at a compound annual rate of about 2 percent, but new applications could increase this markedly. In the United States the five plants accounting for all selenium production are located at the major electrolytic copper refineries of American Metal Climax, American Smelting and Refining, International Smelting and Refining, Kennecott Copper at Garfield, Utah, and Kennecott Copper at Ann Arundel County, Maryland. In Canada, Canadian Copper Refiners operates the largest selenium recovery plant, treating materials obtained from Noranda Mines, Gaspe Copper Mines, and Hudson Bay Mining and Smelting. International Nickel also recovers some selenium. Selenium recovery, of course, represents only a very minor part of the overall operations of these firms.

SILICON

Background. Silicon is the second most abundant element, making up about 27 percent of the Earth's crust. However, it is never found free as a metal but always tightly combined with other elements, with the result that it was not isolated as a metal until 1824, when Berzelius, the Swedish scientist, produced an impure form. There was early interest in using silicon as an alloy in steel. In 1891, a U.S. inventor, E. D. Acheson, accidentally discovered silicon carbide while trying to prepare artificial diamonds in an electric furnace. This led to increased use of silicon, as the carbide proved to be an important abrasive and replaced diamond dust in many operations. Great advances were made in the electrical use of silicon during World War II, but it was not until 1949 that the first silicon meeting the high purity requirements for semi-conductors (transistors) was prepared. Subsequent improvements have allowed silicon to play an important part in the rapid growth of the electronics industry.

Present Demand and Uses. Silicon in various forms enters into many aspects of our technological society, and the demand is steady and growing. The uses are many and some have been alluded to in the preceding paragraph. The question of demand, however, is somewhat academic in that there is no shortage of silicon nor is there ever likely to be.

Sources. Sources of silicon are as abundant as sands on the beach—literally—as most beach sands are quartz, a silicon dioxide. The matter of supply is simply that of finding the highest quality source possible. Usually these are very well sorted, clean quartz sandstones that have been reworked in nature several times (as is the case of the St. Peter Sandstone of the upper Mississippi Valley), or quartzites, which are simply sandstones cemented with silica. Some of these deposits are as much as 99 percent pure silicon dioxide.

Outlook and Investment. Silicon will grow in use about as fast as the gross national product. Supply is no problem; the advantage will go to companies with the highest-quality quartz-sand supply or quartzite deposits. Most glass companies, such as PPG Industries, have their own quartz sand supply. There are a few smaller companies supplying silicon needs locally. It is not a very large field for investment if one restricts it to simply a source for silicon and excludes glass and sand and gravel, which are taken up separately in this volume. No very good outlets for investment in silicon as such are apparent.

SODIUM

Background. Sodium is a soft, waxy, silver-white metal that always occurs naturally in compounds, never as an element. It is chemically very active and will react with water in explosive fashion. The pure metal has been known only in the chemical laboratory.

Present Demand and Uses. Sodium as an element has very little use but in various compounds has many applications. As part of common salt it is used in a multitude of industrial processes. Other sodium compounds are used in glass-making and in the pulp and paper industry. Use, however, has grown rather slowly, barely keeping up with the rate of growth of the economy as a whole.

Sources. Sodium metal is commonly obtained by electrolysis of ordinary salt; sodium compounds are chiefly derived in nature from trona, a hydrous sodium carbonate discussed separately in this book. There is no shortage of sodium. The chief cost is the energy involved in its extraction.

Outlook and Investment. The outlook, based on present uses, is for modest growth. There are, however, some possibilities of using sodium-sulfur batteries in electric cars. The Ford

Motor Company, among others, is conducting extensive research on this. If it should prove to be commercial, the demand for sodium would rise markedly. Three companies produce metallic sodium. These are E. I. du Pont de Nemours and Company, Ethyl Corporation, and Reactive Metals, Inc. Some of the firms producing sodium compounds from trona are listed in the section on "Trona" in this book.

STRONTIUM

Background. Strontium is an alkaline-earth metal and, like calcium and barium, is sometimes classed with the non-metals. It is not found in the free state but always combined in nature. Celestite, a strontium sulfate, and strontianite, a strontium carbonate, are the two chief minerals. They can be converted to compounds and then employed in various ways. Very little strontium metal is used. The element was discovered in 1790, and about 1800 it began to be used for what is still today one of its chief applications—in pyrotechnics, that is to say, fireworks, and now in tracer ammunition.

Present Demand and Uses. Strontium-compound uses are small, with demand in the United States less than 10,000 tons per year. The principal uses are in fireworks, signals (flares), and in tracer ammunition, due to the brilliant crimson color strontium compounds give the flame. It also is used in greases for special purposes, in certain ceramics, in medicines and delipatories, in refining of high purity zinc, and in a variety of other minor ways including in magnets. Some of the uses, although small now, could increase substantially, as with magnets and television.

Sources. Strontium minerals occur both in sedimentary deposits—sandstones and limestones—and also as veins associated with lead and zinc that were deposited from rising hot solutions. Strontium minerals also are known to form around areas of volcanic activity. Most of the world's strontium has come from England. The United States has minor deposits in California, Texas, Washington, Arizona, and several other states that have been mined briefly during wartime. A fairly large discovery was made recently in Canada in southeastern New Brunswick. There is no comprehensive world inventory of strontium deposits, but reserves believed to be substantial relative to expected demand. In the United States the U.S. Geological Survey has estimated deposits to contain at least 1,130,000 tons of strontium, which would be sufficient to last about 200 years. However, they are not economically mineable at present, so total needs are currently imported.

Outlook and Investment. Strontium cannot be effectively replaced in any of its principal uses, and demand will increase more or less steadily. In the United States, however, no very good deposits are known and almost all supplies are imported. It is possible that better-grade deposits might be discovered, as there has not been any very intensive search for strontium. In Canada, Kaiser Strontium, Ltd., subsidiary of Kaiser Aluminum and Chemical Corporation, produces strontium at a plant near Sydney, Nova Scotia. For the forseeable future, however, strontium is likely to be a relatively minor commodity in world trade and not a significant investment outlet.

TANTALUM

Background. Tantalum was discovered by a Swedish chemist, Anders Ekeberg, in 1802 and got its name from being so tantalizingly difficult to isolate. Nothing was done with the metal until beginning about 1903 it was used for a few years as a filament in light bulbs, replacing carbon. But by 1912 tantalum had been replaced by tungsten. In the 1940s, however, when tantalum was used in electronics and as an oxide catalyst in making synthetic rubber, there were temporary shortages of it. More recently tantalum has continued to increase in use in electronics, chemical equipment, and in alloys with high resistance to heat.

Present Demand and Uses. Electronics and alloys still take most of the tantalum produced, the alloys being of particular use in the construction of nuclear reactors. The position of tantalum fluctuates from shortage to oversupply, but underlying this is a moderate growth trend.

Sources. Tantalum is known in placer deposits in Idaho and California but they cannot now compete economically with foreign sources. The United States now imports all its needs. At Bernic Lake, Manitoba, a pegmatite is estimated to contain seven million pounds of recoverable tantalum. Most tantalum now comes as a by-product of tin mining. The Congo and Nigeria have the largest tantalum reserves.

Outlook and Investment. Tantalum has a small but solid position among the minor metals and use of it should grow slowly. In the United States no way is available for putting money into tantalum directly. The Norton Company manufactures tantalum powders but does not control the raw materials source. In Canada, Chemalloy Minerals, Ltd., completely controls Tantalum Mines Corporation of Canada, which has a large deposit in Manitoba.

TELLURIUM

Background. Tellurium was discovered in 1782 but was not of any particular interest until some years later when it was found that tellurium demonstrated both the Seebeck effect (conversion of heat to electricity) and the Peltier effect (conversion of electricity to heat). Tellurium has been and continues to be involved in a variety of research programs that might lead to much greater use than at present.

Present Demand and Uses. In the United States, 100,000 pounds or more are used annually. Tellurium is employed in steel alloys, in plastics, in chemicals, and potentially in certain types of batteries.

Sources. The United States is the world's leading tellurium producer and consumer. About 80 percent of the domestic supply and more than 80 percent of the world supply is obtained as a by-product of copper refining. Tellurium occurs in porphyry copper deposits in the West, and a U.S. Geological Survey report indicates that the largest tellurium deposits in the United States may be in the copper-mining district just west of Ely, Nevada; the mine there (at Ruth, Nevada) is owned by Kennecott. The United States appears to have the world's largest reserves, followed by Chile and the Soviet Union.

Outlook and Investment. Tellurium use is predicted to grow slightly faster than the rate of population growth; if research on batteries using tellurium shows commercial promise, use could grow somewhat faster. There is no direct way of investing in tellurium. The copper companies with the western porphry copper deposits hold most of the U.S. supply. These would include Kennecott, Phelps Dodge, and others.

THALLIUM

Background. Thallium was discovered in 1861 by an English scientist, Sir William Crookes, but thallium compounds were not used until 1896, when they were employed in medicine. In 1919 a photosensitive cell using a thallium compound was patented. Beginning in 1925, thallium was used in rat poison and later in insecticides, and for 40 years this was the chief use. In 1965 the Federal government prohibited the use of thallium in rat poison.

Present Demand and Uses. Since 1965 most thallium has been used in specialized electronic components and in some alloys. If the cost of thallium should rise sharply, it would have many substitutes. Demand currently is only several thousand pounds annually.

Source. Thallium is recovered from zinc ores, and at present thallium metal and compounds are produced by the American Smelting and Refining Company. Foreign thallium operations are likewise related to zinc smelting.

Outlook and Investment. Supply is more than adequate to meet demand. There is neither any specific investment vehicle nor any particular incentive for investors to put their money into thallium as far as can now be foreseen.

TIN

Background. Tin was used in Egypt as early as 600 B.C. and as an alloy in bronze implements many centuries earlier, perhaps 3200 to 3500 B.C. Extensive use of tin, however, is essentially a 20th century fact, Even at present the amount of tin used is not great, but it does have some special important uses.

Present Demand and Uses. The United States consumes about 30 percent of the world's supply of tin. Principal uses, in decreasing order of importance, are tinplate, solders, bearing alloys, bronze, chemicals, and coatings other than tinplate. Aluminum, plastics, and tin-free steel (steel with a very thin coating of chromium) are capturing a large share of the previous tin market, with the result that the growth in tin usage in other ways is about balanced. The resulting slow growth in the demand for tin is perhaps fortunate for North Americans, as tin deposits are very minor here and major supplies come from areas that are politically rather unstable.

Sources. Except as a minor by-product of molybdenum mining in Colorado (American Metal Climax), tin is not produced in the United States, and there are no major deposits known in North America. Some small amounts of the metal have been discovered in Alaska, and past production there has been about 2,000 tons from placers and 350 tons from primary rock.

The chief mineral of tin is cassiterite, a tin oxide. Tin occurs disseminated in certain types of igneous rocks and as veins deposited in fractures by hot waters. In secondary form, tin occurs in placer deposits, just as does gold, and for the same reason—it is heavy, resistant to erosion, and survives in fairly large pieces as a result of weathering from primary rock sources and transportation by streams to where the sands and gravels forming the placer deposits accumulate. About 60 percent of the world's tin supply comes from placers in Southeast Asia. These stream placers, by the way, were formed seaward of the present shoreline, during the time in the recent geological past when removal of sea water to form glaciers of the Pleistocene Epoch (commonly called the "Ice Age") lowered sea level several hundred feet. These old stream deposits are now submerged as sea level has risen with the partial melting of the glaciers around the world, and the tin is obtained by dredging.

Outlook and Investment. The slow growth in use of tin together with the fact that North America has virtually no tin deposits (most are in Asian countries), precludes Canadians and Americans generally from investing in tin. There is the remote possibility that a significant tin deposit can be found in North America, in which case the organization making the discovery would be an interesting speculation. The outlook is for the supply of tin to be equal to demands without any large rise in price relative to other commodities.

YTTRIUM

Background. This metal is named from Ytterby, Sweden, where it was originally discovered. Yttrium has been a neglected element until recently, as can be seen from the uses that are listed in the next paragraph—almost all are recent innovations.

Present Demand and Uses. Yttrium is used chiefly in compounds as host material for color television phosphors, in making microwave equipment, in fluorescent lamps, in certain types of glasses, and in iron-chrome alloys. Demand presently is strong and is likely to continue to the end of this century, with the high end of the growth projection estimated at 5.8 percent compounded annually.

Sources. World yttrium reserves are dominated by India, which has nearly 60 percent of the total, now estimated at about 107,000 tons. However, most of the yttrium mined recently has come from the Elliot Lake district of Ontario. About 13 percent of world supply is in the United States. Most yttrium is obtained as a by-product of certain titanium-bearing minerals or from the uranium mineral, brannerite. Spent uranium solutions from Canada are used by several companies in the United States to produce yttrium. Denison Mines recovers yttrium in Canada.

Outlook and Investment. Yttrium will have a slightly-better-than-average growth rate in use among the minor metals according to present forecasts. Canadian uranium producers such as Denison Mines have yttrium reserves. Also, the companies with titanium deposits have yttrium (see section on "Titanium"). In all instances, however, production of yttrium is but a small part of total corporate operations.

14

Gold, Silver, and Other Precious or Popular Materials

SOME NATURAL RESOURCES have been prized by people but not necessarily or entirely for their industrial value. Even where there is an industrial use for these precious or popular materials, such as gold, silver, platinum, and various gemstones, the value placed on them may be well beyond this level.

The history of world currencies has been a sad one at best, and the recent scene is a prime example. People have been fleeing from paper money, and one of the most obvious directions is toward things that have a high unit value and that can be conveniently stored (indeed secreted) or transported if necessary. The precious metals and gemstones qualify in this regard. Although one would like to see a restoration of confidence in world currencies, and from time to time this will no doubt occur to a degree, the long history of money put out by governments (now chiefly paper declared by a government to be "money") is such as not to inspire much confidence. The result is that precious materials will stay precious. Investment in them will be of keen and, at times, of compelling interest and concern.

GOLD

Gold was probably the first metal to be picked up and prized by people—it is still picked up and prized. Gold is very durable and attractive and can be easily worked into various shapes.

Gold was used very early as a medium of exchange and it remains a substance to which nations turn when they cannot agree on the value of other things, especially each other's currencies. Gold also is a useful industrial metal and has some unique properties. A single ounce can be drawn into a wire 35 miles long without breaking, and it can be hammered into sheets as thin as 1/250,000th of an inch. Gold is remarkably heavy, a cubic foot weighing more than half a ton. This cubic foot, at $200 an ounce, would be worth $3.6 million. Gold is so durable that an estimated 85 percent of all the gold ever produced is still available.

Gold has been used as a medium of exchange for more than 4,000 years. The first gold coins were minted by the Greeks about 560 B.C., and gold coinage soon became a very high art.

Debasement of Coins. This started almost as soon as gold and silver coins were invented. In a visit to the museum in the Old Roman city of Sabratha near Tripoli, Libya, I saw an interesting exhibit of coins. It showed how the earlier coins had a high content of precious metal, but as the Roman empire had to meet its foreign war costs and pay for expensive social programs at home, the currency was debased by putting in more base metals. So as the earlier more precious coins remained in circulation, the people simply filed them down to equal the value of the new coins being issued. Some of the earlier coins were reduced to about half their original size by this process—a graphically honest evidence of inflation in the Roman empire. Unfortunately for honesty, paper money cannot be treated that way; we simply raise prices to compensate for the fact that the government is debasing the currency. Prior to 1966 we still had some silver left in our coins, although the amount had been reduced. Now, all precious-metal backing of currency is gone, and the monetary crises of the past decade are, in part, the result.

Politicians and some economists are fond of minimizing the usefulness of gold as a medium of exchange, and as countries live beyond their means and currencies depreciate it is politically expedient to ignore gold as a standard of exchange. But my own view is that gold is not likely to go out of style. Somebody will always want it at some price, just as has been the case for 4,000 years or more.

As all the gold in the world only amounts to about 2.5 billion ounces—not nearly enough to finance world trade—we probably are not going to return to a gold standard, strictly speaking. But the gold market will always be a "standard" of sorts on the edge of world currencies and against which the worth of a given currency is judged by the cold and very realistic eye of the currency speculator. The currency speculator and the gold trader serve a very useful purpose in this regard.

Where Is the Gold? By this I mean where nature placed it. The answer is "chiefly in Africa." Gold in Africa occurs mainly in South Africa's Witwatersrand (commonly called the Rand) district and was discovered there in 1885. The Rand soon became and has remained the world's largest gold producing area, accounting for about 50 percent of total annual production. Although gold is mined widely around the world—71 countries have recorded some production—large deposits are rare. Only five countries account for 90 percent of production.

The geological reasons for this abundance of gold in South Africa are not entirely known, except that we recognize what are termed "metallogenic belts" around the world. Western North and South America are in the silver metallogenic belt, but the gold belt is chiefly elsewhere. Gold initially is carried up into the outer portions of the Earth's crust by hot solutions that commonly also carry quartz. This gold is then deposited in veins and in other sorts of deposits. In the Homestake Mine of the Black Hills these solutions have deposited gold in very minute particles in a metamorphic rock called a schist, which acted more or less as a sponge to soak up the gold-bearing solutions. In the Newmont Mine near Carlin, Nevada, the gold is disseminated in a black shale. In both cases, gold cannot be readily seen in the rocks and the ore must be very carefully processed to recover it.

Ultimately, many of these primary gold deposits are weathered and the gold, being resistant to weathering and also heavy, tends to survive transportation and be concentrated in certain gravel and sand deposits called placers. Thus the gold-bearing quartz veins of the Sierra Nevada of California yielded their gold to erosion, and the streams carried it to the placers of the upper Sacramento River drainage including at Sutter's Mill.

The gold of the Witwatersrand occurs in a series of ancient sands and gravels that are now solid rock again by compaction and cementation. These sand and gravel beds are called "reefs." One theory holds that the gold (and some uranium with it) was deposited with these sands and gravels initially and thus they are ancient placer deposits. The other theory is that the gold and uranium were introduced by rising mineralizing solutions after the deposition of sands and gravels. In either case, however, South Africa has the bulk of the world's gold. The Soviet Union appears to be next. Canada is third and the United States is fourth. Of the 2.5 billion ounces of gold produced in the last 400 years, South Africa has produced about 37 percent.

In terms of reserves left to produce, it is estimated that total world gold supply is about one billion ounces, of which 60 percent is in Africa. The United States has an estimated 60 to 80 million ounces, or about 6 to 8 percent. It should be noted that "reserves" refers to gold that can be recovered economically with existing technology and at current prices. More gold remains that might possibly be economic at some future time.

Gold in very small amounts is very widely distributed. It occurs geologically chiefly in association with quartz veins in granitic areas or is washed out from such terrains to form placers. Gold also is associated with copper and silver, in some lead-zinc deposits, and in nickel deposits, and is produced as a by-product of these metals.

In summary, gold occurs in primary deposits called "lode" deposits, in secondary deposits called placers resulting from the weathering and erosion of primary deposits, and as a by-product of other metals. The gold is brought to the deposit in the solutions that also brought the copper, lead, zinc, or nickel. In a strict sense this is a primary deposit also.

Investing in Gold. United States citizens can now legally own gold as such. Also, as before, one can buy gold coins. This is a highly specialized business, as the value of the coins involves the rarity of the coin as well as its gold content. (For some excellent advice on this matter, read Hoppe's *How to Invest in Gold Coins*—see the bibliography at the end of this book.) You can also buy into gold-mining shares. The richest gold mines are in South Africa. Shares are traded in the United States chiefly on the basis of what are called American Depository Receipts—otherwise known as ADRs—which simply are receipts for shares kept in South Africa and amount to the same thing as buying the shares. Some stocks are not strictly stocks in gold mines but in gold mining "houses" that finance gold mines, offer technical and legal services for a fee, and own various interests in the mines.

Some of the major gold mining "houses" of South Africa are:

Anglo American Corporation
Anglo Transvaal Consolidated Investment Company
Consolidated Goldfields
General Mining and Finance Corporation
Goldfields of South Africa
Johannesburg Consolidated Investment Company
Rand Mines
Union Corporation

The largest of these, Anglo American Corporation, has historically been mining about a third of the gold in South Africa. It also has substantial copper interests elsewhere in Africa as well as other mining interests.

There also are shares available to North American investors in individual South African gold mines. As the previously mentioned mining-investment houses may have other interests besides gold, one school of gold-investment thought holds that buying the shares of the individual gold mines is the better approach. This, of course, has to be balanced by the problem of having all your eggs in one basket. Some of these gold mines are:

Blyvooruitzicht	President Steyn
Buffelsfontein	Vaal Reefs
East Dreifontein	West Dreifontein
Kloof	Western Deep Levels
President Brand	Western Holdings

Some leading gold-producing companies in the United States are:

Homestake	Kennecott
Newmont	Phelps Dodge
Hecla	UV Industries
Anaconda	American Smelting and Refining

Only Homestake and Newmont mine gold as a primary objective. All the rest produce it as a by-product of other mining operations.

There are numerous gold-mining operations in Canada, some recovering gold as the principal part of their operation and others as a by-product. The primary gold mines are relatively small operations and have had a sporadic history. The more steady producers of gold are those that obtain it from other metal-mining operations and include Cominco, Hudson Bay Mining and Smelting, International Nickel, and Noranda Mines. Campbell Red Lake Mines and Campbell Chibougamau are gold mines as such.

Future of Gold Mining. The future of gold production around the world is clouded by the fact that the easily won gold has already been mined. Special air-cooling equipment has had to be installed in the Homestake Mine, where the shafts are over a mile deep now and temperatures are very warm. The future of South African gold mining will probably be characterized by considerably higher costs as some of the mines there are very deep and mining is increasingly expensive. Raising total gold production in South Africa from present rates will be difficult; in fact, a decline is being predicted shortly barring some new major discoveries. Labor difficulties are also becoming chronic.

Gold Futures Market. As a further note on how to invest in gold, it should be mentioned that in 1975 a gold futures market was established in the United States, where gold, like silver, is traded as a commodity on the futures market.

Find It Yourself. With the rise in price of gold, weekend prospecting has become increasingly popular. The geological surveys of most states with known gold deposits have published useful pamphlets on the technics for panning or sluicing gold, and maps showing known gold localities. Write your State Geologist. The basic tools for such a project are simple—a shovel, a gold pan, and some idea of where geologically the gold might be in your area. It is a good thing to have someone show you initially how to pan for gold, as the technique is somewhat of an art. More sophisticated gold prospectors have devised their own gold "dredges," which are simply suction pumps for sucking out gravel and sand from deep crevices between boulders. Rumor has it that certain enterprising individuals have made rather nice fortunes dredging gold out of some of the rivers in California in this fashion. They visited remote and relatively inaccessible areas by helicopter and found gold that some of the old prospectors had not been able to recover. No doubt some still remains. Not long ago a young fellow showed me several nice gold nuggets he had found in a stream in the Klamath Mountains of southern Oregon. It should be mentioned that gold nuggets have value well beyond simply their gold content, for they are prized in jewelry making and find a ready market in that industry.

In any case, gold panning is wholesome exercise. The chief hazard, from my experience, is the tendency to get arthritis from keeping one's hands and other extremities in the cold stream water for hours at a time.

Investing in Gold Mines. There are a remarkably large number of "gold mines" in existence, according to their owners, and most of them are for sale, in spite of the high price of gold. Accordingly, if someone offers you a "gold mine" to invest in, get the considered opinion of an expert if you are seriously interested. Just a few high-grade ore samples don't make a mine. You have to be able to mine large amounts of ore to make it pay, usually, although the story of a "pocket" of gold yielding $10,000 or so has actually been true in some instances. This is the sort of thing that keeps "gold fever" high. The next round of powder will blow open one of these pockets! Once in a rare instance it does. Good luck!

SILVER

Of the precious metals, silver is the most widely used in industry. As such it has had and will continue to have a very distinguished career. Silver is an essential part of photographic processes and is used in electronics and in many small but individually vital other ways. In the hands of politicians and governments, however, silver has led a hard life. In 1960, a U.S. Government bulletin made the following statement:

World outlook is for continuation of the rising trend in both production and consumption of silver. Notwithstanding that total world consumption exceeds production, large stocks are available to meet anticipated demand and no shortage of silver is expected at least in the near future. Output from domestic mines plus imports and secondary production should be ample for all normal domestic requirements.

Five years later President Johnson signed a law allowing the removal of all silver from coins.

Silver has been used as a medium of exchange in coinage since coins were invented, and some countries continue to try to retain it in their monetary systems. Vast quantities of silver are hoarded in various forms around the world, particularly in France and India and more recently in the United States. Industrial demand and popular demand seem likely to continue to outrun supplies at what have been historically regarded as reasonable price levels, and the price of silver, while subject to some violent speculative fluctuations, is likely to increase at least as fast as that of other commodities and probably somewhat faster. It remains a favorite hedge against inflation.

Where Is the Silver? When nature passed metals around, western North and South America were in line for the silver deposits. Chile, Peru, Mexico, and western United States are on that north-south line, which, as it crosses the border into Canada swings eastward to the great copper-silver deposit near Timmins, Ontario. Canada, Mexico, the United States, and Peru have been the world's leading producers for many years. Some silver deposits were very early known in the Mediterranean region but these were substantially mined out long ago.

Geologically, silver is what is called an epithermal deposit, which means it is deposited out of hot waters in fractures in the rock at relatively shallow depths. Indeed, that has been a control in the history of silver-mining areas. About the time the railroad reached Tonopah, Nevada, to handle the great silver trove there, the shallow silver deposits were exhausted. The shallowness of a typical silver deposit is also illustrated at Treasure Peak, near the old ghost town of Hamilton, Nevada, about 50 miles southwest of Ely. In the early 1860s an Indian, who was befriended by a prospector-trapper, told him that he knew where there was a mountain top "covered with silver." The prospector was skeptical but curious and ultimately went to look. To his very pleasant surprise the Indian was essentially right! A deposit of "horn silver," the mineral cerargyrite (a silver chloride that is soft and can be cut with a knife), was distributed in fractures of a shattered limestone that was a fold and now is a mountain top. In a few years some $30 million worth of silver was taken off the mountain but the pits rarely went down one hundred feet. The diggings are there today for all to see.

At a few places silver is found at depths of several thousand feet, the chief example being in the largest silver mine in the United States, the Sunshine of northern Idaho. The interesting story of this mine was told in the section on "Penny Stocks" in this book.

There are only a few silver mines in the United States; it is obtained to a large extent here as a by-product of other mining operations, notably copper, lead, and zinc. Some silver comes from nickel deposits, and silver is always associated with native gold deposits. Because the major deposits of silver are principally in these other ore deposits, the amount of silver produced is largely the result of the mining done for other metals, notably copper. An increase in the silver price can bring silver out of hoarding but it will not significantly increase the amount of silver that is mined.

World Silver Reserves. Apparent world silver reserves have been estimated by the U.S. Bureau of Mines as follows:

	In Millions of Ounces
United States	1,320
Mexico	730
Canada	640
Peru	530
Other free world	300
Communist countries (except Yugoslavia)	1,980
Total	5,500

Of the reserves in the United States, 65 percent are in ores where silver is recovered as a by-product.

Supply-Demand. Much has been written about supply and demand, which are, of course, functions of price. At some price there would be ample silver for the needs that can afford that price. But looking at the price of silver historically it seems clear that silver prices must continue to rise relative to most other commodities. The U.S. Bureau of Mines states:

In summary, the long-term outlook is that cumulative demand [to the year 2000] can be met from available sources of supply but at a probable increase in price.

There are some large hoards of silver, however, that may tend to modify price increases as this comes to market, although there is a question as to how much of this hoarded silver will ever be sold. An estimated five billion ounces exists in India, where there is an embargo on exports, but some smuggled silver continues to get out.

Silver, much more than gold, is lost over the years to industrial uses. It has been estimated that over 30 million ounces —one-fifth of U.S. industrial needs—are lost each year in the photographic industry because of lack of effective recovery processes.

How to Invest. There are four main ways to invest in silver. These are to buy shares of silver producing companies, buy into a silver mine as such, buy silver coins or bullion, or buy into the silver futures market.

There are very few silver-mining companies as such. Sunshine Mining is one; Hecla, while having other metal interests, is also quite heavily in silver mining. There are a number of small silver mines traded mostly over the counter in the Spokane area and in various areas of Canada (chiefly Vancouver and Toronto).

As most silver is recovered as a by-product of base-metal mining, the silver investment dollar is diluted when one puts it into companies with only some silver production such as Anaconda, Kennecott, Phelps Dodge, Gulf Resources and Chemical, American Smelting and Refining, and Texas Gulf (major holdings in Canada).

In Canada, Ecstall Mining Company, owned by Texas Gulf, is the world's largest single silver producer. Cominco, Hudson Bay Mining and Smelting, Noranda Mines, International Nickel, United Keno Hill Mines, and Agnico-Eagle are silver producers. Rosario Resources, based in New York, is a silver producer in Honduras. American Smelting and Refining Company has substantial silver interests in Mexico, as do two Canadian companies, Tormex Mining Developers and Pure Silver Mines, Ltd.

Buying into an individual silver mine is for the expert or at least some one with expert advice. Silver deposits tend to be shallow although a few can be extremely rich. A vein of almost solid native silver was discovered near Cobalt, Ontario, where, for a length of about 100 feet and a depth of about 60 feet, more than 650,000 ounces of silver were recovered. Slabs of very nearly pure silver were mined and one specimen was five feet long, weighed 1,640 pounds, and contained almost 10,000 ounces of silver. But this sort of thing is the marked exception. If you are considering a silver-property purchase, investigate thoroughly before you buy, not afterward.

Silver coins are perhaps a less complicated investment than are gold coins, for rarity of the coin and therefore the value of the coin as a collector's item rather than for metal content enters into the matter less often. Bags of ordinary silver coins can be purchased through silver brokers who have various arrangements on storage and buying on margin. Ads appear regularly in *The Wall Street Journal* as well as in local newspapers. Silver bullion can also be purchased on the same general basis. At times of rapidly rising silver prices (or a rapidly inflating dollar, which is the same thing) this sort of investment will work out, but the fact that it does not produce any income militates against it. There are also storage charges and insurance costs if delivery of the coins is not taken. However, no doubt there is a "peace of mind" value for some people to have a sack or two of silver coins hidden away somewhere. Once in a while in history, having such a cache proved to be very useful; it could be so again, although one would hope that our social and economic systems would never again be shattered to that degree. But who can say?

The silver futures market has been a wild ride this past decade and probably will continue to be. Here one can buy a contract for future delivery of silver (which you don't take, usually, of course, but simply sell the contract later on again) at some date and at some specified price. These prices on silver futures change daily and indeed minute by minute, and when one combines the rapid changes in price (though there is a daily limit imposed on how much it can move) with the leverage one has in the small investment that controls a large amount of silver, the profit—or loss—potential is great and can be had in a short time. It is my understanding that a majority of persons trading in almost all commodity markets, including silver, ultimately lose money, but the rewards can be large for a few. Your broker can tell you about it. Merrill Lynch and other large firms maintain commodity specialists in most of their principal offices and even in some smaller ones.

Summary.   The price of silver is likely to rise more rapidly than other commodities to the year 2000, and beyond. Silver is an exceedingly useful industrial metal and is used in electrical circuits (it conducts electricity better than any other metal), is the most reflective of all metals, makes numerous useful alloys, and is essential in photographic processes. There are several ways to invest in silver; investing in going silver mines paying dividends is probably the most satisfactory, although speculation in silver futures can result in very large profits, or otherwise. In any event, the demand for silver will continue to be strong for the indefinite future.

PLATINUM-GROUP METALS

Metals of the so-called platinum group are platinum, iridium, osmium, rhodium, and ruthenium. Iridium, incidentally, is the heaviest element in nature. All these metals always occur alloyed together, and of these platinum is the most abundant and important. For practical investment purposes, platinum is the only metal to be considered.

Occurrence.   All these metals are associated with what are called ultramafic rocks, which means they are on the other end of the mineral composition spectrum from granite. Nickel is the chief metal obtained from ultramafic rocks, and considerable platinum-group metals are recovered as a by-product of nickel mining. Platinum, like gold, is heavy and resistant to weathering and tends to accumulate in placers. Many gold placer operations also recover platinum, as has been the case in Colombia. The United States produces only about 1 to 2 percent of its platinum needs, chiefly from copper ores. Platinum placers are known in Oregon and California but the quality is low. In North America, Canada is the major platinum source.

World Reserves.   Total indicated world reserves of platinum are 424 million troy ounces. According to the U.S. Bureau of Mines, the United States has 3 million, Canada 6 million, Colombia 5 million, South Africa 200 million, and the Soviet Union 200 million. At least half of the world's output to date has been produced by the Soviet Union.

Uses.   About 40 percent of the platinum-group metals are used in the production of organic and inorganic chemicals and as catalysts in the refining of petroleum. Electrical applications and the production of glass fibers are the next largest uses.

The Future and Investment. Demand for platinum-group metals will grow steadily and perhaps about as fast as the gross national product as these metals find increased use in sophisticated petroleum-refining techniques. However, the chief metal used is likely to be palladium, and the Soviet Union is virtually the only source in quantity.

In North America, some platinum production comes from the placer operations of Goodnews Bay Mining Company (Alaska) and placers worked occasionally by Yuba Consolidated Industries. Platinum is recovered from sludge and residue by American Metal Climax and American Smelting and Refining incidental to other metal mining operations. Canada is the chief platinum producer, International Nickel providing the most and Falconbridge Nickel lesser amounts. International Mining produces both gold and platinum in Colombia and Bolivia. In South Africa, Rustenburg Platinum Mines, Impala Platinum, and Western Platinum are principal producers and contribute two-thirds of the free-world supply of platinum-group metals.

GEMSTONES AND RELATED MATERIALS

What is a gem is to a considerable extent a matter of opinion. Precious stones are usually the ruby, emerald, sapphire, and diamond, but the semi-precious list is long and according to one's tastes may include such things as agates, petrified wood, and even silicified dinosaur bones, which make very pretty pieces for necklaces and bracelets. Related materials that are not minerals (and gems do have to be of mineral composition and inorganic in origin to qualify as gems) include pearls, coral, amber, and jet (a hard, black variety of coal).

Gems in general have three principal qualities—they are durable, they have some degree of rarity, and they are beautiful. Most gems are used for decorative purposes although some, such as the diamond in cutting and drilling and the ruby more recently in laser work, are used industrially. Most people invest in at least a few gems during their lifetimes. Tradition has it that you give a diamond to the lady of your choice. The diamond producers of Africa are hard at work encouraging this idea, as are lots of young ladies.

A few comments follow in regard to certain gems and related materials.

Diamonds. These are the most popular gemstone but not the most valuable, weight for weight; that distinction belongs to the emerald. Diamonds are by far the hardest substance known and are a form of pure carbon. They occur in diamond-bearing "pipes," which are pipe-like masses of once molten (igneous) rock called kimberlite. Weathering releases the diamonds from this rock, which decomposes to a blue clay, forming the "blue ground" of the diamond fields. Some diamonds have been transported by water to river beds and some to the sea where diamonds are recovered by dredging.

Of the several hundred kimberlite pipes found in South Africa to date, only 27 are known to contain diamonds. Of these, 11 are too lean to be commercial. Outside South Africa, only in the Soviet Union has kimberlite been discovered rich enough to be mined. Even the richest kimberlites, however, contain relatively few diamonds. For each carat of diamonds recovered—and a carat weighs only 7/1000ths of an ounce—three tons of rock must be processed.

The first people to know diamonds were the Dravidiands of India about 800 B.C. They balanced diamonds on scales against the seeds of the carob tree, the "cattie" or "carat" that gives us the name origin of this unit of measure of diamond weight.

Most diamonds now come from South Africa, where De Beers Consolidated Mines controls over 80 percent of the world diamond output. Brazil, Venezuela, the Soviet Union, and India also have some deposits. Investing in diamond mines essentially means investing in De Beers; its shares are quoted daily in the foreign list of securities in *The Wall Street Journal.* Diamonds are also advertised as investments. For certain periods in history, diamond prices may rise more rapidly than those of other materials. But over the long run the fact that you get no interest on your investment, the cost of insurance, and the fact that diamonds are a very specialized market would suggest that the average investor would generally do better in other things.

Diamonds in North America. Diamonds do occur here in two different situations. In Pike County, Arkansas, is a diamond deposit that is privately owned and where tourists are allowed (indeed, encouraged) to dig for a fee. An occasional good diamond has been found. A more intriguing situation is the presence of diamonds in the glacial deposits of northern United States, in Wisconsin, Ohio, and West Virginia—somewhere to the north is an undiscovered diamond mine! Copper nuggets in the glacial drift of Finland were ultimately traced to where the glacier had obtained them, leading to the discovery of one of the better copper mines of Europe. A few people have tried to apply this same concept to the diamonds of the northern United States, but so far the diamond mother lode has eluded them.

Synthetic Diamonds. Because of the great demand for diamonds for use in drills for cutting hard rock as well as for many other industrial applications, there have been attempts to make them synthetically. General Electric synthesized diamonds in 1955 and now is making them in quantity for industrial use. Synthetic diamonds now are also made in Ireland, Japan, the Soviet Union, Sweden, and South Africa.

Emeralds. These are a form of beryl, which is a beryllium aluminum silicate. Some of the best came from upper Egypt in "Cleopatra's Mines." More recently most of them come from Colombia, where emerald mining and the initial sales are a government monopoly. Emeralds have been found in the United States at Hiddenite, North Carolina. Emeralds can be made synthetically and I have seen stones made by a man in California that were difficult to tell from the natural product. He has not patented the process because of fear that once the patent was on file, those countries that do not honor U.S. patents would steal the method. Emerald investment, like that of diamonds, is a special field and hardly one for the average citizen, but the general appeal of a high unit value, easily transported, is there.

Rockhounds. We could pursue the matter of gemstones at greater lengths, but it is a very specialized area of investment. For most people the closest approach that collecting and/or dealing with rocks and minerals might be to an investment is in the general area of "rockhounding"—collecting, working on, and marketing various rocks, minerals, and fossils. There are hundreds of rock and mineral clubs around the country; most of them put on annual shows where the products are sold. Agates are a popular item and a great variety of other rocks, minerals, and fossils also find a ready market. It is a fine way to capitalize on a pleasant and wholesome hobby. For some it has become a profitable, full-time occupation.

A fossil-fish quarry west of Kemmerer, Wyoming, was a valuable deposit worked by an old German gentleman in Kemmerer for many years; I have one of his fine fish fossils. Near South Hadley, Massachusetts, a dinosaur-track quarry was opened, and for years tracks from this quarry were sold to adorn fireplace mantels and other showplaces around the world. The tracks were advertised occasionally even in *The Wall Street Journal.* As a matter of information, dinosaur tracks are sold by the "foot," so to speak. A good track used to fetch about $20, but no doubt inflation has caught up with that market also.

Land with interesting rock, mineral, or fossil deposits can be a good investment and a source of income. Quite a number of areas, especially in the West, which have agates or other such rocks on them, have been opened to collectors for a fee. The Priday Agate Beds, an excellent locality for the famous Oregon "thunderegg" agate, are an example.

I have no estimate of the dollar volume involved in various sorts of rocks and minerals sold across the country in various ways, but I am sure it must be considerable. I personally know a number of people who pursue the matter part-time and have a nice supplemental income. At the same time they enjoy both the collecting of the materials and the processing of them afterward.

15

Nonmetallic Materials

THE NONMETALLIC MINERALS are rather less glamorous than gold and silver or even copper and tungsten. The nonmetallics include sulfur, gypsum, phosphate, crushed rock, the materials for making cement, and such everyday items as sand and gravel. Yet, the value of sand and gravel far exceeds the value of all the gold and silver produced in the United States each year. Total value of sand and gravel is now well over $1 billion annually.

These nonmetallics may be less exciting but they are certainly no less essential to our civilization than are the metallics. Fertilizers (for example, from phosphate) are the basis for our agriculture, and we are in the "Age of Cement" as much as we are in the Atomic Age or the Iron Age.

Some of these nonmetallics have the potential of becoming quite distinguished in their own right because of certain special properties. Boron is one such material that may be on the verge of much wider uses than at present. With the advent of production of synthetic gas and oil from coal in volume and the production of oil from oil shale, the demand for hydrogen will greatly increase.

These nonmetals are woven into the fabric of our civilization in myriad ways. The very solid spectrum of investment opportunities they offer the investor is discussed in subsequent pages.

AGRICULTURAL LIMESTONE AND DOLOMITE

Background. Soil conditioners have been used for hundreds of years as part of the evolution of our agricultural practices. More recently, as food supply is becoming critical, the proper care of soils is receiving much more attention. Agricultural limestone and dolomite (which besides the calcium carbonate of limestone also contains magnesium) are used to treat soils that are acidic or that have had their calcium content leached out by heavy rainfall.

Present Demand and Uses. Limestone and dolomite are used generally throughout most farming regions where cropping is intensive (as compared with the more lightly farmed areas of the western Great Plains winter wheat belt). Much "agricultural lime" is really finely crushed limestone or dolomite. This is entirely satisfactory, however, as the fine rock particles weather into the soil over a period of several years, thus providing a continuous supply of calcium. Demand for agricultural limestone and dolomite is steady and growing slowly.

Sources. About 3.6 percent of the Earth's crust is calcium, much of it in the form of bedded limestone and dolomite deposits left on the continents by ancient seas. However, the deposits are not always located where they are needed. In western Oregon, for example, soils are quite acid but there are no good local limestone sources. Generally, however, limestone suitable for the low-quality needs of agriculture is available at no great distance. These materials are widely distributed around the world and supplies are ample for the indefinite future.

Outlook and Investment. Use is dependent upon agricultural demand, which is steady and slowly growing as soils become depleted of their natural mineral content. There are many companies producing agricultural limestone and dolomite; most of them are privately held. A supply of good-quality (relatively pure, not full of silica in particular) limestone or dolomite adjacent to a substantial agricultural area is always worth investigating. Your state geological survey can help you evaluate it.

ASBESTOS

Background. Asbestos is both one of the most unusual minerals and also one of the most useful. It is unusual in that it is fibrous and looks more like silk than a mineral. Its fibers, up to six inches long, can produce more than six miles of thread from one pound. Certain types of asbestos can stand temperatures up to 5,000° F.

Present Demand and Uses. To fully list the more than 2,000 uses of asbestos would take many pages. Principally it goes into wallboards, insulating materials, fire-proof cloth, shingles, brake linings, asbestos cement pipe, and in floor tile. Demand, largely related to the building industry, is steady and growing. At the present time the United States uses about one-fifth of world production.

Sources. The largest known asbestos deposits in the world are in the Thetford district of Quebec, an area about 6 miles wide and 70 miles long that extends into Vermont. Other deposits are known in Ontario, British Columbia, and the Yukon. Both the Soviet Union and Africa have large deposits. The United States has substantial amounts, chiefly in Vermont and North Carolina and also in California, where there was a modest "asbestos rush" in 1959. Geologically, asbestos occurs chiefly as a result of the metamorphism (heat, hot solutions, and pressure) of what are called ultrabasic rocks—dark-colored igneous rocks. To put it simply, asbestos occurs where these sorts of rocks have been throughly chewed up and worked over by natural processes to the point where the original rocks can hardly be identified.

Outlook and Investment. Asbestos demand in the United States is expected to double by the end of this century. World demand will probably rise even more rapidly because the developing countries have a larger new construction potential. An average annual growth rate of about 4.2 percent has been projected. United States and Canadian asbestos resources are more than ample to meet the high end of the forecast for the United States to the year 2000 without affecting the Canadian ability to supply the major part of demand for the rest of the world. Currently the United States supplies about 15 percent of its needs.

There are a number of asbestos-mining companies in the United States and Canada. The more important ones include Johns-Manville Corporation, Atlas Mineral Corporation, Union Carbide, General Aniline and Film (GAF Corporation), Cassiar Asbestos, and Asbestos Corporation. Turner and Newhall of England runs a fully integrated asbestos operation worldwide.

BORAX AND BORON

Background. Boron, an element that stands between the metals and the nonmetals, sometimes is called a "semi-metal." It can combine with both metallic and nonmetallic elements. Boron is light and strong and when combined with certain epoxy compounds can be made into materials that are lighter than aluminum and stronger than steel. Although known for nearly 200 years, boron is still being researched and it seems likely that substantial new uses will be found for it. In synthetic compound form, cubic boron nitride is the second hardest known substance, being about half as hard as diamond—this is pretty hard, as diamond is five times as hard as the next naturally occurring substance, corundum.

Present Demand and Uses. Boron is now used chiefly in such compounds as the well-known boric acid and borax. The largest single use for boron is in glass-making, where boron compounds add strength. Other uses include soaps and detergents, metal fluxing, and agricultural chemicals.

The present, rather prosaic uses of boron compounds may be eventually overshadowed by new applications such as in atomic energy control rods, jet and rocket fuels, and motor-fuel additives, and as the stiffening agent in extremely strong, lightweight, composite structural materials. Much study has already been given to the wide use of boron compounds in the aircraft industry.

Sources. About half of the total estimated world supply of boron is in the United States, in dry lake beds and brine lakes in southeastern California. Other minor deposits are in lake beds in Oregon and Nevada. Turkey and the Soviet Union are next but with substantially lesser amounts.

Outlook and Investment. The old 20-mule-team Borax Company, U.S. Borax and Chemical, is now a wholly-owned subsidiary of the British firm, Rio Tinto-Zinc, which has a predominant position in borax through worldwide holdings. American Potash and Chemical, now a subsidiary of Kerr-McGee, has sizeable boron holdings, as does Stauffer Chemical.

The outlook for boron is good if not excellent; its conventional uses are in basic and growing industries, and current research may turn up substantial new uses for this interesting material.

BROMINE

Background. Bromine is one of two elements, the other being mercury, that is liquid at room temperature. Bromine is so very active chemically that it is highly corrosive and exists naturally only as compounds.

Present Demand and Uses. Bromine's chief use now is in leaded motor fuels, where bromine serves as a scavanger of combustion products, mainly lead. However, as leaded gasoline is phased out, this use of bromine will drop substantially. Some 14 percent of bromine is used in various sanitary ways such as in disinfecting agents, bleaching agents, fumigants, and swimming pool sanitizers. About 5 percent is used in preparing fire-fighting compounds. There are a number of minor but vital uses for bromine in certain specialized products including pharmaceuticals.

The demand for bromine will probably grow somewhat less rapidly than the rate of growth of the total economy unless it becomes used more widely than at present as a basic chemical raw material to compensate for reduced consumption in motor fuels.

Sources. Bromine occurs in brine wells in Michigan, the same brines from which magnesium is produced. It also exists in brines in Searles Lake, California, and in oil-well waters in Texas and Oklahoma. At a concentration of 65 parts per million, there are virtually limitless quantities in sea water. The bromine resources of the United States are virtually inexhaustible at foreseeable rates of U.S. expansion of demand. Worldwide the situation is the same. The Dead Sea, for example, has about a 1-percent bromine content.

Outlook and Investment. Demand for bromine may be less

in the future as leaded fuel is phased out. Dow Chemical holds large reserves, as does Kerr-McGee through its ownership of part of Searles Lake, California. Dow Chemical is engaged in a continual program of bromine research designed to find new uses for this abundant material.

BUILDING STONE AND SLATE

Background. Some early people lived in a natural stone house called a cave. Then they moved out, presumably to something a bit more luxurious. But the low maintenance costs of the cave (it didn't need to be painted) and the excellent insulating qualities of rock were so appealing that they now have rebuilt their rock houses around them by cutting stone and using it in construction of homes and office buildings. Stone is durable; it costs little to keep up. On the other hand it is heavy, and its durability is well beyond what it needs to be—that is, the structures become obsolete in terms of design and function before the stone is destroyed by weathering. If you wanted to build a house with no exterior maintenance and that would last indefinitely, you would build a house out of quartzite with a slate roof. Quartzite is chemically inert, very tough, harder than steel, and should last you 100,000 years or more with no difficulty, However, the demand for that sort of durability is limited, so building stones have to compete with other, less durable but more economic materials. There are a great variety of building stones; granite, marble, slate, sandstone, dolomite, and limestone are the more common.

In spite of the weight, some expecially beautiful stones are shipped great distances—for example, the Italian travertine (a hot-spring deposit), which is used in buildings all over the world. The beautiful Morton gneiss from western Minnesota likewise is widely used because with the quality of taking a high polish but of being resistant to weathering, it can be used as a striking exterior finish. This is in contrast to marble, which takes a fine polish but if used outdoors, particularly in wet climates, quickly looses this finish. Marble, therefore, is more adaptable to interior uses.

The Bedford Limestone of Indiana is unique in that when it is first quarried it is relatively soft and can be readily carved with a knife to all sorts of forms and images. When it drys out, however, it becomes as hard as other limestones. This limestone, incidentally, is made of myriad tiny fossils, which give it a uniform but somewhat "sandy" looking texture.

Present Demand and Uses. Good quality building stone, particularly near markets, is in steady demand. Its uses do not need to be elaborated on. The decorative and durable qualities of this natural material are pleasing to our senses and it remains a favorite construction material.

Outlook and Investment. In spite of the many new materials being used in construction, stone continues to be popular. There are, however, several factors that determine the value of a deposit. Desirability of appearance, of course, is a major factor, but the ease with which it may be quarried and worked also are important. The high cost of quarrying a hard rock like granite is a limiting factor in its use. Other rocks such as dolomite, limestone, marble (simply a recrystallized limestone), and travertine are considerably softer and easier to work. Colorful and durable rough stone for use in fireplaces is an item in considerable demand, and a good local source of this sort of material is always worth pursuing.

There are no major companies into which investments can be made in building stone or slate. Many stone companies are privately or closely held. A few are traded over the counter. If there are stone quarries in your area and you are interested in such an investment, no doubt the local bank would know the ownership. Ownership of a good stone quarry has sometimes been an incidental feature of owning country property, and if such a quarry or potential site exists on property you are considering it should be evaluated carefully. The state geological survey can help you in this matter.

Slate presents too specialized a situation to merit much discussion. Its chief use has been in roofing, both in large sheets and ground up as surfacing for asphalt shingles. In large sheets, slate roofs are quite heavy, and their great durability is somewhat countered by the fact that additional money must be spent to build a strong-enough support. A slate roof will outlast several wooden buildings underneath it, and slate roofs have been transferred from one building to another as the building below fell apart. In one case, to my knowledge, a slate roof became part of the family inheritance, being passed along to the eldest sons. A slate roof can last 1,000 years or more but there is not much demand for that kind of durability. Slate is also used as flooring, particularly in entrance ways. Slate in crushed form is used as an aggregate in cement.

Slate is not a very profitable item at present. In shingle form it is expensive because it requires hand-quarrying; no one has figured out yet how to quarry and split slate by machine very effectively. Simply as crushed rock it has lots of competition and loses its primary advantage—that it can be split into sheets.

Slate is simply shale that has been further compressed (metamorphosed), while shale is simply compacted clay. So they are part of a single rock series. Slate occurs in areas where the rocks have been folded tightly and subjected to heat and pressure. Like marble it is classed as a metamorphic rock.

CALCIUM, LIME, AND CEMENT

Background. Calcium is a metal, but it never occurs naturally in native metal form and is rarely used that way. In compound form, such as in limestone, it is usually classed with the nonmetallic materials. That is why I have included it here with the nonmetals. The use of calcium in various natural rocks as a soil conditioner and the use of calcium as cement date back at least 2,000 years. The Romans made puzzolan cement (so named from Puzzouli, Italy, where a volcanic ash called puzzuolana has been dug). The cement was formed from quicklime mixed with this volcanic ash; the baths at Pompeii were built of this material and are in as good condition today as when they were buried by the eruption of Mt. Vesuvius in 79 A.D. The Romans used cement in construction throughout the Mediterranean world; some of it still remains.

The discovery of Portland cement, which constitutes 99 percent of present cement production, was made by an English bricklayer, Joseph Aspdin, and named for rock that it resembles on the island of Portland.

Lime (also called quicklime, burnt lime, or caustic lime) is simply calcium oxide formed by burning calcium carbonate (limestone). Cement is formed by the burning of limestone to form lime with the addition of clay in the process. The whole mass is fused and then ground to a powder (cement). The addition of water and various aggregates such as sand, gravel, or pumice produces concrete when it sets. There is no precise chemical composition of cement; its content varies with the quality of the raw materials used.

Present Demand and Uses. It would be superfluous to belabor the reader with a list of the uses of cement. Suffice it to say that cement literally forms much of the visible structure of our civilization. Demand is closely related to the growth of the gross national product. Consumption is increasing more rapidly (from a lower base, of course) in the underdeveloped countries as industrialization takes place and as housing in particular is improved. The United States and the Soviet Union are the largest producers and consumers of lime and cement.

Being the chief ingredient in plaster, lime also, is used in construction. Some lime is used for agricultural purposes, although much "lime" used in that fashion is simply finely ground limestone (see section on "Agricultural Limestone and Dolomite"). Lime also is used as a soil stabilizer for roads, airports, and building foundations.

Pure calcium is a soft, silvery-white lightweight metal related to barium, magnesium, and other alkaline-earth elements. It is the fifth most abundant element in the Earth's crust but occurs only in compounds. Pure calcium is used in some chemical processes and is combined with other materials to form medicinal preparations. But altogether these uses are very minor compared to the use of relatively impure calcium in cement and plaster and as a soil conditioner.

Calcium in the form of limestone is used as a fluxing material in steel operations. This is one of the reasons why the steel industry of the United States centered originally around Pittsburgh, where coal and limestone were available to mix with the iron ore brought in by low-cost water transport on the Great Lakes.

Sources. About 10 percent of the surface of the continents is covered with deposits of limestone and dolomite. Pure limestone is calcium carbonate, but there is no pure limestone in nature; common impurities are quartz sand, clay, silt, and silica. Depending on the end uses, various grades of limestone can be mined. Also, oyster shells are a local source of lime along coastal areas, especially the Gulf Coast. This material is used for agricultural lime and for road materials particularly in places such as southern Louisiana, where gravel deposits are rare.

Some of the more-nearly pure limestones are formed by the deposition of calcium carbonate by marine organisms such as corals. The cement plants at Mason City, Iowa, are based on the existence of abundant coral-rich limestones. Here they are making cement out of old coral reefs.

There is no shortage of calcium around the world, but locally there may be problems of distance to quality supplies.

Outlook and Investment. Continued growth in use of calcium-based materials, including lime and cement, is assured. Several factors contribute to profitability of these sorts of operations. One of the chief costs of making cement and lime is fuel for burning the limestone. As fuel costs rise and as there also are maladjustments in distribution of fuel supplies, this will be an increasingly important item affecting efficiency and cost of operation. Any investment in cement manufacturers should include consideration of the future fuel situation. Overcapacity has also been a chronic problem in the cement business; more recently shortages have occurred. Historically, capacity, added in large increments, has contributed to these imbalances. This cyclical nature of the business will probably continue but to a lesser extent.

Another factor creating imbalances between production and demand has been the differing rates of building activity in various parts of the United States at different times. As cement cannot be economically hauled great distances, the matter of local sources is important. From time to time, as some areas of the United States have had construction booms and other areas have lagged, so too have the local cement industries waxed and waned.

In dollar volume the cement business is one of the largest segments of the mineral industry. About a dozen companies in the United States account for more than half of the cement production. These include Kaiser Cement and Gypsum Corporation, Lehigh Portland Cement, Ideal Basic Industries, Lone Star Industries, Flintkote, U.S. Steel, General Portland, Texas Industries, Martin Marietta, Giant Portland Cement, and Penn-Dixie Industries. In Canada, Canada Cement Lafarge and Genstar are important producers. Lime producers in the United States include Allied Chemical, PPG Industries, Bethlehem Steel, United States Gypsum, National Gypsum, Phizer, Inc., and Dow Chemical. In Canada, Texas Lime, Algoma Steel, Reiss Lime of Canada, The Steel Company of Canada, and Dominion Lime are major producers.

Comment. Mining limestone is done mostly by open pit; only a small percentage is from underground operations. These pits in some areas become sites of attractive lakes; in other places they mar the landscape and create environmental problems. Future cement operations will no doubt have to take into account what costs are involved in reclaiming these limestone-mining sites. Also, cement manufacturing involves finely grinding the product. This can result in a very dusty operation, covering considerable areas of the countryside with the material. This form of pollution has already caused lawsuits, and controls are being instituted in that regard. Many cement plants are obsolete today in terms of both the fuels they use and the lack of pollution-control systems. Many of them will have to be rebuilt or replaced over the next decade and beyond.

CARBON

Background. Carbon is an element occurring in such diverse forms as the diamond and graphite (the "lead" in the lead pencil). It is the chief constituent of coal and a major constituent of oil, natural gas, and wood. It is used chiefly in its various compound forms as fuels and raw material for a variety of industries.

Present Demand and Uses. Carbon as carbon, not as a compound, is used in the form of charcoal, carbon black, petroleum coke, and coal coke. Of these, only carbon black is relatively pure. The end uses of lower grades of carbon are chiefly in the production of aluminum, phosphorus, and steel. More than 90 percent of carbon black goes into rubber manufacturing; the rest is used chiefly in ink, paint, and plastics and as a filtering agent. Some carbon is combined with silicon to make silicon carbide, an exceedingly hard abrasive. Demand for carbon products tends to follow the growth curve of the steel industry, on which it is largely dependent. High-grade carbon black is dependent chiefly on the rubber-tire industry as an outlet.

Sources. Carbon can be obtained from coal, petroleum, natural gas, and wood. The resources are enormous.

Outlook and Investment. Carbon demand will continue to grow with the economy. Virtually no industry makes carbon except for carbon black. Even this is a very small part of the activities of several companies, one being Cities Service. Carbon used in the steel industry is made by that industry. Carbon, as such, is not an investment medium of consequence.

CHLORINE

Background. Chlorine is a highly toxic and volatile gas, always found combined. It was discovered in 1774, although alchemists who experimented with aqua regia (a mixture of hydrochloric and nitric acids, so named "royal water" because it will dissolve gold and platinum) knew of some properties of chlorine from hydrochloric acid, which contains chlorine (HCl). An early use of chlorine was to bleach textiles. Chlorine was first produced commercially in the United States Maine in 1892. Growth of chlorine production the past few decades has been exceptionally rapid—an 8.1-percent compound rate.

Present Demand and Uses. The principal use of chlorine is in the bleaching of pulp and paper. Large amounts are also used in plastics manufacture ("teflon" uses chlorine in its production). Other uses include chlorinated solvents employed in dry-cleaning, in pesticides, in various sanitation disinfectent processes including water and sewage treatment (which account for about 4 percent of total chlorine production), and in pharmaceuticals. Demand follows the pulp and paper industry cycles somewhat, but as other uses tend to flatten out these cycles the demand for chlorine shows a fairly steady growth pattern.

Sources. Chlorine is produced in three ways, all using common salt, or sodium chloride, as the basic raw material. There being no shortage of salt (see section on "Salt"), there is no shortage of chlorine. The only critical factor in chlorine production is the amount of energy used; most chlorine is produced by electrolysis.

Outlook and Investment. Outlook is for a steady growth,

somewhat faster than the growth of the gross national product. To invest in chlorine as a basic material, one simply invests in salt. It is estimated that the chlorine contained in the salt reserves of the United States amounts to at least 36 trillion tons. Chlorine producers in the United States include Stauffer Chemical, Dow Chemical, and Hooker Chemical, now a division of Occidental Petroleum.

CLAY

Background. The earliest human use of clay is lost in antiquity, but it is surely one of the first Earth materials used. It is still used in vast quantities. In the United States each year we use the equivalent of about a quarter of a ton of clay per person. It is a high-volume, low-value item, except for certain special high-quality clays. There are many kinds of clay. The U.S. Bureau of Mines recognizes six principal categories:

1. Kaolin (also called china clay and other names). Used for china, in rubber, paper, refractories.
2. Ball clay (so-named because of its plasticity). Used for china and ceramics in general and for fillers.
3. Fire clay. Used in refractories (brick linings in blast furnaces, for example), for crocks, jugs, jars.
4. Bentonite. A weathered volcanic ash. Two types exist—a swelling and a non-swelling variety. Some swelling types increase up to 15 to 20 times over their dry volumes. Used in making special muds for oil-well drilling, as grouting to prevent leaks in certain structures, and in foundry (casting) sands. It is also used in the process by which low-grade iron ore (taconite) is made into pellets of higher quality.
5. Fuller's earth. Used as an absorbent and as a cleaning agent.
6. Miscellaneous clays. Includes brick, sewer pipe, and common clay tile. These uses account for most clay production.

Shale is simply the hardened rock form of clay. In industry the terms clay and shale tend to be interchanged.

Clays are heavy, and so transportation costs enter into the economic picture. Only a few very special purpose clays can be shipped very far and still meet competition successfully. For common clay and clay products it is estimated that the effective economic radius is about 200 miles. Almost all clay is mined by open-pit methods.

Present Demand and Uses. Most clay is used in structural products (brick, pipe, tile) and ceramics. Pipe and lightweight aggregates are major end products, but clays are also used as fillers for paint, paper, and rubber, in drilling muds for oil-well operations, for absorbent uses of various kinds, in chemicals, and in a variety of other ways. Growth of use for individual clay types differs considerably, but overall the growth is about consistent with that of the gross national product.

Sources. Clays are a group of very fine-grained non-metallic minerals that are mostly hydrous aluminum silicates. Clays form chiefly from the weathering of a common group of minerals called feldspars, which make up some 60 percent of granite and many other igneous rocks. They are the product of chemical weathering and, as such, form in granitic and other igneous rock areas where there is abundant rainfall and a moderate climate. Georgia is such a place and has some of the best clay deposits in the United States. Certain other clays have special sources. One of them is bentonite, which is formed from the weathering of volcanic ash and so is widely distributed across western United States, particularly in Wyoming, Colorado, and Montana. Volcanoes to the west contributed ash that fell on Kansas, and substantial bentonite deposits exist in that state. Clay deposits are widely distributed around the world. The only problems of source involve special-purpose clays that may not be well-located relative to their greatest demand.

Outlook and Investment. Clay usage has a slow but steady increase, and it is unlikely that any new demand would substantially change this trend. It is a low-margin business in general, although some special clays command a substantial premium in price. If one has a clay deposit that appears to be of value, usually the geological survey of the particular state is in a position to test the material and offer some opinion as to what the demand might be. There are more than 1,200 clay mines in the United States. Many of them are privately owned or closely held. Some of the major construction-materials companies have clay deposits, but these are usually a small part of total operations as is the case of U.S. Gypsum. Companies that are somewhat more specially concerned with clay production include Glen-

Gery Shale Brick Corporation, Ferro Corporation, and General Shale Productions Company.

Comment. The problems of shipping clay products very far are important. Urban sprawl has been encroaching upon clay deposits located convenient to large areas of use. Preservation of these local clay sources is important and calls for proper zoning. There is a continuing need to search for new clay deposits that can provide a local source for materials now shipped in from some distance. If such deposits are found they should be readily marketable to established clay-processing companies.

CORUNDUM

Background. Corundum first came into substantial demand about 1860, when the bonded grinding wheel was developed. To meet that demand, commercial mining of corundum began in the United States in 1871 in North Carolina. Since that time, output has been sporadic from several mines in Georgia, North Carolina, and Montana. There has been no consistent U.S. production since 1906 except for short periods during World War II. Emery is a dark, granular variety of corundum.

Present Demand and Uses. The development of fused aluminum oxide, which is a synthentic corundum, has largely replaced the natural material.

Sources. There are no appreciable economic deposits of corundum in the strict sense known either in the United States or Canada. However, there are sizeable deposits of emery near Peekskill, New York, and in Virginia and elsewhere. South Africa, Southern Rhodesia, and India have extensive deposits, with cumulative reserves of several million tons. The Soviet Union is believed to have large deposits.

Outlook and Investment. The development of synthetic corundum has largely displaced the natural product although minor amounts are imported. The outlook is for limited demand and it is not a significant outlet for investment capital for North American investors.

CRUSHED ROCK

Background. Broken rock has been used by many civilizations to surface their roadways, and it is still in great demand for that purpose today. In the very wet areas of the Pacific Northwest, large amounts of crushed rock are used to surface logging roads. They must have a solid base to stand the great weight of the log trucks during the rainy season, which in Oregon, where I live, can be nine months long on occasion. Broken rock used on roads is commonly called "road metal," a term that probably should be abandoned in favor of simply calling it what it is—crushed rock—as no metal is involved. Broken rock can be of most any origin. Generally it is desirable to have rock that in total is fairly soft, at least softer than the rock crusher. Limestone fits this description. When used to surface roads, limestone also tends to weather and lose lime to the underlying soil, causing the soil to stabilize and thus improve the road condition.

In some areas, however, only hard rocks are available, as is the case in much of the Pacific Northwest, where the predominant rock is basalt. This is considerably harder than the rock crusher and occasionally it is the rock crusher that is crushed rather than the rock. Granite is also harder than steel, but unlike basalt, which is fine-grained, granite is coarse-grained with a multiple mineral composition. Granite lends itself more readily to crushing and makes fine road surfacing as well as good roofing material.

Present Demand and Uses. Crushed rock is used for roadways, as ballast along railroad tracks, and in construction of buildings in various ways. Demand is fairly steady but tends to fluctuate considerably with the work on major projects such as construction of a new access-road network to the back country. Location is very important, as hauling crushed rock very far is expensive and its unit value is low.

Sources. Stream gravels and glacial gravels are common sources of rock from which to make crushed gravel (as opposed to natural gravel, which is simply sized by screening). Otherwise, a great variety of rocks are used for this purpose, the chief qualification being generally that the rock is locally available to the project that needs the rock.

Outlook and Investment. Continuing steady but with no great growth in demand is the rather obvious outlook for crushed rock. Most companies are locally owned and investment would have to be largely on that basis. However, Flintkote and Rosario Resources are two major firms that have crushed rock operations. A piece of land with a potential site for a rock crushing operation might have special investment value.

Comment. Rock crushers are noisy and the operation is also dusty. A rock-crushing area tends to be unsightly both during and after the operation. Zoning laws and environmental restrictions must increasingly be considered in this sort of enterprise.

DIATOMITE

Background. Diatomite is a rock made of the accumulated silica shells of an interesting little plant called a diatom, which has lived and still lives in both lakes and oceans in fantastic numbers. It is an unusual plant, by the way, in that it swims around and is not stationary. A single cubic inch of diatomite has been estimated to contain the shells of as many as 25 million individual diatoms. At such places as Lompoc, California, diatomite deposits can be measured in cubic miles! Diatomite is a porous material, being about 90 percent space, and will easily float on water. It has very high volume for its weight and is fireproof and an excellent insulator. Diatomite production began in the United States in 1884 in Maryland. The very large, high-quality deposits at Lompoc, California, were first mined in 1890. The United States is both the world's largest producer and consumer of diatomite.

Present Demand and Uses. Diatomite enters into many products and processes. There are more the 12,000 species of diatoms known, with a wide variety of size ranges and shapes. Certain species have particular characteristics of their porous shells, which make them useful filtration especially. Machines have been devised that actually sort out various species of diatoms. Diatomite is used in water purification, in refining various foods such as sugar, and in oil refining. It is also used as a mild abrasive and as a filler and extender in plastics, paints, and paper. It is used in thermal insulation in construction. Johns-Manville uses the trade name "Celite" for diatomite insulating materials. Demand is strong and fairly steady at present and can be expected to continue so.

Sources. Diatoms live in both salt and fresh water. Their shells are therefore found in both lake and marine deposits, but they are in greatest abundance where there is an excess of silica in the water. This condition had occurred in certain ocean areas and also in a number of ancient lakes in western United States where for the past several million years volcanic ash was spread widely over the landscape and provided a ready source of the silica needed for the diatom shells. In diatomaceous earth the diatoms were not abundant enough to form pure deposits but were mixed to a greater or lesser extent with clay and silt that washed into the lakes, bogs, or ocean embayments in which the diatoms lived. "Diatomaceous earth" and "diatomite" are actually synonyms, but commonly the term "diatomite" is used for the more nearly pure deposits.

Diatomite is widely distributed in the United States, both on the East and West coasts, and also in certain interior areas of Nevada, Arizona, Oregon, and Washington. The most notable deposits are those at Lompoc, where the beds are about 1,000 feet thick.

Outlook and Investment. The outlook for diatomite is good for both the near and more distant future. It is useful in a wide variety of processes and materials, and its use promises to increase at least as fast as the economy as a whole. Johns-Manville mines the deposits at Lompoc, California, and Basalt, Nevada. Eagle-Picher Industries mines Nevada deposits also. A number of smaller companies, some privately owned, also have diatomite in various parts of the United States. Supplies are ample for world use to the year 2000 and well beyond.

Comment. Beyond the usual reclamation needs associated with open-pit mining, there are no particular environmental problems with diatomite production. The large moisture content of the crude diatomite makes for a fairly dustless operation.

FELDSPAR

Background. In certain relatively rare forms feldspar has been known and used for a long time as a gemstone. Its use, however, for the porcelain on the bathtub is relatively recent, although feldspar as a distinct ingredient in ceramics dates back to at least the Tang Dynasty of China (A.D.621–945). Feldspars are a group of minerals that are sodium, calcium, and potassium aluminum silicates. On weathering they produce clay, and extreme weathering of certain feldspar-derived clays produces the aluminum ore, bauxite. Feldspars are the most abundant mineral "building blocks" of the Earth's crust; the average granite is about 60 percent feldspar.

Present Demand and Uses. Most feldspar is used as a flux in glass-making and in ceramics, with minor amounts going to such things as porcelain enamels, scouring soaps, welding rod coatings, and artificial teeth. Demand is quite closely related to the demand for glass in various forms, including containers.

Sources. Feldspar is an exceedingly abundant mineral, and no firm estimates have been made of total supplies. However, they are huge and obviously adequate to meet any forseeable demand for centuries ahead. In the United States, California and North Carolina have accounted for more than half of the output. Other major producing states are South Carolina, South Dakota, Georgia, and Virginia.

Outlook and Investment. The outlook for feldspar consumption appears to be one of slow and steady growth. However, increased recycling of glass containers may reduce this growth rate somewhat. Freight rates are a principal factor in feldspar economics as supplies are fairly widely distributed. Any given deposit is subject to considerable competition, especially as feldspar is a low-unit-value material. It also has strong competition from deposits of nephline syenite (a form of feldspar) developed recently in Canada, some of which is shipped across the border to the manufacturing states of the North and Northeast. International Minerals and Chemicals, The Feldspar Corporation, Ferro Corporation, and Wedron Silica of California are major feldspar producers in the United States. In Canada not much feldspar is produced, but what is mined comes chiefly from operations of International Minerals and Chemicals (Canada), Ltd.

FLUORINE AND FLUORITE

Background. Fluorine is an extremely active gas found only in nature in the combined form. Its chief source is the mineral fluorite (sometimes called fluorspar), in which it is tied to calcium. The name comes from a Latin word meaning "a rock that flows" and refers to its use back as far as the 16th century as a flux in metallurgical processes.

Present Demand and Uses. Fluorine is used principally in the forms of fluorspar and cryolite for the smelting of steel and aluminum. Cryolite is a sodium aluminum fluoride mineral vital in aluminum smelting. Only one source has been known in the world—at Ivigtut, Greenland. After 100 years of production the deposit was mined out in 1963. Cryolite is now made synthetically, but a new natural source would be a most welcome and valuable discovery. Other uses of fluorine are in various chemical compounds, including refrigerants, aerosols, solvents, and plastics, and in the manufacture of hydrofluoric acid, an acid that can etch glass. Demand is growing somewhat faster than the gross national product.

Sources. Fluorite, the chief source of fluorine, occurs in the middle Mississippi Valley, in Kentucky, Illinois, Missouri, Arkansas, and Oklahoma. There are smaller deposits known in the West. Reserves about equal to those of the United States exist in Canada and Mexico. Geologically, fluorite occurs disseminated as small grains through certain igneous rocks, as veins in various kinds of rocks, and as bedded deposits (as in the major source areas mentioned above) interstratified with limestones. Origin of this last sort of deposit has been the source of considerable speculation. Current thought is that fairly hot brines circulating up into these bedded rocks brought the fluorite.

Outlook and Investment. The outlook is for continued strong demand for fluorine and therefore fluorite. At present prices it seems certain that world supplies will be depleted before 1990. Therefore appreciable price increases can be expected to bring more marginal properties into production. There are no substitutes for fluorine in the manufacture of hydrofluoric acid or in the various fluorocarbon chemicals (of which "teflon" is one example). In other uses the substitutions are only limited. Thus fluorine and fluorite are critical materials, and any new deposits of size would surely have a ready market almost irrespective of their locations.

At higher prices, some fluorine can be obtained from phosphate rock, and it is speculated that large deposits of fluorapatite (a calcium phosphate mineral with fluorine attached) may exist in marine phosphate rocks that lie beneath the sea extending east from known phosphate deposits in North Carolina,

South Carolina and Florida. Fluorine might also be recovered directly from sea water and from certain lake brines. Companies holding fluorite deposits can look forward to somewhat higher prices of fluorite relative to other commodities.

There are no very large fluorite-mining operations in either the United States or Canada; production is obtained from a number of smaller operations, some privately held. Among publicly held companies, NL industries and Cerro Corporation are producers of fluorite as a minor part of their total operations. In Canada, Newfoundland Fluorspar, Ltd., a wholly-owned subsidiary of Alcan Aluminum, is a major producer.

GARNET

Background.   The term garnet includes a group of closely related minerals some of which are extraordinarily beautiful and have been used for thousands of years as gemstones. The most important industrial variety of garnet is almandite, a reddish iron aluminum silicate that is, like all garnets, relatively hard. It is substantially harder than steel but not so hard as corundum. The wide use of garnet in industry is fairly recent (since about 1880) as compared with the long history of garnet as a gemstone.

Present Demand and Uses.   Garnet is used almost exclusively as an abrasive. It also has minor other applications, such as in crushed form in non-skid paints. It is used in lens and metal grinding, in sandpaper for wood furniture, and for sand blasting. Demand is steady and growing about with the economy.

Sources.   The United States is by far the dominant world producer and consumer of abrasive garnet, accounting for nearly 95 percent of world output and for more than 90 percent of consumption. Garnet occurs as a metamorphic mineral—that is, formed from pre-existing rock materials through heat, pressure, and perhaps added hot solutions. Garnet is a widespread mineral and fairly common, but there are only two major sources in the United States, New York and Idaho. The Barton Mine of Barton Mines Corporation, New York, is the largest domestic producer and has been owned continuously by the same family since production began.

Outlook and Investment.   Demand for garnet appears to

have grown rather consistently with the gross national product and will probably continue to do so. It has competition from synthetic abrasives and has no special properties likely to create a sudden larger demand in the future. It is a stable industrial commodity. Domestic sources of high-quality abrasive garnet are estimated to be about 200,000 tons, which is less than the projected demand to the year 2000. So if additional sources can be found, it may be somewhat more profitable than the sand-blasting grade of garnet, which has very large reserves. Garnet mines of the United States are privately held and unavailable to the investing public. Discovery of an additional good-quality deposit would be welcome and profitable. Gem-quality garnet deposits, of course, are always to be sought.

GRAPHITE

Background. Natural graphite is the mineral form of elemental carbon. It is the "lead" in the lead pencil. Graphite mining in the United States has always been on a small scale, and most of the needs have been supplied by imports, except during the world wars when domestic production was increased.

Present Demand and Uses. United States demand tends to be about 5 to 15 times domestic graphite production, as production costs are higher and ore-quality lower than they are abroad. Graphite is used mainly in foundry facings, where it is mixed with clay and used to coat molds for a clean and easy recovery of metal castings. It is also used in refractories, which are materials used in smelting metals. Graphite is used directly in steel making and also as a lubricant, in brake linings, and in dry cells. Demand is reasonably steady but tends to follow the cycles of heavy industry and metal production.

Sources. Graphite deposits have been reported in 25 states and commerical quantities have been produced in 17 states, including Alabama, California, New York, and Pennsylvania. Probably the largest U.S. deposits of graphite are in the Seward Peninsula of Alaska, but at present they are not economic. The most important deposits in the western hemisphere are in the state of Sonora, Mexico, where, in an area 20 miles by 10 miles, millions of tons are known. The world's largest reserves are in Malagasy, where deposits occur in an area nearly 600 miles long and 100 miles wide. Graphite layers here are usually continuous for lengths up to 4,000 feet. A few deposits are 350 feet thick. Elsewhere graphite is widely distributed. There is no anticipated shortage.

Outlook and Investment. Graphite has some competition from other materials, and artificial graphite is now being manufactured in quantity. The result is that the future demand for natural graphite appears to be one of slow growth. Recently there has been only one producer in the United States, Southwestern Graphite Company, near Burnet, Texas, where graphite is mined by open-pit. Slow growth in demand, severe competition from foreign sources, and relatively low-grade deposits here make the outlook for graphite investment in the United States and Canada relatively unattractive.

GYPSUM

Background. Gypsum was used by some of the earliest civilizations for artistic purposes in carvings of alabaster, a compact, very fine-grained variety of gypsum, and also for building purposes. The Egyptians used gypsum as mortar in construction of the pyramids about 3000 B.C. Gypsum continued to be used in various ways through the Middle Ages, and in the late 18th century it began to be used as a soil conditioner and fertilizer in Europe. It was used for this purpose early in the settlement of North America.

Present Demand and Uses. Gypsum is chiefly used now in the construction industry and demand follows the pattern of activity there. Its use includes that of a retarder in cement, as gypsum building board, and in plaster. About 25 percent goes for agricultural purposes, and 2 percent for various other applications.

Sources. Gypsum is precipitated from solution out of sea water or saline lake waters that are entrapped or embayed and therefore attain a greater-than-normal salinity. Gypsum is a very abundant material in many parts of the world including the United States, where it occurs in the Southwest in large quantities. It also is found in New York, Michigan, Iowa, and elsewhere. At White Sands, New Mexico, beds of gypsum have been reworked by the wind to form a dune area of 270 square miles with an average thickness of 20 feet. In the Maritime Provinces of Canada, beds of gypsum 40 to 100 feet thick are common. Gypsum is mined by both open-pit and underground methods.

Outlook and Investment. Gypsum as a basic building material and also as a soil conditioner and fertilizer is assured of a steady but not particularly fast growth in demand. Transportation is an important factor, and gypsum deposits near the ultimate place of use have a substantial advantage over more remote sources. However, the various modes of transport, such as cheap ship transport versus rail, offer offsetting advantages to distance. Gypsum from Nova Scotia can be laid down in New York City competitively by ship in spite of gypsum deposits located within 200 miles of New York City.

The future of the gypsum industry should be good, but it may grow slightly less rapidly than the gross national product. Ample supplies are available for the foreseeable future both domestically and abroad. Gypsum appears to offer a solid sort of investment if the record of the leader in the field, U.S. Gypsum, which has paid dividends continuously since 1919, is an indication. Gypsum is mined in the United States by nearly 50 companies from about 70 mines in 21 states. Three of these companies, however, account for about two-thirds of the production and through subsidiaries are also the dominant ones in Canada. They are U.S. Gypsum, National Gypsum, and the Gypsum Division of Georgia-Pacific Corporation. Along with Kaiser Gypsum Company and the Flintkote Company, they also own or have investments in gypsum mines in Nova Scotia, Mexico, and Jamaica, from which come most of the imports to the United States.

HELIUM

Background. In the universe, helium is in great abundance; the Sun contains vast amounts. On Earth it is a rare element and occurs only as a gas. It results from the radioactive decay of uranium and thorium, which occur in several kinds of rock, including dark, organic-rich marine shales, which are common source rocks for oil. Accordingly, helium occurs in trace to minor amounts in certain natural gas fields, especially those in the Panhandle regions of Oklahoma and Texas.

Present Demand and Uses. Helium is a light, inert gas and does not burn. Therefore it can be a safe substitute for hydrogen in lighter-than-air craft. It is used in the space program and also in various industrial applications, including creating a controlled and inert atmosphere in which to weld certain metals, for growing crystals, for heat transfer in atomic reactors, and also in cryogenics research and engineering where liquid helium is used to obtain temperatures close to absolute zero. In its special functions it has no substitute. Demand is growing fairly rapidly and could rise even faster if certain uses now in the research stage, chiefly those related to nuclear plants, would become commercial.

Sources. The only sources of helium at present are certain natural gas fields, notably in southwestern United States. After helium-bearing natural gas is liquified, the residue gas is helium-rich. From this, crude helium is recovered and further refined. Other countries may have substantial helium resources, but there appears to be no information on this, as it is not a commonly recovered material from natural gas. In the United States large amounts of helium are lost annually to the atmosphere, as much natural gas containing helium is not processed for that element.

Outlook and Investment. Demand for helium will probably continue to rise fairly rapidly, as a number of new uses are on the verge of becoming commercial. Companies holding sizable natural gas reserves in helium-rich areas recover the helium in some instances, but at best it is only a small part of their revenues. Kerr-McGee Industries is one such company. Helium has to be sold to the U.S. Government, which is stockpiling it.

Certain areas of the Rocky Mountains have gas deposits that are not usable as natural gas but do contain some helium. There has been no drilling for helium as such but conceivably an exploration program could be conducted for it. This would be done in the uranium country, where helium is produced from the natural degeneration of uranium. However, barring some very major development, supplies in sight appear to be adequate for expected demand to the year 2000.

IODINE

Background. Iodine was discovered in France in 1811. Its importance in medicine was early recognized and it has been used in that capacity since 1829. Its light sensitivity in compounds was discovered shortly thereafter, and in 1851 the photographic wet plate was introduced using silver iodine. Iodine was early used also in a variety of chemical processes and as reagents. It has the ability to form compounds with nearly all elements.

For many years the only commercial source of iodine was the ashes of seaweed harvested along the coasts of France and Scotland. This seaweed industry declined after 1868, when iodine production began from Chilean nitrate deposits. The United States produced some iodine from seaweed in World War I. Recovery of iodine from oil-well brines began in 1928 in Louisiana and a year later at the Signal Hill oil district of California, where United States iodine production was centered until 1960. At that time the brine wells of Michigan replaced those of California as the principal source.

Present Demand and Uses. Iodine and its compounds have numerous uses in agriculture, industry, and medicine. About 20 percent of U.S. iodine demand is for disinfectants. An important use of iodine is for iodizing salt for human and animal consumption, as small quantities of iodine are essential for the proper function of the thyroid gland and for promoting the general health of humans and the higher animals. Iodine enters into many industrial products, including dyes, photographic materials, resins, and some metal compounds, and in the manufacture of high-purity metals such as titanium, zirconium, boron, and hafnium. It also has been used in cloud-seeding operations to induce rainfall. For some uses, iodine can be replaced by chlorine or bromine, although they are commonly less desirable than is iodine. For many uses, however, iodine has no competition. Demand is strong and growing.

Sources. Iodine is a widely distributed element but only in a few circumstances is it concentrated in commercial amounts. Sea water contains about 5/100ths of a part per million of iodine. Brines in wells in the United States run from about 38 parts per million to more than 500 parts per million. Chilean nitrates contain about 0.04 percent iodine. Natural gas well brines of Japan are reported to contain an estimated 500,000 tons of iodine reserves. Seaweed in various areas contains enough iodine to be regarded as a potential source. There appear to be ample world sources to supply all needs to the year 2000 and beyond.

Outlook and Investment. Dow Chemical at Midland, Michigan, is the only domestic producer of iodine. Much of what the United States uses is imported. Japan is an increasingly large supplier. Oil companies with iodine-bearing brines in their wells in southern United States and California have iodine reserves but these are not now being utilized.

Comment. The disposal of brines from wells producing iodine constitutes a modest environmental problem.

KYANITE, SILLIMANITE, AND ANDALUSITE

Background. These minerals all have essentially the same chemical composition (aluminum silicate) but different physical properties. Industrial interest in them is rather recent and involves their use chiefly as very-high-quality refractory (firebrick) materials and in other ceramic products. The United States the past two decades has gone from nearly total dependence on imports to a position as the world's largest producer and exports considerable quantities of these materials. Very large resources have been discovered, particularly in southeastern United States.

Present Demand and Uses. Demand has grown at a rate of about 8 percent a year since 1945, by far the greatest increase being in the refractories industry. Demand remains strong, and uses are increasing, including in a variety of ceramics such as spark plug insulation and wall tile. Other uses include brake linings, welding rod coatings, and blown aluminum silicate high-temperature insulation.

Sources. Very large deposits are known in Virginia, North and South Carolina, Georgia, Idaho, and Colorado. Altogether they constitute the world's largest resources. South Africa, the Soviet Union, and Canada, in that order, also have substantial deposits. Geologically, these minerals occur in areas of metamorphism, that is, where the rocks of the Earth's crust have been altered by heat and pressure.

Outlook and Investment. The outlook for kyanite and related minerals appears to be good, and present growth rates exceed by a substantial amount the rate of growth of the gross national product. Chief use at present is in refractories for the steel industry, although possible changes in steel-making may somewhat reduce the need for them. On the other hand, research is being conducted on the use of these minerals in metal-fiber-reinforced ceramic parts for aircraft and spacecraft and in the production of aluminum-silicon master alloys. Although these uses are small at present they have an important growth potential. Combustion Engineering, Inc., has two mine operations, one in Georgia and one in South Carolina. Babcock and Wilcox Company operates a plant in Georgia. The Kyanite Mining Corporation has mines in Virginia.

MICA

Background. Mica is an interesting and unusual mineral in several respects. Some of its forms are very plate-like and can be split almost indefinitely into very thin translucent to transparent sheets (the "isinglass" of the old wood stoves). It is flexible and is a dielectric material used in capacitators and electronic tubes for element spacers. Early in the 1800s mica was used to fabricate such things as lamp chimneys and lamp shades. Sheet mica and ground mica have different end uses and the demands for these two types of products differ widely.

Present Demand and Uses. Mica is used chiefly in electrical-appliance manufacture and in the electronics industry. Some mica is used in the manufacture of roofing and asphalt shingles and in paint. The rubber industry uses mica as an inert filler in rubber and as a mold lubricant in the manufacture of molded rubber products such as tires; the plastics industry uses mica in a similar manner. There are numerous other minor uses. Sheet mica demand is low, but demand for ground mica is slowly increasing.

Sources. Sheet mica comes from certain coarsely crystalline rocks called pegmatites, some of which occur in the United States, but at the present time these deposits are not competitive with sheet mica in India, Brazil, and the Malagasy Republic. Mica in small flakes is very widespread around the world, so abundant in fact that there has been no effort made to estimate reserves.

Outlook and Investment. Demand for mica, except sheet

mica, will rise about with the growth of the economy. Sheet mica demand is declining. Several small companies produce mica, chiefly in North Carolina and New Hampshire. In Canada there are substantial mica deposits also owned by several small firms. Mica has only a limited investment potential.

NEPHELINE SYENITE

Background. Nepheline syenite, a rock something like granite, is mined for its feldspar content. It has been of only minor commercial interest to date but has a variety of small uses and possible uses that may bring it greater prominence.

Present Demand and Uses. Nepheline syenite is becoming increasingly important as an industrial material in glass-making. In the Soviet Union it is used not only as a source of ceramic materials but also chiefly as an ore of aluminum. It is not used for that purpose yet in the United States.

Sources. Principal deposits are in Canada, Norway, and the Soviet Union. The United States has some reserves.

Outlook and Investment. Use of nepheline syenite is likely to increase only slowly unless it becomes used in North America as a source of aluminum. Falconbridge Nickel and International Minerals and Chemical operate mines in Canada, but there are no mines in the United States. It is not a significant outlet for investment at present.

NITROGEN

Background. Nitrogen is a gas in elemental form and makes up nearly four-fifths of the air. Nitrogen is a relatively inert gas but will react with a few other elements under certain conditions. It is important to plant growth, and one of the problems involved in intensive agriculture is to get nitrogen into the soil. Seventy-five percent of the demand for fixed nitrogen in the United States is for fertilizer use. Elsewhere in the world, because of historically longer cultivation of the soils and their relatively greater exhaustion, the demand for nitrogen in the soil is even larger.

Present Demand and Uses. Principal use of nitrogen is in fertilizer. It is also used as an inert "blanketing" gas to prevent oxidation in the chemical, metal, glass, and food industries, and especially in the storage of gasoline, phosphorus, and other chemicals that should be kept out of contact with oxygen. It is a basic component of ammonium nitrate, a widely used explosive. Nitric acid reacts with ammonia to form ammonium nitrate, which when mixed with fuel oil is a very effective explosive used in the mining industry. There are many minor uses of nitrogen such as in synthetic rubber, dyes, weedkillers, and pharmaceuticals. There is no substitute for nitrogen as a plant food.

Sources. Nitrogen is chiefly produced through the process of liquifying air, and therefore the supply is virtually limitless. It also can be obtained in compound form from nitrate deposits in Chile.

Outlook and Investment. Projected growth rate in the use of nitrogen is slightly higher than the general growth of the economy (about 4 percent). However, a greater-than-expected demand for ammonia as fertilizer would raise this rate somewhat. An even more dramatic rise in nitrogen demand could come if research, now in very early stages, proved that ammonia could be used as a substitute for gasoline. On the other hand, research is being conducted on ways in which bacteria can be utilized to capture and fix nitrogen in the ground and thus generate nitrogen *in situ.* If this technology became a reality on a wide scale, it would significantly reduce the demand for nitrogen in its chief use as fertilizer. However, this development on any large scale is probably far in the future at best.

Most elemental nitrogen is produced in the same air-separation plants that produce oxygen. The largest producers include Union Carbide Corporation, Airco, Air Products and Chemicals, National Cylinder Gas Division of Chemetron Corporation, Liquid Carbonic Division of Houston Natural Gas, American Cryogenics, Inc., and Big Three Industrial Gas and Equipment Company.

OXYGEN

Background. Oxygen, a gas in elemental form, is the most abundant element in the Earth's crust, making up 47 percent by weight. It forms almost one-fourth of the Earth's atmosphere by weight. Commercial production of oxygen did not begin until after the development of the first continuous machine for liquifying air in 1895.

Present Demand and Uses. The chief use of oxygen is in steel-making. It is also used widely in the manufacture of industrial chemicals, in metalworking and aerospace industries (liquid oxygen as a fuel oxidizer for rockets), and in many other ways, including in the field of medicine and therapy. Demand is strong and rising rapidly as many new applications are being discovered.

Sources. Air at present is the chief source, but theoretically oxygen can be recovered from many Earth materials, including water. Supply is unlimited.

Outlook and Investment. The oxygen industry has been one of the fastest-growing raw-material resource industries in the United States, as well as in many other countries. This growth is likely to continue and probably accelerate to the end of this century. The United States oxygen-producing industry is dominated by six firms, which account for more than 80 percent of the total production. Seven of the larger steel firms and about 100 smaller companies provide the rest of the output. The six major companies are Union Carbide, Airco (formerly Air Reduction Company) Air Products and Chemicals, Inc., National Cylinder Gas Division of Chemetron Corporation, Big Three Industrial Gas and Equipment Company, and Liquid Carbonic Division of Houston Natural Gas Company. The competition is obviously considerable in this business, but the demand also is very strong. The more efficient companies should be good investment vehicles in this vital raw material.

PERLITE

Background. Perlite is a glassy volcanic rock containing about 2 to 5 percent water, which on heating expands or "pops" to a frothy mass of low-density material. The term perlite also includes the expanded commercial perlite product. Perlite has high volume, low heat and sound transmission, and is chemically inert. Perlite is a relatively recent addition to the commercial mineral scene, coming into substantial production in the United States only about 1946. Use grew rapidly until about 1958, since when there has been a slower growth in demand.

Present Demand and Uses. About two-thirds of perlite consumption is related to construction, principally as an aggregate for plaster, concrete, and insulating board, and for loose-fill thermal insulation. The remaining major use is in filtration where it competes well. Smaller quantities are consumed in agriculture and as fillers or extenders in various industrial products. Potential substitution by competitive materials exists for all uses of perlite. Demand is related chiefly to the fortunes of the construction industry.

Sources. Perlite is associated with areas of geologically recent volcanic activity, and in the United States this is the West, where New Mexico is the dominant producer. There are "perlite belts" around the world that follow the zones of recent volcanic activity such as through Japan to New Zealand and from Iceland extending southeasterly through Scotland, Italy, Sardinia, and the Aegean Islands. Total reserves have never been closely estimated but must be in the billions of tons.

Outlook and Investment. Perlite use will grow slowly, closely atuned to the construction industry. Leading companies are Johns-Manville, United States Gypsum Company, Grefco, Inc., and United Perlite Corporation. These companies account for about 90 percent of the perlite mined and about half of the expanded perlite production.

PHOSPHORUS AND PHOSPHATE

Background. The world has lots of problems. Keeping phosphorus in circulation is one of them. There is only so much available and it has the unfortunate habit of getting locked into rocks of various kinds. All vertebrates, including humans, must have phosphorus as a major structural element, for in the form of calcium phosphate it makes teeth and bones. It has been suggested that one reason why the Chinese are generally small of stature is that there is not enough phosphorus available to supply their basic needs. In any event, phosphorus and phosphates are vital to agriculture and ultimately to the growth of animals. Use of it as a fertilizer goes back at least to 200 B.C. Phosphorus is one of three major and vital food elements (nitrogen and potassium, which are more abundant than phosphorus, are the others). For many years phosphorus has been removed from agricultural land by cropping faster than it could be re-placed by natural means, with the result that the demand for phosphorus in fertilizer compounds has been growing rapidly.

Phosphorus is never found free in the uncombined state in nature; it has great affinity for oxygen. In the Earth it occurs in several minerals, but chiefly as phosphate rock, which is a collective term for commercial phosphate ores, or calcium phosphate mixtures with other materials. A variety of other elements, including vanadium, uranium, and rare-earths, as well as gypsum and fluorine, tend to accumulate also in these ores.

The first phosphate was mined in the United States in 1867 in South Carolina, and use has increased every year since.

Present Demand and Uses. Most phorphorus is used in the form of processed rock for fertilizer. Other uses are as animal-feed supplements, in electroplating and polishing of metals, and in a great variety of other ways, including medicinal, as insecticides, and as incendiary bombs. It is used in making washing powders (detergents), but the ecological effects of this are being questioned as it has promoted excessive algal growth in lakes and has other undesirable effects. Phosphates in washing products, however, are very useful, so their ultimate fate in this capacity will probably be debated for some time. However, as there is no substitute for phosphorus as a plant food, there it has an assured and steadily increasing demand.

Sources. Phosphorus occurs commonly in the mineral apatite, which is a minor constituent of certain igneous rocks such as granite. Small quantities occur in guano obtained from islands off the coast of Peru and in certain other localities including caves (bat guano). Digging dried guano on treeless tropical islands is not high on the list of desirable occupations, and prisoners have occasionally been used for this labor. However, the chief source of phosphorus is in the form of phosphate rock, which was formed in certain special ocean environments. Some of the deposits are still on the ocean floor, but others, by uplift of continents, are now on land, as is the case of the large phosphate deposits of western United States, chiefly in Idaho, Montana, Utah, and Wyoming. One of the interesting aspects of these deposits is the large number of fossils in them, including an unusual shark called *Helicoprion,* which had a median jaw process shaped something like a toothed pinwheel. These shark remains have been found in western United States, Australia, and the Soviet Union, giving firm evidence that these regions were once all interconnected by ocean waterways. To these ancient oceans we owe our great and vital phosphate reserves.

The world's largest phosphate deposits are in Morocco, which is credited with about 9.2 billion tons, followed by the United States with 6.8 billion and the Soviet Union with 2.6 billion. A number of other countries have deposits but very much smaller than those just cited. In the United States, deposits are known in 23 states, but Florida and North Carolina produce most of the phosphate, with the Western Phosphate Field of the northern Rocky Mountains next. Submarine phosphate deposits are also known in several parts of the world, including off the coasts of California, the Carolinas, and Florida, but these have not been exploited so far.

Outlook and Investment. The United States is the largest producer of phosphate (as phosphate rock) in the world, and is also the largest consumer, using about one-fourth of world output. Phosphorus is used in myriad ways and its use is certain to increase for the foreseeable future. There is ample phosphate in the world to supply needs to the year 2000, but there will be some shifts in supply patterns as large unexploited deposits of the Sechura Desert of Peru, Spanish Sahara, Australia, and several other areas come into production. From time to time imbalances of supply and demand have occurred, with temporary overproduction a result. But the long-term growth in use of phosphorus is certain, with the rate about equal to or slightly greater than that of the economy as a whole. The chronic world food shortage will focus increasing attention on and demand for phosphates.

A substantial number of firms produce phosphate. Among the larger ones are American Cyanamide and Kerr-McGee (in partnership in Florida), Borden, Inc., Cities Service, FMC Corporation, W. R. Grace, International Minerals and Chemicals, Kennecott, Mobil Oil, Monsanto, Occidental Petroleum, Stauffer Chemical, and Texas Gulf. In Idaho, the J. R. Simplot Company is an important producer but remains a privately held corporation as of this date. Phosphate is not produced commercially in Canada.

Comment. Disposal of waste water and slimes from phosphate processing, particularly in Florida and North Carolina, is becoming an increasing problem. Also, residential areas are impinging on the Florida deposits in particular, causing a variety of conflicts. Western phosphate deposits have fewer current problems but may be forced to go from open-pit to more costly underground operations as the easily reached phosphate rock is mined out. In all cases, higher operating costs will result, which may make these deposits somewhat less competitive with foreign sources as time goes on.

POTASSIUM AND POTASH

Background. The term "potash" is loosely applied to a variety of compounds of potassium—an element which is fundamental to all life. Every living cell contains a minute amount of this substance. The term "potash" was derived from the residues—pot ashes—originally obtained by evaporating solutions leached from wood ashes. Worldwide food shortages, which are likely to persist, indicate that potash will be in strong demand for the indefinite future. However, it should be noted that supplies also are very large, and simply the existence of deposits does not insure profitability. There are other factors, including competition from deposits closer to places of use, quality of deposits, and types of mining that must be employed (open-pit, underground, or by solution through wells).

Present Demand and Uses. Demand has been growing about 7 to 8 percent a year, almost entirely due to increased use of potash in fertilizers, which accounts for about 95 percent of consumption. This trend will continue, as there is no substitute for potassium in agriculture. Minor uses of potash are in soapmaking, synthetic rubber manufacturing, and glass-making. However, demand and supply have been out of balance in times past, with overproduction a common situation. The United States uses about one-fourth of the world output of potash.

Sources. Potash comes chiefly from two sources, bedded salt deposits left behind from ancient seas, and brines in salt lakes such as in Utah and California. Potash deposits are known from many places in the world. The major ones, in order of size, are in Canada, the Soviet Union, East Germany, West Germany, and Israel. The United States has relatively small deposits. However, total world reserves are sufficient for several hundred years, and if potassium can be recovered economically from sea water, as is magnesium, the available resources would be enormously larger. Energy to do this would be the limiting factor.

Outlook and Investment. Growth in potash use will continue strong for the foreseeable future, or as long as populations continue to grow or even maintain present size. That would appear to be a long time unless there are some highly unlikely reversals of current trends. Agricultural lands around the world are being taxed to capacity to produce foodstuffs, and shortages seem inevitable. However, the overall very large supplies of potash insure competition and mean that it will be the efficient producers, those most accessible to major markets and cheap transportation and that have the most economically exploitable deposits, who will prosper. In this regard, the deposits in the United States, largely in Utah and New Mexico, must be considered marginal.

Search for new potash deposits, therefore, is not a particularly promising endeavor and no large additional North American deposits are likely to be discovered, as this part of the world has been rather thoroughly perforated with drill holes. Any appreciable deposits probably have already been found. Canadian deposits, located chiefly in Saskatchewan, are in the strongest position in the Western Hemisphere. Eastern United States is being supplied from German sources, but recent discoveries in New Brunswick a few miles from ocean transportation will offer strong competition. The great Midwest agricultural area can most cheaply be supplied by Canadian potash from Saskatchewan.

Companies holding major potash deposits include Noranda Mines, Hudson Bay Mining and Smelting, Cominco, Swift and Company and Homestake (joint operation in Saskatchewan), International Minerals and Chemicals, Kaiser Aluminum and Chemical, U.S. Borax and Chemical (now a subsidiary of Rio Tinto-Zinc), Ideal Basic Industries, American Potash and Chemical (subsidiary of Kerr-McGee), American Metal Climax, and Texas Gulf, which is a producer in Utah and owns a 40-percent interest in Allen Potash Mines of Canada.

Comment. Most potash mining is underground, and one company in Canada produces potash by circulating water down bore holes and recovering the dissolved potash salts through other wells. The environmental effects of potash production are slight. The chief problem facing the industry is how to translate the large surplus productive capacity into shipments to countries in need of potash. Most of these are the overpopulated, underdeveloped nations with few means to pay for the fertilizers they urgently need. Large surpluses of potash fertilizer in some countries, and its scarcity in other parts of the world, tend to create political and social problems. Chief cause of overproduction has been the rapid development of the very large and rich deposits in Canada. This flood of low-cost potash is causing a continual shift in supply patterns as marginal producers, including those in the United States, cannot meet the competition. The Saskatchewan government has put some controls on potash production to alleviate this problem somewhat. The United States does not have high-grade potash deposits sufficient for its needs beyond perhaps 20 years, and so increasing amounts will have to be imported.

PUMICE

Background.   Pumice is volcanic rock "froth" formed by gases diffusing through rocks, so that it is sometimes blown by volcanic eruptions for distances of 20 miles or more. Pumice is light and floats on water and has been known to float downstream and eventually cause "pumice-jams" just as logs will cause log-jams. Occasionally this has resulted in damming of streams and floods during volcanic eruptions.

The commercial use of the term "pumice" includes pumice, pumicite (volcanic ash), volcanic cinders, and scoria. Strictly speaking geologically, pumice is a light-colored silica-rich volcanic rock froth such as forms from rhyolite (which are the flows of Yellowstone National Park). Scoria forms as a volcanic rock froth from darker lava flows such as basalts on the Hawaiian Islands or at Craters of the Moon, Idaho.

Pumice is a classic construction material. It was used in the form of pozzolan cement in Roman structures such as the Pantheon and in later European construction. Pumice was used widely as a lightweight concrete aggregate in Europe in the 19th century. Pumice was first used in the United States in 1851, when it was quarried in California for building blocks. Demand for it grew slowly, however, until after World War II, when consumption, chiefly for use as a concrete aggregate, grew rapidly. Over the years pumice has also been used as an abrasive, including being the "lava" in Lava soap.

Present Demand and Uses. Pumice continues to be used chiefly as a lightweight concrete aggregate, and therefore demand follows rather closely the construction industry where more than 95 percent of pumice is used. It is also used for road material and as railroad ballast.

Sources. Pumice production in the United States is confined to the 15 western states, including Hawaii. Arizona, California, and Oregon, in that order, produce about 72 percent of the supply. There is no shortage of pumice for the foreseeable future. Nature even manufactures new supplies occasionally in active volcanic areas such as Hawaii. Elsewhere around the world, pumice deposits are also very large.

Outlook and Investment. Pumice will continue to be a basic raw material for construction, including roads, as well as being used as an abrasive. Growth in use is related chiefly to construction. A pumice deposit located close to major areas of use can be quite valuable, although the quantities must be large, as it is a low-unit-value material. Numerous small companies in western United States produce pumice. Most are closely held.

Comment. Pumice is mined open-pit, and the operations tend to be dusty for some types of deposits.

QUARTZ CRYSTAL

Background. Quartz crystals in various colors (such as amethyst) have been used as ornaments for thousands of years. The industrial use of quartz began about 1921 in electronics when it was discovered that a quartz crystal could be used to control the frequency of a radio oscillator circuit. A quartz plate of a particular area and thickness serves as a piezoelectric resonator with a fixed mechanical vibration frequency of the driving circuit.

Present Demand and Uses. Almost all quartz crystals are used in electronic frequency control or selection. A very few are used for prisms, wedges, lenses, and other special optical purposes. Demand for the natural quartz crystals is possibly good but is hard to determine, as synthetic quartz crystals now offer severe competition to the natural ones. It is a matter of availability and price, with the natural quartz losing out.

Sources. The United States and Canada have virtually no electronic or optical grades of quartz. Small deposits have been found in Arkansas and in a few other localities that have been briefly worked, particularly during wartime. Most of the world supply comes from Brazil.

Outlook and Investment. Because of problems of adequate supply, a great deal of research has been done on replacing natural quartz crystal with a suitable synthetic product. The communications industry is particularly concerned, and the Bell Telephone Laboratories has been able to grow quartz crystals that are satisfactory substitutes for natural quartz. The outlook is for a continued decline in production of natural quartz crystals in the face of this competition. At best, production of natural quartz crystals for industry has been very modest. There appears to be no appreciable opportunity for investment here.

QUARTZ SAND, QUARTZITE, AND MASSIVE QUARTZ

Background. Strictly speaking, "sand" is a size term, but much sand is quartz sand because of the durability (chemical inertness and hardness) of quartz, which allows it to survive transportation when weathered out of igneous rock sources such as granite. Quartzite is simply a rock composed of quartz sand grains that have been so firmly cemented together with silica that the cement is just as hard as the quartz grains. When broken, the fracture will go through both the quartz sand and the cement, rather than through the cement and around the quartz grains.

Massive quartz is quartz occurring in large veins and irregular masses originating from silica-bearing solutions that moved up into fractures in the Earth's crust. These materials are all potential sources of silica, chiefly used in glass but also in other industrial products. In actual practice nearly all silica comes from quartz sand, because it is easier to mine than is the case of massive quartz or quartzite.

Present Demand and Uses. Most nearly-pure quartz sand

is used for glass-making. Some is used for abrasives, for filtering, and for molding sands in foundry work. There are a number of lesser uses. Use in glass-making has been growing with the general rate of the gross national product. However, it is possible, with the new energy economics upon us, that an increased interest in solar heating will create a substantially larger demand for glass.

Sources. Most high-quality quartz sands are obtained from sandstones derived from previous sandstones, with perhaps even three or four cycles of reworking involved in the geological past. Starting with an impure weathering product from an igneous rock containing quartz, the material must be transported and winnowed and worked and reworked several times to obtain the 99-percent-pure quartz sand that characterizes such deposits as the St. Peter Sandstone of the upper Mississippi Valley. This formation is widely used as a source of glass sand. Locally in other parts of the country, good-quality glass sands also occur. Worldwide there is no shortage of quartz sand, but very pure deposits such as the St. Peter Sandstone are relatively rare. Quartzite occurs in vast quantities, entire mountains being made of it in some places. Massive quartz is less widely distributed but is not uncommon.

Outlook and Investment. Demand for quartz sand and other relatively pure quartz deposits is steady and relates chiefly to the glass-making industry. Most companies that produce glass, such as PPG Industries, Corning Glass Works, and Anchor Hocking, have their own mines. A very clear, pure quartz-sand deposit, especially if it is located near population centers, can almost always find a market. The plastering trade makes use of this material in quantity, as does the glass industry.

SALT

Background. There are many kinds of salts, but when we say "salt" we almost always mean common salt, sodium chloride. The mineral name for this compound is halite—so "please pass the halite." Salt is one of the most useful natural resources. Highly prized in ancient times, camel caravans went long distances to the salt deposits of India and other places to obtain this indispensable material. The Huns and others fought over the possession of salt deposits in Europe. We cannot live without salt, yet it is an interesting fact that it is composed of two very poisonous elements, sodium and chlorine. Salt is used in thousands of chemical processes, and the demand for salt is one of the most steady and predictable among minerals.

Present Demand and Uses. The demand for salt grows about as fast as the economy, for salt is involved in what amounts to nearly a total cross-section of our industrial world. To list uses would be superfluous, and lengthy; salt is basic.

Sources. You might guess that a substantial part of the salt used in the United States would come from such an obvious source as Great Salt Lake in Utah, where it can be had by the millions of tons just for the shoveling. But this is not so. Salt occurs in great quantities in many places, including the area that was once the bed of a shallow sea stretching across parts of what are now New Mexico, Texas, Oklahoma, and Kansas during Permian time (about 250 million years ago). Here, more than 100,000 square miles of salt deposits exist with an average thickness of 200 feet. Similar buried salt deposits, residual from ancient seas, are known in Michigan, Ohio, and New York. There is a salt mine 1,000 feet beneath Detroit producing from a 20-foot-thick bed. Elsewhere, salt is produced as a brine from wells where water is circulated down into the salt deposits and then returned to the surface and evaporated.

Salt also is produced by solar evaporation of sea water in the San Francisco Bay area and in many other parts of the world. Tremendous salt domes have been squeezed up along fractures in the Earth from deeply buried salt beds on the Gulf Coast. (More nearly correctly, they "floated up" along fractures due to the fact that salt is lighter than the surrounding sediments.) These domes are believed to have originated from salt deposits about eight miles below the present Gulf coastal plain. Several hundred domes from Alabama to Mexico have been identified. They are from a few hundred feet to several miles across and may be a mile or several miles vertically.

Oil and gas are produced from the flanks and the tops of many domes; sulfur comes from the top of some domes. Salt-mine shafts penetrate some of the shallower domes such as at Avery Island, Weeks Island, and Jefferson Island in Louisiana (so named "islands" because these domes, protected by an insoluble residue, stand up as hills in the southern Louisiana swamp country). I have been inside all three of these domes, 600 feet below the surface of a Louisiana swamp, and I have never been in a drier environment. Salt deforms easily, and as a result great taffy-candy-like patterns in the banded salt deposits are visible in the walls of the mines, showing how the salt has flowed to its present position—a striking sight.

In Canada, underground salt deposits have been found in all provinces except British Columbia and Quebec. In some places the salt beds are 1,500 feet thick.

Outlook and Investment. The future of the salt business is assured and stable but hardly outstanding as a growth situation. Still one could do worse than buy into as solid, basic, and steady a business as is this one. There is considerable merit in the fact that a major salt producer, Pennwalt Corporation, has paid dividends every year uninterruptedly since 1863.

Several companies mine salt as part of their operations. Akzona (the old International Salt Company in merger form) is one. There are several small salt companies in the United States; some are closely held.

Canadian salt producers include Domtar Chemicals, Allied Chemicals Canada, and the Canadian Salt Company.

The U.S. Bureau of Mines estimates that the known salt reserves of the United States are sufficient to last for more than 100,000 years, even assuming a rate of consumption 100 times greater than at present. Canada is equally well supplied. The key factor in economically developing salt deposits is distance to markets. Salt is sold on a "delivered" basis, and that is why the Great Salt Lake area accounts for only a small percentage of the salt used in the United States. Freight costs are more important than having a large quantity of salt at any one place.

SAND AND GRAVEL

Background. Would you rather have a gold mine or a gravel pit? I suppose there is more glamour to owning a gold mine, and who would decline one? But good gold mines are rare. Good gravel pits are much more common and they can be highly profitable. The sand and gravel business is thought to be a rather commonplace enterprise and this it may be, but the value of sand and gravel represents about one-fifth of the total value of all nonfuel nonmetallic minerals produced in the United States. A well-situated gravel pit (especially with regard, for example, to a new expressway construction project) has been a "gold mine" for many people, and this will no doubt continue. Urban sprawl is covering over many valuable gravel deposits, but the demand for gravel continues to be steady and rising.

Sand and gravel are made of a variety of materials, but silica in various forms (such as quartz sand and chert) is a predominant constituent because of its hardness and chemical inertness.

Present Demand and Uses.   Construction makes use of all but a very small percentage of the average sand and gravel produced. Certain high-quality sands are used for other end purposes and have been treated in the section on "Quartz Sand, Quartzite, and Massive Quartz." Demand grows approximately with the economy and is likely to continue to do so.

Sources.   The northern half of the United States, thanks chiefly to glaciers of the past, is plentifully supplied with sand and gravel deposits. In other areas, stream beds, both ancient and modern, are major sources. Only southern Louisiana and adjacent areas and Florida have an insufficient local gravel supply. Elsewhere around the world, sand and gravel generally are in ample quantities.

Outlook and Investment.   The outlook is for sand and gravel demand to increase at least as fast as the rate of growth of the gross national product. There are no supply problems except locally, but environmental problems are increasing as no other mining activity is beset with as many land-use conflicts as are sand and gravel operations. Urban growth depends on nearby sources of low-cost construction materials, and as urban areas grow and encroach on gravel pits, land becomes zoned in ways that preclude these operations. Zoning authorities should be fully aware of the economic costs to a community of their decisions when they eliminate very large deposits of gravel and sand from further use.

Land rehabilitation also is becoming more costly. Then too, sand and gravel operations tend to be dusty and create local nuisances. Nevertheless, it seems certain that accommodation has to be made to allow the low-cost recovery of sand and gravel.

There are nearly 5,000 commercial sand and gravel operations in the United States, most of them locally owned. Flintkote is an example of a larger, publicly held company with sizable sand and gravel interests.

A well-located sand and gravel deposit can be very profitable. Should you become aware of or own a good source of sand and gravel, an evaluation of the market potential is surely worthwhile. Your state geological survey, which most likely has an inventory of known deposits, can help by giving you the broad economic realities of the matter rather quickly.

SULFUR AND PYRITES

Background. Sulfur is widely distributed both in the elemental and combined states. It has been known for thousands of years—the Egyptians bleached their linens with it in 2000 B.C. Use of sulfur in making sulfuric acid was begun in 1793. By about 1880, it was used chiefly for gunpowder, bleaching agents, and medicinal compounds(*e.g.* sulfur and molasses). In 1894, Dr. Herman Frasch successfully mined sulfur in Louisiana by pumping hot water down into a sulfur deposit and recovering the dissolved sulfur. The Union Sulphur Company, organized by Dr. Frasch, produced the world's first sulfur by this process in 1895. During the next 25 years and more, sulfur mining by the Frasch process became common in salt domes along the Gulf Coast and continues to the present time. Of the more than 230 salt domes known in Texas and Louisiana, sulfur deposits have been found in 24 of them. By 1913 the United States had become the world's largest sulfur producer, and it has maintained that position ever since.

Pyrites are iron sulfide minerals such as pyrite (the common name of which is "fool's gold"), marcasite, and chalcopyrite, from which sulfur can be recovered by roasting. About one-fourth of the world supply comes from this source. From the smelting of chalcopyrite, a principal ore of copper, sulfur is recovered as a by-product. Pyrites have been used as alternate sources of sulfur where elemental sulfur was not available.

Present Demand and Uses. The uses of sulfur are legion but chiefly include the manufacture of phosphatic mineral fertilizers (by far the largest demand), in the pulp and paper industry (sulfite process), petroleum refining, refining of metals, production of cellulose fibers such as rayon, in the preparation of inorganic pigments, in food preservatives, and in the manufacture of tires and synthetic rubber in general. The uses of sulfur are so diverse and touch so many industries that sulfur consumption can be taken as a reliable indicator of industrial activity. Demand is strong, steady, and growing, especially with the increased use of fertilizers. Almost 90 percent of sulfur is used in the form of sulfuric acid in preparing various products.

Sources. Sulfur is obtained from many sources, ranging from deposits around volcanoes to the cap rock of salt domes in the Gulf Coast and elsewhere. Very large bedded deposits of sulfur also exist in southwestern United States. In some cases the elemental sulfur is mixed with other sediments such as sand and clay; in other cases it is combined as in the form of gypsum, which is a calcium sulfate.

Sulfur is an objectionable ingredient in coal, oil, and gas. Some oil has as much as 5½ percent sulfur by weight, and sulfur is recovered from these "sour crudes" (sour crude being any oil with more than ½ of 1 percent sulfur) as a by-product. Substantial sulfur is recovered in Canada from petroleum. Sulfur is produced from a variety of ore minerals, chiefly those of copper, lead, and zinc. Sulfur lost up the chimney during the smelting of these ores combines with moisture in the air to form sulfuric acid. In some areas of the United States "sulfuric acid rain" has devastated the landscape. Efforts are now being made, and indeed are required, to remove sulfur from stack discharges. As a result, recovery of sulfur from smelting processes is increasing.

World sulfur reserves are very large and can supply any probable demand to well beyond the year 2000. All continents are potentially self-sufficient in supply. Sea water is a possible large source of sulfur but none is presently recovered.

Outlook and Investment. Sulfur is a basic raw material for our modern industrial society, and its future is assured. Sulfur has historically suffered from oversupply, but there also have been brief shortages. Activity in the fertilizer industry, which consumes about 50 percent of total sulfur production, controls sulfur demand. World crop surpluses seem less likely to occur in the future than in the past, and the demand for sulfur henceforth should be relatively more steady.

Many companies produce sulfur; some produce it simply as a by-product of other major activities as is the case of metal-mining and oil companies. Companies whose activities are relatively more concerned with native sulfur production include Texas Gulf, Freeport Minerals (formerly Freeport Sulfur), and Jefferson Lake Sulfur (now a subsidiary of Occidental Petroleum).

Sulfur from oil and minerals is called "recovered sulfur" and accounts for about 20 percent of sulfur produced in the United States. Companies producing it include Standard Oil of Indiana, Getty Oil, Shell Oil, Stauffer Chemical, Kennecott, and American Smelting and Refining. In Canada, world's second largest producer, sulfur is recovered both from sulfide ores and crude oil. International Nickel, Cominco, and Noranda Mines are major producers of recovered sulfur, and some 20 oil companies obtained it from petroleum.

Exxon Corporation recovers large amounts of sulfur from Venezuelan crude oil at a refinery on Aruba in the Caribbean.

TALC AND SOAPSTONE

Background. Talc is a hydrous magnesium silicate, which, in specific samples, has quite a range of composition. Talc is soft (can be cut with a fingernail) and has a greasy feel. Soapstone is the term used for a massive and less-pure form of talc. High-purity massive talc is called steatite. Pyrophyllite is similar to talc but contains aluminum instead of magnesium. The end uses of these materials, however, are all quite similar; precise use is determined by the quality of the substance. Soapstone is commonly used for decorative facings on interior portions of buildings. It can be carved by hand very readily. Certain native crafts in various parts of the world (*e.g.* by Eskimos) are based on soapstone, and the products are sold to tourists. Carved soapstone objects are found among the artifacts of ancient peoples.

Present Demand and Uses. Demand for talc and related products is increasing in general about as fast as the growth of the economy, but certain specialized uses are increasing more rapidly. Talc is used in ceramics, paints, roofing materials, insecticides, rubber (as a filler in their compounding formations), paper, and in cosmetics such as talcum powder. This last grade of talc must be of very high quality, as impurities tend to be abrasive, and the market for sandy talcum powder is limited.

Sources. Talc and related materials occur in metamorphic rocks—rocks that have been altered very substantially by heat, pressure, and hot water. Talc is widely distributed around the world. Domestically, large deposits are in Alabama, California, Georgia, New York, North Carolina, and Texas. No very detailed estimate has been made of talc and related resources around the world, but a rough calculation places reserves at over one billion tons. There is no anticipated shortage of these materials against any foreseeable demand to the year 2000 and beyond.

Outlook and Investment. Talc demand appears to be steady and growing at least as fast as the economy. As with other bulky, low-unit value materials, location of deposits relative to places of principal use is an important factor. Additional good talc and related mineral deposits may yet be discovered in the United States and could be of considerable value if they are situated so they can compete favorably with presently known supplies. The five largest producers of talc in the United States account for about half of the total output, and the remainder is divided among about 35 smaller companies. Only two well-known companies have divisions that produce talc. These are Cyprus Mines and Chas. Pfizer and Company. In Canada, only a few companies produce talc, including Canadian Talc Industries, Broughton Soapstone and Quarry Company, and Baker Talc.

TRONA

Background. Trona is a naturally occurring soda ash—a hydrous sodium carbonate. Its use in quantity is a relatively modern event, and early people were probably not even aware of its existence.

Present Demand and Uses. About 40 percent of the sodium compounds derived from trona are used in glass-making; lesser amounts are used in making chemicals and in the production of pulp and paper. The remainder is consumed in various ways such as in water treatment, aluminum production, and the manufacture of soap and detergents. Metallic sodium, obtained from trona, is used primarily in the manufacture of tetraethyl lead, which has been used in gasoline but now is being phased out to some extent.

Sources. Trona deposits are reasonably widespread in western United States, occurring in Utah, California, Colorado, and Wyoming, among other places. The deposits are chiefly related to saline lake beds. Trona is in ample supply.

Outlook and Investment. Use of trona has not kept pace with the gross national product. Slow growth is likely to continue although experimental lightweight batteries using sodium or lithium as an electrode show some promise. If this development became commercial it could materially increase sodium demand. However, sodium can be obtained from other sources, including common salt.

Principal companies producing trona—but only as a small part of their total operations—include Allied Chemical, FMC Corporation, Stauffer Chemical, and Hooker Chemical, which is a subsidiary of Occidental Petroleum, with production at Searles Lake, California.

VERMICULITE

Background. Vermiculite was discovered in Massachusetts in 1824. Its name was based on the Latin word "vermiculari," meaning "to breed worms," because of the unique property of expanding into long worm-like pieces when heated. Vermiculite was discovered and subsequently mined in Colorado about 1915, but the major find in the United States was in Montana in 1921. This deposit is still the principal U.S. source.

Present Demand and Uses. Vermiculite's use is based on its properties of high bulk, good thermal-insulation values, chemically inert composition, fireproof nature, and high absorption of liquids. Construction materials using vermiculite account for about 80 percent of production. Vermiculite aggregates mixed with gypsum plaster and plaster or clay and asbestos form an excellent plaster fireproofing that is sprayed or troweled onto steel or concrete structures. There also is a large reduction in weight, which permits savings in structural steel and foundation costs. Vermiculite's other major uses is in soil conditioning, as a plant-growing medium, and as packing material for nursery stock. There is a fairly steady and growing demand for vermiculite. Increasing amounts are being exported to Canada and overseas.

Sources. Vermiculite appears to be the product of the alteration of the mica mineral, biotite, by heat or hot water or both in the Earth's crust. The major United States deposits are in Montana and South Carolina, with smaller amounts in other states, including Arizona, Texas, Colorado, and North Carolina. The United States produces about 70 percent of the world supply, with the remainder coming chiefly from South Africa. Supplies appear to be adequate to take care of projected demand to the year 2000 and beyond. Apparent U.S. reserves are in excess of 300 million tons. Current demand is substantially less than one million tons annually.

Outlook and Investment. Vermiculite is a very useful product, but as it is tied chiefly to the construction industry the demand for it is related to the cyclical nature of that industry to a large extent. Other uses, such as in agriculture, however, tend to stabilize demand, which is expected to grow about 3 to 4 percent a year to the year 2000. The Zonolite Division of W. R. Grace and Company operates mines in Montana and South Carolina and dominates the industry. Several smaller companies, however, also have production, including Patterson Vermiculite Company of South Carolina. Vermiculite does have competition from a variety of other materials, including perlite and pumice, but its properties allow it to compete well.

ZEOLITES

Background. Zeolites have been known since the 1750s. They are a group of some 20 minerals, aluminum silicates, chiefly of sodium or calcium with large amounts of water in their crystal structure. The origin of the name comes from the fact that zeolites, when heated, give off this water and appear to boil. The Greek words "zein" (boil) and "lithos" (stone) are the roots of the name. Zeolites are very widely distributed, but deposits of commercial quality are not common. Though not very hard, some forms such as Thompsonite are occasionally used as gemstones.

Present Demand and Uses. The natural zeolite industry is

in an early stage of development. It also suffers from the fact that zeolites can be produced artificially. However, zeolites have several interesting properties that suggest they will be increasingly in demand. In particular, the porous framework of zeolites enables them to act as molecular sieves. They also exhibit cation-exchange and reversible-dehydration properties that can be useful in pollution control, particularly in the removal of objectionable gases. Zeolites are also used in oil refining and have considerably increased the production of gasoline from crude oil. Ninety percent of the petroleum catalytic cracking installations in the United States use zeolites. Demand currently, however, is only a few hundred tons a year, but it is growing.

Sources. Zeolites occur in many geological settings, including in saline lake beds, in cavities in lava flows (as in Oregon and Washington), and in metamorphic rocks (as in New Zealand, where the deposits average more than 10,000 feet thick and locally are as much as 40,000 feet thick. Most zeolites in the United States are related to volcanic ash and other volcanically derived rocks in the West. The U.S. Geological Survey states that "identified, hypothetical, and speculative resources of zeolites in the United States are conservatively estimated at more than 10 trillion tons." Total resources of zeolites in the rest of the world have not yet really begun to be catalogued.

Outlook and Investment. The outlook for zeolites appears promising, but the industry is in its infancy. The future of zeolites depends almost entirely on research for new uses rather than in locating any additional deposits, as supply is no particular problem. Union Carbide Corporation, through its Linde Division, is one of the companies interested in zeolite research and production.

16

Water

Nothing, absolutely nothing, can live without water. We may live on land but in many ways our civilization is built on water. How much water do you account for each day? Most people, in answer, will merely add up what they drink, use for washing their face and hands and for other sanitary purposes, and perhaps use for washing the car and watering the lawn. In geology classes I have taught, the students generally guess from 15 to 50 gallons a day. But the answer is probably closer to 15,000 gallons! If you want to run around naked you can cut your water consumption; otherwise you have to figure in the fact that it takes 800,000 gallons of water to grow an acre of cotton from which to make your clothes. If you wear wool clothing the proportionate figure (for raising sheep per acre) comes out even greater. When you eat a quarter-pound hamburger you are consuming 725 gallons of water, for it takes about 3,000 gallons to raise one pound of beef in the form of a two-year old steer.

It takes about 65,000 gallons of water to make a ton of steel that goes into your car, refrigerator, and the office building where you may work. It takes 70,000 gallons to make a ton of high quality paper and about 64,000 gallons to make a ton of rayon. People are busy inventing things that take more and more water, and they ardently save money so they can buy things such as automatic dishwashers, washing machines, and backyard swimming pools.

Supplying the water we need is a very large business, and it seems likely that our national investment in water- producing and transporting facilities will have to more than double by the year 2000.

Investment. Many water supplies are owned by municipalities. Investors may be well advised therefore to consider investing in water-revenue bonds, which have attractive, tax-exempt features in some cases. Historically, water-revenue bonds have been relatively safe. However, there are more than 3,500 investor-owned water utility companies. Most of them are small and locally owned and are worth inquiring about in your area. Shares in these companies are commonly traded on a local or even personal basis, just as are shares of local banks and telephone companies. The return on investment has been good in many cases. These are utilities, subject commonly to rate regulation, but they do not have the problems of great capital needs or fuel costs that electric utilities have. Furthermore, people apparently tend to regard the water bill as one of the first they should pay.

Some of the larger investor-owned water companies are listed below.

American Water Works	Indianapolis Water
Bridgeport Hydraulic	Jamaica Water Supply
California Water Service	Philadelphia Suburban Water
Elizabethtown Water	San Jose Water
General Waterworks	Southern California Water
	Utilities and Industries

Hydropower. In a sense you can invest in water when you invest in those utilities that derive their electrical generating capacity from waterpower. Electricity, of course, is not a primary energy source but has to be produced by something else. A few utilities derive a very large part of their power from damsites. So if one wished to regard that as a method of investing in water, these utilities would be a vehicle. They include chiefly Idaho Power, Puget Sound Power and Light, and Washington Water Power. Montana Power, Utah Power, Pacific Gas and Electric, and certain other utilities derive a small percentage of power from hydro facilities also. Those companies that get a substantial amount of power from damsites are in a relatively strong position for, unlike utilities dependent on fossil fuels and in many cases on foreign supplies of oil, the hydropower companies get their power with every rain. It is a renewable power source and they don't have to argue with the Arabs about it.

Water—A Renewable and Reusable Resource. The amount of fresh water in the world is strictly limited at any one time and quite unequally distributed, but, unlike oil, water is a renewable and also a reusable resource. It comes to us in every rain so that companies dealing in this resource have a perpetual supply. Water also can be reused many times after it is here. Water going down the Ohio River has been estimated to be used more than 100 times before it joins the Mississippi. More than 50 million people in the United States now drink reused water.

Investment in Water Processing. Because of the reusable nature of water, investing in firms that make and service water-processing equipment and supplies may also be thought of as investing in water. In some cases, water that is unused but is initially unsuitable for industrial or domestic purposes is processed to usable form. This includes desalinization of sea water. In any event, water treatment is a logical and growing avenue of water investment. Firms involved in this are many and include Crane Company, American Standard, Foster Wheeler, Nalco Chemical, and FMC Corporation. Westinghouse Corporation has been a leader in desalinization plants. Fluor Corporation, Foster Wheeler, General Electric, Koppers Company, and Combustion Engineering build desalinization equipment. A General Electric official states, "There's a profitable multi-million dollar market in desalinization in the years to come."

Water Permeates Many Investments. In a sense, when you invest in a great variety of things, you are also investing in water. Water supplies control the growth of industries and populations. As an application of this concept, I once took the U.S. Geological Survey figures on available fresh water in each of two states and then divided the total number of shares of stock in all the banks of these states into the total amount of water available. In this way, I found how much water in the state was behind each share of stock. The theory is that banks depend on local industrial and population expansion for their growth, and, other things being equal, the state with bank stocks having the most water behind them would show the better growth. In this case the connotation of "watered stock" is a good one. I might add that one of the states was Florida, and the growth of the banking industry there has been excellent.

In a broader sense one can apply this principle to regions. If you locate places where the average temperature is about 65° F (the optimum temperature for human activity) and where the annual average precipitation is 30 inches or more, you have pretty well pin-pointed regions that have adequate water supplies and a mild (low space-heating energy requirements) climate. This combination certainly seems fundamental to future growth as energy costs rise and water supplies become short. It makes an interesting study.

Summary. Water is a basic resource and there are many opportunities to invest in it, both directly in water-supply or water-treatment companies and indirectly in hydroelectric companies. More broadly, water supplies underlie all economic growth and should be factored into many investment decisions, particularly those with longer-range commitments.

17

Air

You don't have to drill or prospect for air—it's readily available. But what do you do with this vast resource? The answer is quite a lot. Demand for air-derived products is growing rapidly. Production of oxygen and nitrogen are a big and important business and these gases have been discussed earlier in this book.

An "ocean of air" is the expression sometimes heard. But the atmosphere and the oceans are different, partly in the fact that almost every element on Earth occurs in the ocean, whereas air has a relatively simple composition: nitrogen 78 percent, oxygen 21 percent, argon 1 percent. This adds up to 100 percent, but before the figures were rounded there was enough space in the decimal points to allow for traces of carbon dioxide, neon, helium, and several other gases in very small quantities.

A brief note here is made of the minor gases—argon, neon, xenon, and krypton. Of these, neon is the most familiar, in the form of neon signs. Neon ionizes and glows with a reddish color when an electric current is passed through it. Argon is an inert, colorless gas that is used in light bulbs and radio tubes. Krypton is an inert gas used in high-power electric light bulbs. Xenon is an inert gas used in various types of special lights such as strobe lights and in certain scientific equipment such as bubble-chambers.

Investment. Reducing air to liquid form and, in the process, separating out its various gaseous components is a big business. The most valuable end products are nitrogen and oxygen, which were discussed in this book earlier. However, the minor gases have important uses and are a valuable by-product of nitrogen and oxygen production. Firms that recover these rare gases include Linde Division of Union Carbide, Airco, and Air Products and Chemicals, Inc.

18

The Oceans—Last Great Physical Frontier on This Earth

THE OCEANS COVER 71 percent of the Earth's surface, but we know the details of the surface of the moon better than we do that of the ocean floors. We can see the moon and map it easily with cameras, but the ocean bottoms can be studied in detail only with some difficulty. Yet there is great interest in the oceans and the ocean floors because of their sheer magnitude, among other things. The amount of potentially useful materials that exist in the oceans in various forms is staggering. But to a large extent these resources have not yet been utilized.

An increasingly vexing problem to those concerned with developing ocean resources is the question of "Who owns the oceans?" The old "three-mile limit," based on how far a cannon could hurl a cannonball and thus control the area, has long since gone, and some countries now claim a 200-mile limit. The problem of who owns the deep ocean basins in particular is unresolved. Conferences have been held where the participants have agreed chiefly to disagree. Ultimately it is probable that "ocean sectors" will be assigned, but then the question comes up about the interests of those countries that are entirely landlocked and do not have an ocean coastline. Are they left out? The argument seems sure to continue.

In the meantime, as food, energy, and mineral resources are depleted on land, we are turning to taking resources from the oceans on the basis of the very rough existing rules of ownership. Quite a few conflicts are arising in this regard, but the necessity of obtaining these resources is causing a number of nations and industries to push ahead with exploitation of the seas.

Marine resources can be considered in five categories: ocean mining, recovery of dissolved minerals from sea water, fishing, mariculture or "sea farming," and energy from the ocean. Each of these, with some comments on the apparent and possible investment opportunities, is briefly considered.

OCEAN MINING

There is nothing new about mining the oceans. Shallow waters have been mined by dredging for gold, tin, rutile, diamonds, sand and gravel, oyster shells, and iron ore for many years. The continental shelves are simply extensions of the continent and mineral deposits on land can and do extend under the sea. By entrance from the mainland or artificial islands, coal, tin, copper, and other minerals have been obtained from the continental shelf. At one time Alaska Juneau, a gold mine, operated its workings beneath the sea from a shaft on an adjacent hillside. Of the small amount of platinum produced in the United States so far, more than 90 percent of it has come from old buried river-channel placer deposits under the shallow waters of Goodnews Bay, Alaska. Sulfur from salt domes has been mined offshore by the hot-water Frasch process for many years. Phosphate nodules are known in a number of places on the ocean floor but have not yet been mined in any quantity. More than 1.5 billion tons lie off the Southern California coast.

The relatively new concept in ocean mining is that of obtaining minerals from the deep sea and possibly from certain mineral-rich brines and muds. Also, there is the more remote prospect of eventually operating mines on the ocean floor, just as we operate mines on land today.

In general, it can be said that the ocean basins are made out of basalt, a rock that does not normally carry a great variety of mineral wealth. There are only a relatively few small areas in the ocean where there are rocks more like the granitic rocks of the continents, and more useful metals such as copper, lead, zinc, and silver might theoretically be found in any abundance. .

However, on many parts of the ocean floor there are vast quantities of manganese nodules. They are as big as several inches across, and they contain manganese, nickel, copper, and cobalt. They apparently are forming today, and it is estimated that the nickel in them is accumulating at a rate several times greater than current world consumption. This is an intriguing situation—a mine where the metal forms faster than it is being used. That is about as close to a renewable metal resource as one can get.

Studies show that the major and most valuable concentrations of manganese nodules in the world occur in the North Pacific, forming a broad east-west band about 500 miles south of the Hawaiian Islands. In fact, this is the only place in the world where manganese nodules exist with the minimum quality of 1-percent metal content used for both nickel and copper. This deposit is significant also in that its geographic position is midway between the United States and Japan, two of the major markets for manganese.

In the Red Sea and in certain other areas, brines of copper and other metals are known that may in the future be exploited. There also are metal-rich muds in the Red Sea and elsewhere.

Investment. There is a great deal of activity at present in ocean mining. Large barges and special mining equipment are being built. Hughes Tool Company has a barge in operation. Tenneco, Lockheed, Deep Sea Ventures, Inc., International Minerals and Chemicals, Global Marine, Kennecott, and Zapata, as well as other companies have been developing ocean mining techniques. Substantial profits from mining the deeper ocean areas have yet to be realized, but the potential would appear to be very large. Aside from the companies just mentioned, there is a general way in which investors can participate in the exploitation of ocean resources, including offshore drilling and mining; it is by mutual funds such as Oceanographic Fund, Inc.

It is probable that ocean mining will occur on a large scale before the end of this century and will offer a variety of investment opportunities.

DISSOLVED MINERALS IN SEA WATER

The figures in regard to total dissolved mineral material in sea water both stagger and whet the imagination. The basic problem, of course, is the economics of recovery; cheap energy would be the key that would unlock many of these materials for our use. So that developments in the recovery of these dissolved materials can be put in the perspective of the relative amounts of them available, I have included here a fairly complete tabulation of what sea water contains.

Sea water contains an average of 35,000 parts per million of dissolved solids. In a cubic mile of sea water, which weighs 4.7 billion tons, there are about 165 million tons of dissolved matter. Most of it is the chlorine and sodium that make up the common salt in the sea. The volume of the oceans in total, is about 350 million cubic miles, giving a theoretical mineral reserve of about 60 quadrillion tons. What is in this mineral reserve besides common salt?

Listed in the table below are 56 elements that occur in sea water. Of these, only common salt, magnesium, and bromine are now being extracted in significant amounts. (The data in the table are from Edward Wenk, "The Physical Resources of the Ocean," *Scientific American*, vol. 221, no. 3).

Element	Tons per Cubic Mile	Element	Tons per Cubic Mile
Chlorine	89,500,000	Zinc	47
Sodium	49,500,000	Iron	47
Magnesium	6,400,000	Aluminum	47
Sulfur	4,200,000	Molybdenum	47
Calcium	1,900,000	Selenium	19
Potassium	1,800,000	Tin	14
Bromine	306,000	Copper	14
Carbon	132,000	Arsenic	14
Strontium	38,000	Uranium	14
Boron	23,000	Nickel	9
Silicon	14,000	Vanadium	9
Fluorine	6,100	Manganese	9
Argon	2,800	Titanium	5
Nitrogen	2,400	Antimony	2
Lithium	800	Cobalt	2
Rubidium	570	Cesium	2
Phosphorus	330	Yttrium	1
Iodine	280	Silver	1
Barium	140	Lanthanum	1
Indium	94	Krypton	1

Element	Tons per Cubic Mile		Element	Tons per Cubic Mile
Neon	0.5		Lead	0.1
Cadmium	0.5		Mercury	0.1
Tungsten	0.5		Gallium	0.1
Xenon	0.5		Bismuth	0.1
Germanium	0.3		Noiobrium	0.05
Chromium	0.2		Thallium	0.05
Thorium	0.2		Helium	0.03
Scandium	0.2		Gold	0.02

Outlook and Investment. It is obvious that one cannot buy these mineral resources as such. But you can buy into the technologies that will allow these elements to be economically recovered. The fact, however, that magnesium can be obtained profitably from sea water now is encouraging in that although the concentration is only 0.13 percent it can compete with the vast deposits on land that contain 30 percent magnesium. The economics of recovering these metals is complex. Much study is being given the matter and it surely is a field worth watching for major developments and investment opportunities.

At the present time Dow Chemical is a leader in this research and is the source of most of the magnesium of the United States produced from sea water.

FISHING

For centuries the seas have yielded their fish products to us. At times the yields have been very large, only to have them drop off very rapidly as a result of overfishing, or sometimes for causes not known. These cycles are still with us in large part because we do not have adequate international agreements on the exploitation of our fish resources. Hopefully, the problem will be resolved. In the meantime it may be noted that Americans and Canadians have done relatively less with ocean fisheries than have many other countries. However, interest is increasing as food supplies become more of a concern. Much fishing is done by individual fishermen or by small private fishing companies. The fishing interests of larger firms are modest compared with their other activities. Therefore, investing in fishing enterprises is somewhat difficult for the average investor. Zapata Corporation is an example of a company whose ocean fisheries contribute only about 5 percent of its profits. However, this could be enlarged.

One cannot, of course, buy the fish resources of the sea directly, but only the equipment and technology to capture these resources. In total, fishing has been a fairly marginal pursuit, subject to many changes. It is a field to be watched, perhaps, but does not appear to be very attractive for investment at present or in the near future.

MARICULTURE—OR "SEA-FARMING"

Four-fifths of all living organisms on Earth live in the sea. Fish and shellfish attract most of the interest in food from the sea, but certain forms of algae, plankton, and other ocean organisms are edible and contain certain high-grade nutrients suitable for human consumption.

Oceans occupy more than two-thirds of the Earth's surface and therefore receive twice as much solar energy as does the land. Sunlight is the basic energy source for growing food, so oceans have a food potential greater than land. However, 90 percent of the ocean area is a relative biologic desert because there are not sufficient nutrient materials in the euphotic zone (the zone to which light penetrates sufficiently to allow photosynthesis) to support the level of planktonic life essential to the high productivity of fish resources. The bulk of the organisms live where runoff from the land or the upwelling of nutrient-rich deep water fertilizes the surface water and stimulates the growth of marine life. Many of these areas are adjacent to land. River estuaries are notably rich in marine life, and land-enclosed areas such as Puget Sound are highly productive of fish and shellfish.

These facts suggest that rather than trying to become more efficient in fishing the open oceans, the logical answer is to make the fertile areas along the coast even more efficient producers by farming them, even as land is farmed to make it a more efficient producer of food than it is in its natural state. Puget Sound is an example of an area with great potential. It is the nation's biggest inland sea. It has 2,300 miles of coastline and waters both shoal and deep. In its estuaries, vigorous tidal action mixes fresh and salt water and the nutrients essential to life. Its latitude brings sunshine at a direct-enough angle to stimulate growth of tiny organisms that in turn become food for higher forms of sea life.

Acre for acre, properly cultivated sea water can produce far more protein than can land. In small areas of Japan's Inland Sea, suspension cultures of oysters annually yield 46,000 pounds of shucked meats per acre of cultivated area. Japan, incidentally, had laws concerning oyster-farming well back before the time of Christ. Aristotle discusses the cultivation of oysters in Greece, and Pliny has described oyster-farming during the early part of the Christian era.

Outlook and Investment.   Mariculture is in its infancy, but already a number of companies have had stock offerings. No doubt more investment opportunities will come as people now being trained in our expanding schools of oceanography and marine biology (and we now have Sea Grant universities just as we have Land Grant schools) seek to capitalize on their training to produce food from the sea in a controlled and scientific manner.

At the present time, oysters and certain forms of algae are among the chief resources farmed. A good start has been made on raising salmon commercially. Union Carbide and Marine Protein Company are working on this as well as on other mariculture projects. Other companies that have recently gone public are Marifarms and Oceanography Mariculture Industries. Marine Colloids Company processes red seaweed into materials used not only in foods but in toothpaste and in air fresheners. There will no doubt be many abortive attempts to capitalize on the concept of marine farming, but the very high productivity per acre and the high quality of protein produced are so attractive that it seems impossible for this business not to become a major industry in this century. The worldwide food shortage will certainly be another factor encouraging mariculture.

The key to the success of any such enterprise will be a good location and, above all, technically competent people. The right technological team at the right location should make for a very profitable enterprise.

ENERGY FROM THE OCEANS

The major future oil provinces of the free world lie in shallow and not so shallow marine waters. Already a substantial portion of U.S. oil production comes from offshore. This portion will climb markedly in the next decade and beyond as land areas become thoroughly drilled up and we develop the capabilities of moving economically into deeper waters in search of oil. Oil and gas have been treated in earlier sections of this book as have tides and waves.

The two other ocean energy sources are the use of water-temperature differentials to generate steam and ultimately electricity through very-low-pressure power plants and the possibility of using ocean-current flows, such as the Gulf Stream, to generate power.

In both cases, of course, one would buy into the technology and not the resource as such. So far, both ideas appear to be a considerable time away from application. The concept of water-temperature differential might possibly be a reality before the end of this century.

Theoretically, mechanical energy, and from it electrical energy, can be developed from heat being passed from a body of water with a higher temperature to one with a lower temperature. The less the temperature differential between the two bodies, the more difficult and less efficient is this process. In the case of the oceans this is compensated for somewhat by the tremendous amount of water of two different temperatures available. The idea is to bring up cold ocean water from great depths and warm it with the heat of the warmer surface waters. A huge pipe would have to be installed, and only certain basins adjacent to land areas have a suitable topography. This limitation, however, might be solved with floating power plants. Also, mixing the mineral-laden, cold, deep waters with the sunlit surface waters probably would cause a considerable increase in organic productivity of the ocean in that region, and thus there would be some beneficial side effects.

However, the whole idea is just that so far—an idea—but it is an intriguing one that is being pursued and could eventually become a reality. How one would invest in it is hard to predict at this time, but presumably it would be in the firm or firms with the technology.

The other concept, that of intercepting ocean currents and using their energy in some fashion to run power plants, has possibilities in the sense of the amount of power theoretically available. If the Gulf Stream, for example, were impounded in some fashion the energy produced would be very large. However, the climatic effects of tampering with the Gulf Stream or other ocean currents might be catastrophic. The Scandinavian peninsula and the British Isles are heated by the Gulf Stream. London, with the same latitude as the southern portion of Hudson Bay, would be much colder if the Gulf Stream were even partially blocked. Accordingly, it seems unlikely that harnessing the major ocean currents to produce energy is really very attractive when all considerations are weighed.

19

Summary and Conclusions

THE UNITED STATES AND CANADA, the last major lands to be discovered and exploited, retain a mineral, forest, and agricultural vitality beyond that of any other comparable area in the world. Also, the potential for renewable natural resources, in a balanced blend of agricultural and forest lands, is without peer. These facts, together with the growth of populations both here and abroad, make it inevitable that the resources of these two countries will increasingly be drawn upon to sustain humanity. To accomplish this the capital requirements will be very large.

But let it be clearly stated that this is not to infer that our population growth can be long sustained. The population problem overshadows all else. There simply are not the resources available under existing or foreseeable technologies to bring much of the rest of the world up to the standard of living of the Western industrialized nations. Lower-grade deposits of mineral ores involve vastly greater amounts of energy to process. The same is true in finding and producing the deeper oil from tighter formations. Furthermore, many of these resources are non-renewable in the sense that nature renews them so very slowly that in the foreseeable future of the human race there will be no appreciable additional supplies beyond those that exist today, examples being oil, gas, and coal.

Ultimately, it is necessary that the world come to an almost completely recyclable economy based on renewable resources.

Gradually, capital investment should shift toward the concept of living on a finite Earth where resources have to be used and reused, with only a modest amount of "income" from solar energy or perhaps from, for all practical purposes, the infinite source of hydrogen in the sea. This adjustment in our outlook is already beginning to take place and it will continue indefinitely. But even with the recognition of this as an imperative goal, as we move toward this objective the need to continue to develop the resources we now have is evident.

We are, admittedly, buying time to make the changes in our economies and our ways of life and time to find the technologies to launch us on a firmer renewable-natural-resource path. One of the important tasks as we do buy time by exploiting our finite and non-renewable resources is to begin the process of national and international education toward the goals of a recyclable steady-state economy compatible with living on this finite spaceship Earth. Even the arrival of fusion and the hydrogen economy, if that can ever be accomplished, will not eliminate the need to continue to move toward a closed-system economy, because that is what we really have. We see this now as we end one era of history and enter another. But in this transition (and here we are looking at hundreds of years), there continues to be a great need to develop our conventionally used resources. Old materials must be united with new technologies to produce oil from oil shale, gas from coal, and energy from the atom in advanced reactors. Also, new exploration techniques, including Earth-scanning satellites, are locating natural resources that we had not suspected before. And there are still a few physical frontiers to be explored on this Earth. The ocean basins are one, the continent of Antarctica is another, the 800,000 square miles of Greenland is a third, and there are others beneath the Brazilian jungle, the muskeg of Canada, and the glacial deposits of northern United States.

So, as the dedication states, this book is directed toward the cause of conscientious and intelligent investing, wherein a balance between the needs of today and the trends of tomorrow are achieved. We have the resources for enabling us to enter the 21st century with a higher standard of living than we have today. But it should be made clear to those in political control that the mover under our system of personal and economic freedom is the opportunity to make a fair profit. It is most important that capital in the area of natural resource investments be treated fairly in the remaining decades of this century and beyond, for the capital needs are enormous. Money must be attracted to this basic purpose.

The great natural resource base represented by Canada and the United States, together with free men and their savings, have combined to produce an economy second to none in this world. We can continue to enjoy a fine standard of living if we preserve the system that has brought it to us. But as we do this we must also recognize that our resource base is changing and our non-renewable resources are diminishing. To be successful, an investment program must take this fact into account, and capital increasingly must be diverted toward the end of a steady-state, recyclable economy.

The challenges are greater than ever before because the stakes are so large. Hopefully, this book offers some positive and tangible guidelines to investors of today and tomorrow as we face both the problems and the opportunities in natural resource development to the end of this century and beyond.

General Bibliography

The literature on natural resources is vast and is growing rapidly. For the purpose of this book I have simply selected some general and relatively easily available reports that may be of interest to the reader who wishes to pursue these matters. This literature has been listed under seven headings—land, renewable natural resources, energy sources, mineral resources, mining and prospecting, marine resources, and the longer, broader view.

Land

Boudreau, Eugene. *Buying Country Lands*. New York: Collier Books, 1973.

Cooley, L. F., and Cooley, L. M. *Land Investment*. Los Angeles: Nash Publishing, 1973.

Rickert, D. A., and Spieker, A. M. *Real-Estate Lakes*. U.S. Geological Survey, Circular 601-G, Washington, D.C., 1971.

U.S. Department of Agriculture. *Land*. U.S. Department of Agriculture Yearbook, Washington, D.C., 1958.

U.S. News and World Report. *How to Buy Real Estate*. Books by U.S. News and World Report, Washington, D.C., 1970

Renewable Natural Resources

U.S. Department of Agriculture. *Trees*. U.S. Department of Agriculture Yearbook. Washington, D.C., 1949.

———. *Crops in Peace and War*. U.S. Department of Agriculture Yearbook. Washington, D.C. 1951.

———. *Water*. U.S. Department of Agriculture Yearbook, Washington, D.C., 1955.

238

————. *Timber Resources for America's Future.* U.S. Department of Agriculture Forest Resource Report Number 14, 1958.

————. *Food for Us All.* U.S. Department of Agriculture Yearbook, Washington, D.C., 1969.

Vardaman, J. M. *Tree Farm Business Management.* New York: The Ronald Press Company, 1965.

Energy Sources

Ayers, Eugene, and Scarlott, C. A. *Energy Sources—the Wealth of the World.* New York: McGraw-Hill, 1952.

Daniels, Farrington. *Direct Use of the Sun's Energy.* New Haven, Conn.: Yale University Press, 1965.

Gray, T. J., and Gashus, O. K. *Tidal Power.* New York: Plenum, 1972.

Hammond, A. L. *et al. Energy and the Future.* Washington, D.C.: American Association for the Advancement of Science, 1973.

Hottell, H. C., and Howard, J. B. *New Energy Technology: Some Facts and Assessments.* Cambridge, Mass.: MIT Press, 1971.

Kruger, Paul, and Otte, Carel (eds.). *Geothermal Energy: Resources, Production, Stimulation.* Stanford, Calif.: Stanford University Press, 1973.

National Petroleum Council. *U.S. Energy Outlook.* Washington, D.C.: National Petroleum Council, 1972.

————. *U.S. Energy Outlook: Fuels for Electricity.* Washington, D.C.: National Petroleum Council, 1973.

————. *U.S. Energy Outlook: Oil Shale Availability.* Washington, D.C.: National Petroleum Council, 1973.

————. *U.S. Energy Outlook: Coal Availability.* Washington, D.C.: National Petroleum Council, 1973.

————. *U.S. Energy Outlook: Nuclear Energy Availability.* Washington, D.C.: National Petroleum Council, 1973.

————. *U.S. Energy Outlook: New Energy Forms.* Washington, D.C.: National Petroleum Council, 1973.

Savage, H. K. *The Rock That Burns.* Boulder, Colo.: Pruett Press, 1967.

Theobald, P. K., *et al. Energy Resources of the United States.* U.S. Geological Survey, Circular 650, Washington, D.C., 1972.

Mineral Resources

Cameron, E. N. (ed.). *The Mineral Position of the United States, 1975–2000.* Madison: The University of Wisconsin Press, 1973.

Dickinson, J. Y. *The Book of Diamonds.* New York: Crown Publishers, 1965.

Flawn, P. T. *Mineral Resources. Geology. Engineering. Economics. Politics. Law.* New York: Rand McNally, 1966.

Hoppe, D. J. *How to Invest in Gold Coins.* New Rochelle, N.Y.: Arlington House, 1970.

Lamey, C. A. *Metallic and Industrial Mineral Deposits.* New York: McGraw-Hill, 1966.

Persons, R. H. *The Investor's Encyclopedia of Gold, Silver, and Other Precious Metals.* New York: Random House, 1974.

Schlegel, D. M. *Gemstones of the United States.* U.S. Geological Survey Bulletin 1042-G., Washington, D.C., 1957.

Sinkankas, John. *Gemstones of North America.* Princeton, N.J.: Van Nostrand, 1959.

U.S. Bureau of Mines. *Mineral Facts and Problems.* U.S. Bureau of Mines, Washington, D.C., 1970.

————. *Minerals Yearbook.* U.S. Bureau of Mines, Washington, D.C., (in three volumes), 1971.

U.S. Geological Survey. *United States Mineral Resources.* U.S. Geological Survey Professional Paper 820, Washington, D.C., 1973.

Mining and Prospecting

Northern Miner Press. *Mining Explained.* Toronto: Northern Miner Press, 1968.

Pearl, R.M. *Successful Mineral Collecting and Prospecting.* New York: Bonanza Books, 1961.

————. *Handbook for Prospectors.* 5th ed. New York: McGraw-Hill, 1973.

Sinkankas, John. *Gemstones and Minerals, and How and Where to Find Them.* Princeton, N.J.: Van Nostrand, 1961.

————. *Mineralogy for Amateurs.* Princeton, N.J.: Van Nostrand, 1964.

Wolff, Ernest. *Handbook for the Alaskan Prospector.* Fairbanks: University of Alaska, 1964.

Marine Resources

McKelvey, V. E., *et al.* *Subsea Mineral Resources and Problems Related to Their Development.* U. S. Geological Survey, Circular 619. Washington, D.C., 1969.

McKelvey, V. E., and Wang, F. F. H. *Preliminary Maps of World Subsea Mineral Resources.* U.S. Geological Survey, Miscellaneous Geologic Investigations, map I-632. Washington, D.C., 1970.

Mero, J. L. *The Mineral Resources of the Sea.* New York: Elsevier, 1965.

Pinchot, G. B. "Marine farming." *Scientific American,* vol. 223, no. 6, 1970.

Trumbull, J. V. A., *et al.* *An Introduction to the Geology and Mineral Resources of the Continental Shelves of the Americas.* U.S. Geological Survey Bulletin 1067, Washington, D.C. 1958.

United Nations. *Mineral Resources of the Sea.* New York: United Nations. 1970.

The Longer, Broader View

Borgstrom, Georg. *Too Many: An Ecological Overview of the Earth's Limitations.* New York: Collier Books, 1969.

———. *The Hungry Planet.* New York: Collier Books, 1972.

Daly, H. C. (ed.). *Toward a Steady-State Economy.* San Francisco: W.H. Freeman and Company, 1973.

Dubos, Rene, and Ward, Barbara. *Only One Earth: The Care and Maintenance of a Small Planet.* Middlesex, Eng.: Penquin Books, 1972.

Ehrlich, P. R. *The Population Bomb.* New York: Ballantine Books, 1968.

———, Ehrlich, A.H., and Holdren, J. P. *Human Ecology.* San Francisco: W. H. Freeman, 1973.

Hardin, Garrett. *Exploring New Ethics for Survival: Voyage of the Spaceship Beagle.* New York: Viking Press, 1972.

Herfindahl, O. C. *Natural Resource Information for Economic Development.* Published for Resources for the Future, Baltimore: Johns Hopkins Press, 1969.

Lapp, R. E. *The Logarithmic Century.* Englewood Cliffs, N.J.: Prentice-Hall, 1973.

McHale, John. *World Facts and Trends.* New York: Collier Books, 1972.

Meadows, D. H., *et al. The Limits to Growth.* New York: Universe Books, 1972.

National Research Council. *Resources and Man.* San Francisco: W.H. Freeman, 1969.

Park, C. F. *Affluence in Jeopardy: Minerals and the Political Economy.* San Francisco: Freeman, Cooper, 1968.

Skinner, B. J. *Earth Resources.* Englewood Cliffs, N.J.: Prentice-Hall, 1969.

Index

Gibraltar Mines, 100
Gilsonite, 55–56
 uses, 56
Glen Gery Shale Brick Company, 183–84
Global Marine, 50
Globe-Union, Inc., 70
Gold, 154–60
 gold futures market, 159
 gold mining "houses," 158
 history of use in coins, 154–55
 investing in, 157–59
 location of deposits, 156–57
 mining future, 159
 prospecting for, 159–60
 South Africa gold mines, 158
 U.S. producers, 158
Goodnews Bay Mining Company, 166
Gould, Inc., 70
W. R. Grace and Company, 203, 218
Grahamite; *see* Gilsonite
Graphite, 191–92
 background, 191
 outlook and investment, 192
 present demand and uses, 191
 sources, 191–92
Gravel; *see* Sand and gravel
Great Canadian Oil Sands, Ltd., 55
Great Northern Iron Ore, 105
Grefco, Inc., 201
Gulf Oil, 48, 55, 58, 64, 68
Gulf Resources and Chemical, 10, 121,
 131, 138, 163
Gulf Stream, 233–34
Gulf and Western Industries, 121
Gypsum, 192–93
 background, 192
 outlook and investment, 193
 present demand and uses, 192
 sources, 192–93

H

Hafnium, 136
 background, 136
 outlook and investment, 136
 present demand and uses, 136
 sources, 136
Hanna Mining, 105, 114–15
Harris, Upham and Company, 13
Hecla Mining, 108, 121, 126, 158
Helium, 193–94
 background, 193
 outlook and investment, 194
 present demand and uses, 193–94
 sources, 194
Holmium, 141
Homestake, 64, 108, 115, 158–59, 205
Honeywell Corporation, 70

Horizon Corporation, 21
Horn silver, 161
Houston Natural Gas Company, 199–200
Hudson Bay Mining and Smelting, 100,
 108, 121, 131, 146, 159, 205
Hugoton Field, 51
Hydroelectric power, 8, 221–22
Hydrogen, 65–66
 companies in production, 66
 growth in demand, 65
 "hydrogen economy," 65–66
 investment in, 66
 uses, 65

I

Idaho Bureau of Mines and Geology, 65
Idaho Power, 221
Ideal Basic Industries, 179, 205
Illinium, 141
Impala Platinum, 166
Imperial Oil, 55
Indium, 136–37
 background, 136
 outlook and investment, 137
 present demand and uses, 136
 sources, 136–37
Inspiration Consolidated, 100
International Minerals and Chemicals,
 188, 198, 203, 205
International Mining, 142, 166
International Nickel, 100, 113, 115, 133,
 146, 159, 163, 166, 215
International Smelting and Refining, 146
Iodine, 194–96
 background, 194–95
 outlook and investment, 196
 present demand and uses, 195
 sources, 195–96
Iridium, 165
Iron, 2, 91, 102–6
 background, 102–3
 hematite, 104
 outlook and investment, 105–6
 present demand and uses, 103
 sources, 103–4
 taconite, 104–5
Iron Age, 76
Iron-Aluminum Age, 76
Iron Ore Company of Canada, 106

J

John S. Herold, Inc., 13
Johns-Manville Corporation, 173, 186–87,
 201

K

Kaiser Aluminum and Chemical Corporation, 93, 115, 149, 205